RIGHTS AND COURTS IN PURSUIT OF SOCIAL CHANGE

Over the past few decades, European countries have witnessed a proliferation of legal norms concerning marginalised individuals and minorities who increasingly invoke them in front of courts to assert their rights and claim protection. The present volume explores the relationship between law, rights and social mobilisation in Europe. It specifically enquires into the extent and ways in which legal processes and entitlements are mobilised by less privileged social actors to advance their rights claims and pursue social change. Most distinctly, it explores such processes in the context of the multi-level European system, characterised by the existence of multiple legal and judicial arenas at the national, subnational and supranational/transnational level. In such a complex system of law and governance in Europe, concepts like legal opportunity structures, as well as the factors shaping them need to be reconceptualised. How does the multi-level European context distinctly shape the nature and salience of rights, as well as their mobilisation by individuals and minority actors?

Oñati International Series in Law and Society

A SERIES PUBLISHED FOR THE OÑATI INSTITUTE FOR THE SOCIOLOGY OF LAW

Recent titles in this series

Emotions, Crime and Justice
edited by Susanne Karstedt, Ian Loader and Heather Strang

Mediation in Political Conflicts
Soft Power or Counter Culture?
edited by Jacques Faget

Criminological and Legal Consequences of Climate Change
edited by Stephen Farrall, Tawhida Ahmed and Duncan French

Shooting to Kill: Socio-Legal Perspectives on the Use of Lethal Force
edited by Simon Bronitt, Miriam Gani and Saskia Hufnagel

Managing Family Justice in Diverse Societies
edited by Mavis Maclean and John Eekelaar

Making Human Rights Intelligible
Towards a Sociology of Human Rights
edited by Mikael Rask Madsen and Gert Verschraegen

European Penology?
edited by Tom Daems, Dirk van Zyl Smit and Sonja Snacken

For the complete list of titles in this series, see 'Oñati International Series in Law and Society' link at www.hartpub.co.uk/books/series.asp

Rights and Courts in Pursuit of Social Change

Legal Mobilisation in the Multi-Level European System

Edited by

Dia Anagnostou

Oñati International Series in Law and Society

A SERIES PUBLISHED FOR THE OÑATI INSTITUTE FOR THE SOCIOLOGY OF LAW

·HART·
PUBLISHING
OXFORD AND PORTLAND OREGON
2014

Published in the United Kingdom by Hart Publishing Ltd
16C Worcester Place, Oxford, OX1 2JW
Telephone: +44 (0)1865 517530
Fax: +44 (0)1865 510710
E-mail: mail@hartpub.co.uk
Website: http://www.hartpub.co.uk

Published in North America (US and Canada) by
Hart Publishing
c/o International Specialized Book Services
920 NE 58th Avenue, Suite 300
Portland, OR 97213-3786
USA
Tel: +1 503 287 3093 or toll-free: (1) 800 944 6190
Fax: +1 503 280 8832
E-mail: orders@isbs.com
Website: http://www.isbs.com

British Library Cataloguing in Publication Data
Data Available

ISBN: 978-1-84946-390-4

Typeset by Compuscript Ltd, Shannon
Printed and bound in Great Britain by
CPI Group (UK) Ltd, Croydon CR0 4YY

Acknowledgments

Books and research projects make their own journeys, which are grafted onto people's professional as well as personal trajectories. This book's journey has involved stays in, and support from, different institutions, where it was conceived, developed and prepared. The initial basis for it was laid at an exploratory workshop held in Athens in October 2010, which was funded by the European Science Foundation (ESF). Some of the participants in that workshop gathered again for a follow-up workshop at the International Institute for the Sociology of Law (IISL) at Oñati in the Basque Country in June 2012. The IISL not only funded the workshop but also provided an idyllic setting to convene and discuss rights and legal mobilisation in Europe. This book was conceived and planned during that workshop. I would like to thank both the ESF and the IISL for funding the two workshops on law, rights and legal mobilisation, without which this book would not have been possible.

On my part, work on this project, as well as on the book, extended over a period of time that in part coincided with my stay at the European University Institute (EUI) Department of Law as Marie Curie Research Fellow. I would like to specifically thank Bruno de Witte, who has provided me with invaluable advice and input at various stages of this project, besides himself participating in it. My work on the book continued beyond the EUI once I returned to my home institution, the Hellenic Foundation for European and Foreign Policy (ELIAMEP) in Athens. Even though ELIAMEP is not specifically linked with this book project, I owe it a lot for being such a hospitable and congenial place, supporting my research endeavours in the area of European integration in a variety of ways since 2004.

As a collective effort, this book has been completed through the ongoing, smooth and exemplary collaboration with the authors who wrote the chapters in it. They patiently worked with me to revise their contributions at different stages, without complaining about the repeated suggestions and requests for revisions. Thanks must also be extended to Hart publishers, and especially to Rachel Turner who has been my constant contact with Hart for her responsiveness and patience during the book's preparation. I would also like to thank the two anonymous reviewers who gave an initial positive assessment of the book proposal, and made useful suggestions that were taken on board.

Contents

Acknowledgments v
List of Contributors ix

1. Law and Rights' Claiming on behalf of Minorities in the Multi-level European System 1
Dia Anagnostou

Part I: Law, Rights and the Politics of Minorities in National Context

2. Linguistic Minorities in Western Europe: Expansion of Rights Without (Much) Litigation? 27
Bruno de Witte

3. Legal Mobilisation at the Subnational Level: The Case of Language Rights in the Spanish Autonomous Community of Navarre 53
Xabier Arzoz

4. Rights on the Left? Social Movements, Law and Lawyers after 1968 in France 79
Liora Israël

Part II: European Courts as Arenas for Legal Mobilisation

5. A Tool-box for Legal and Political Mobilisation in European Equality Law 105
Mark Dawson, Elise Muir and Monica Claes

6. European Courts and the Rights of Migrants and Asylum Seekers in Greece 129
Evangelia Psychogiopoulou

Part III: The Role of NGOs and Transnational Human Rights Networks

7. From Belfast to Diyarbakir and Grozny via Strasbourg: Transnational Legal Mobilisation Against State Violations in Contexts of Armed Conflict 157
Dia Anagnostou

8. Activists and Lawyers in the ECtHR: The Struggle for Gay Rights 181
Loveday Hodson

9. Law and Rights as Opportunity and Promise for Minorities in Europe? Concluding Observations and Research Agendas 205
Dia Anagnostou

Bibliography 219
Index 237

List of Contributors

Dia Anagnostou is Assistant Professor of Comparative Politics at Panteion University of Social and Political Sciences; and Senior Research Fellow at the Hellenic Foundation of European and Foreign Policy (ELIAMEP) in Athens.

Xabier Arzoz is Professor of Administrative and EU Law at the University of the Basque Country, Bilbao; and Legal Clerk at the Spanish Constitutional Court in Madrid (since March 2011).

Monica Claes is Professor of European and Comparative Constitutional Law, Law Faculty, Maastricht University.

Mark Dawson is Professor of European Law and Governance, Hertie School of Governance, Berlin.

Bruno de Witte is Professor of European Union Law at Maastricht University and at the European University Institute (Florence).

Loveday Hodson is Senior Lecturer in Law, University of Leicester.

Liora Israël is Associate Professor of Sociology, École des Hautes Études en Sciences Sociales (Paris, France), Centre Maurice Halbwachs (CNRS, ENS, EHESS).

Elise Muir is Associate Professor of European Law (Maastricht Centre for European Law) Faculty of Law, Maastricht University.

Evangelia Psychogiopoulou (Ph.D EU law) is a lawyer and Research Fellow at the Hellenic Foundation for European and Foreign Policy (ELIAMEP) in Athens; and legal officer at the Hellenic Ministry of Culture and Sports.

1

Law and Rights' Claiming on behalf of Minorities in the Multi-level European System

DIA ANAGNOSTOU

OVER THE PAST few decades, Europe has witnessed the emergence of a notable and far-reaching 'rights revolution'.[1] Law and rights have spread across different issue areas and domains of State action. They have become increasingly relevant and salient for the demands advanced by different social groups, but also for the political strategies that they craft. Individuals from, and at times on behalf of, various social and marginalised groups, invoke legal norms in front of courts—domestic, European and international—or quasi-judicial bodies to assert their rights and claim protection vis-à-vis State action or private parties. By resorting to litigation, individuals and social or interest groups have sought to claim and enforce rights emanating from national, European Union (EU) and international law. They have done so in areas encompassing environmental protection,[2] social rights,[3] and gender equality,[4] among others. With the exception of gender equality though,[5] much less attention has been paid to marginalised individuals and minorities who resort to courts, and to the implications of such legal action for democratic participation, State policy and social reform.

[1] C Epp, *The Rights Revolution* (Chicago, The University of Chicago Press, 1998); M de S-O-l'E Lasser, *Judicial Transformations: The Rights Revolution in the Courts of Europe* (Oxford, Oxford University Press, 2009).

[2] T Börzel, 'Participation Through Law Enforcement—The Case of the EU' (2006) 39 *Comparative Political Studies* 128.

[3] L Conant, 'Individuals, Courts and the Development of European Social Rights' (2006) 39 *Comparative Political Studies* 76.

[4] K Alter and J Vargas, 'Explaining Variation in the Use of European Litigation Strategies' (2000) 33 *Comparative Political Studies* 452.

[5] See D Anagnostou and S Millns, 'Gender Equality, Legal Mobilisation and Feminism in the European Multi-level System' (2013) 28 *Canadian Journal of Law and Society* 1.

In seeking to fill this gap, this book explores the causes and consequences of legal mobilisation by individuals from various kinds of minorities and vulnerable groups. Examples of minority-related legal action abound. Individuals from ethnic or religious minorities have claimed their right to practise their religion, to establish their own political parties or to receive social benefits, among other things. Alone or with the support of organisational actors, they have also sought protection against discriminatory treatment and from abuses by the police or security forces. In such cases, the failure of the State to take positive action to prevent discrimination or to punish those who are responsible for abuses has increasingly been recognised to undermine the protection of human rights. Immigrants or asylum seekers have also had recourse to national and European courts to claim a variety of social rights, to condemn conditions of detention or to suspend their expulsion to countries where they are likely to be at risk. Last but not least, gays and lesbians have resorted to courts to challenge differential ages of consent, the ban of homosexuality in the military or to gain recognition of their rights as same-sex partners.[6]

Through such legal actions, courts have become important venues where individual and collective actors seek redress, contest policies and pursue social reform. They are also arenas where some of the most sharply contested societal issues today, concerning sexuality, migration, ethnic diversity and social integration, are debated and fought. Individuals engaging in litigation though are usually not motivated by these larger issues but by the determination to seek a remedy for an injustice or wrong that they suffered. To be sure, the pristine association between judicial affirmation of rights, their actual realisation in practice and their contribution to social change—the so-called 'myth of rights'[7]—has been widely deconstructed and dispelled. Nonetheless, there is a strong enough core belief in the tendency and ability of courts to vindicate the weak.

Scholars have thoroughly questioned the tangible benefits of pursuing rights through courts for the individuals concerned, especially in light of the costs and the amount of resources that litigation drains. They also strongly disagree about the potential of judicially pronounced norms to independently instigate progressive social reforms, as well as legal and policy change.[8] Yet, a significant body of scholarship suggests that the effects of litigation and court rulings on legal reform, policy and social change

[6] See D Anagnostou and E Psychogiopoulou (eds), The European Court of Human Rights and the Rights of Marginalised Individuals and Minorities in National Context (Leiden, Martinus Nijhoff Publishers, 2010).

[7] See SA Scheingold, *The Politics of Rights—Lawyers, Public Policy and Political Change*, (New Haven, Yale University Press, 1974).

[8] G Rosenberg, *The Hollow Hope: Can Courts Bring About Social Change?* (Chicago, University of Chicago Press, 1991).

are profound and multifaceted, even if highly contingent, incremental and often mixed.[9]

While claiming rights on behalf of minorities through courts and quasi-judicial bodies is a well-known phenomenon in countries like the US and Canada, its significance has more recently gained momentum in Europe. The resort to law and legal processes to pursue individual justice or broader social reform has for a long time now been recognised as a form of political participation. Unlike lobbying the government or Parliament, litigation is unhampered by collective action problems and can therefore be more diffused.[10] It tends to emerge and grow in contexts where traditional avenues of electoral politics or interest group representation are inhospitable or closed to the needs, interests and demands of certain social and minority groups; their attainment of rights may be impeded by insufficient or absent majoritarian support.

When both domestic political *and* legal opportunities are limited or closed, individuals from minorities and vulnerable groups may view a transnational tribunal as an appealing alternative to national remedies, or indeed as the only avenue for seeking justice.[11] International courts' decisions may supply leverage and a way to publicise the treatment that minorities receive in particular countries,[12] thereby bringing pressure to bear upon national governments. The resort of vulnerable and marginalised individuals and groups to legal action though is not a mundane but a notable phenomenon, considering that such individuals often have limited access to the substantial resources that going to court requires.[13]

Why and under what conditions then, are individual and social actors from various kinds of minorities and vulnerable groups likely to claim their rights through courts? And what are the consequences of such legal action for law, policy and social reform? This book explores these broad questions by primarily focusing on courts as central, even if not exclusive, venues where rights mobilisation takes place. The contributions specifically inquire into the extent and ways in which legal processes and entitlements

[9] MV Tushnet, 'Litigation Campaigns and the Search for Constitutional Rules' (2004) 6 *Journal of Appellate Practice & Process* 101–11. From a different constitutive perspective on the impact of litigation and court rulings, see M McCann, *Rights At Work* (Chicago, University of Chicago Press, 1994).

[10] F Kahn Zemans, 'Legal Mobilization: The Neglected Role of the Law in the Political System' (1983) 77 *American Political Science Review* 690, 691–93; J Grossman and A Sarat, 'Litigation in the Federal Courts: A Comparative Perspective' (1975) 9 *Law and Society Review* 321, 375.

[11] K Sikkink, 'Patterns of Dynamic Multilevel Governance and the Insider–Outsider Coalition' in D della Porta and S Tarrow (eds), *Transnational Protest and Global Activism* (Lanham, MD, Rowman & Littlefield Publishers, 2005) 157–58.

[12] L Hodson, *NGOs and the Struggle for Human Rights in Europe* (Oxford, Hart Publishing, 2010) 81.

[13] Conant (n 3) 77; M Galanter, 'Why the "Haves" Come out Ahead: Speculations on the Limits of Legal Change' (1974) 9 *Law & Society Review* 95.

are mobilised in national and European courts by less privileged social actors, who seek to advance their demands and rights and to pursue social change. They probe into the factors that motivate individual and organisational actors to engage in legal battles (or to refrain from doing so), the (shifting) relationships and dynamics between lawyers and activists, as well as the political and social mobilisation that takes place alongside or 'in the shadow of' resorting to courts.

Legal mobilisation refers to the invocation of legal rules and conventions (such as rights, constitutional provisions), both substantive and procedural, as well as formal processes, by individual or collective actors in courts and quasi-judicial bodies. The purpose is to gain access to various social goods, and more broadly to regulate, order, legitimate or delimit relations between citizens and the State, as well as relationships between private parties. Besides invoking rights before courts, legal mobilisation can also encompass the use of and appeal to legal entitlements in political discourse and social action to advocate and support specific demands, in the context of advocacy campaigns or in lobbying and pressuring the government. This volume though mainly focuses on litigation. Rights' claiming in courts is a central avenue for enforcing or contesting the application of 'law on the books' in specific sectors, and in established practices and areas of action. At the same time, most of the contributions in this volume explore litigation in tandem with, and as part of, broader frames of social and political action, in which rights' claiming is variably incorporated; in this sense, they explore both litigation and legal mobilisation.

A significant amount of minority-related litigation is strategic: it invokes rights in the legal and judicial system in order to pressure for broader social change. While the individual's interest may be an objective too, legal action in this sense is centrally interested in law and policy reform, with case selection aimed at bringing to the surface broader problems. Besides seeking to challenge existing laws and policies, strategic litigation can have less ambitious but equally important goals such as to clarify laws, to promote human rights consciousness and public attitude change, to document injustices, or to empower vulnerable groups and pressure governments for change. While rights are often mobilised in pursuit of reformist goals, they can also be appealed to in courts by actors to resist progressive social change.

The 'rights revolution' in Europe is closely linked with the emergence of a multi-level system of fundamental rights norms and (quasi-) judicial institutions existing at different levels of law and government. A variety of fundamental and human rights frames at the European and international levels exists alongside bills of rights enshrined in national constitutions. Apart from strongly entrenched principles of civil and political rights, these norms also comprise a contested array of social and cultural rights, and an old but also newly emergent, rich body of equality and anti-discrimination law. While they do not amount to minority rights as such, national and

European courts have progressively (re)interpreted existing or newly established norms to respond to claims raised by individuals from ethnic, racial, sexual or religious minorities and other vulnerable groups. They have done so amidst growing processes of legal mobilisation.

This volume explores legal mobilisation in the context of the multi-level European system of rights protection. It comprises at least three legal-judicial systems and sources of norms at the national, subnational and European levels: constitutional norms that are enforced by national higher and/or constitutional courts, the EU law and the Charter of Fundamental Rights (CFR) to be upheld by national courts and the Court of Justice of the EU (CJEU) in areas linked to the application of EU law; and the European Convention on Human Rights (ECHR or Convention) interpreted by the European Court of Human Rights (ECtHR) but also by national courts through its incorporation domestically. By adopting the CFR and foreseeing the accession of the EU to the ECHR, the Lisbon Treaty in 2008 has further bolstered the arsenal of EU- and ECHR-derived rights available to individuals. Both systems form an 'overarching "constitutional" structure, comprised of fundamental rights and the shared authority of judges to adjudicate individual claims'.[14]

The multi-level structure is further shaped by the processes of federalisation and decentralisation within states, where variable and asymmetrical frames of rights protection may exist.[15] Competence in and jurisdiction over different areas of policy and rights get entangled with contested issues of devolution and national/ethnic or regional identity. Conflicts arise as to which level of government should have jurisdiction over areas in which rights issues figure prominently. Comprising a variety of normative, legal and judicial structures above and below the State, this multi-level European frame distinctly shapes the possibilities and constraints for individuals who selectively invoke norms and engage judges on questions of rights, social inclusion and justice.

The expansion of legal mobilisation of rights is inseparably linked with the growth of judicial power in Europe. Both have far-reaching implications for democratic participation and social and institutional reform, as well as the nature of the policy process in Europe.[16] The pursuit of rights through courts at the national or supranational level can create a space for discourse and social mobilisation, and in this way, it can influence the current or future policy agenda. This is especially significant at the EU level, where it

[14] A Stone Sweet, 'A Cosmopolitan Legal Order: Constitutional Pluralism and Rights Adjudication in Europe' (2012) 1 *Global Constitutionalism* 53, 55.

[15] M Shapiro and A Stone Sweet, 'The New Constitutional Politics of Europe' (1994) 26 *Comparative Political Studies* 397, 402.

[16] DR Kelemen, 'Eurolegalism and Democracy' (2012) 50 *Journal of Common Market Studies* 55–71. See also the special issue of *Comparative Political Studies* (2006) 39 on Courts, Democracy and Governance.

can broaden the space for the participation of citizens, civil society actors and interest groups, and their influence over policy making. Litigation and legal mobilisation on the part of individuals and civil society, including on the part of vulnerable groups, has contributed to the expansion of rights domestically, but also beyond the national community.[17] Such mobilisation has arguably also been instrumental in transforming the EC/EU from an international treaty governing economic cooperation, as it was originally, to a quasi-constitutional polity granting fundamental rights to individuals.[18] All together, litigation and legal mobilisation have the potential to shift the balance of power between citizens, governments and organisations of regional and international governance.[19]

The existence of judicially enforceable rights emanating from the EU and the ECHR, which provide a check on State actions, can also be seen as a legal and institutional frame for post-national citizenship in Europe.[20] By extending the application of human rights into claims raised by minorities, immigrants and asylum seekers, the ECtHR, for instance, has become a transnational legal system where the fundamental rights of every person deserve protection without regard to nationality or citizenship.[21]

The first part of this chapter describes the multi-level legal system and the judicial structures in Europe, in which individuals from minorities and vulnerable groups take recourse. By reviewing existing scholarship related to the North American and European integration context, the second part identifies and discusses analytical perspectives and research issues to guide the study of litigation and legal mobilisation in Europe. The last part of the chapter defines the purpose and approach of this volume and provides an overview of the contributions.

I. RIGHTS, COURTS AND JUDICIAL REVIEW: THE EUROPEAN CONTEXT

Over the past 20 years, a number of developments have contributed to a growing phenomenon of rights' claiming through courts in Europe, including on the part of individuals from minorities and vulnerable groups. In the first place, many countries have bolstered judicial review of legislation or public acts by establishing constitutional courts with extensive rights

[17] Conant (n 3) 95.

[18] RA Cichowski, *The European Court and Civil Society* (Cambridge, Cambridge University Press, 2007).

[19] RA Cichowski, 'Introduction. Courts, Democracy, and Governance' (2006) 39 *Comparative Political Studies* 3, 4.

[20] Y Nuhoglu Soysal, *Limits of Citizenship—Migrants and Postnational Membership in Europe* (Chicago, University of Chicago Press, 1994).

[21] Stone Sweet (n 14) 53.

jurisdiction. This development has substantially augmented the role and influence of courts and judges in politics and policy making.[22] Rights issues have increasingly come to dominate the cases and complaints that are reviewed by constitutional courts in Europe, as levels of rights-related litigation have grown over time.[23] The increasing salience of rights review in continental Europe has gone hand in hand with instances of judicial activism, both of which are considered among 'the most significant developments of the last decades'.[24] They are arguably bound up with the efforts of judges to counter charges of legislative usurpation by relying on constitutional rights.[25] At the same time, judicial activism is both a cause and a consequence of the fact that law and rights are increasingly mobilised by individual and social actors.

A variety of constitutional rights and principles such as equality, family life, respect for one's personality or education and other social rights, among others, can be claimed by individuals from ethnic-racial or sexual minorities before domestic courts. The nature and scope of such rights and their judicial protection vary significantly across different legal systems and constitutional traditions. For example, in Poland, the constitutional definition of monogamous heterosexual marriage spills over into the right of family life, which as a result, is less extensively protected than under Article 8 ECHR. The rights of ethnic, linguistic and cultural minorities receive greater protection in countries like Hungary, Belgium and the Czech Republic.[26] Constitutional and legal guarantees of equality and non-discrimination also display a great deal of diversity across states, notwithstanding a process of convergence evidenced since the 1990s. Differences exist as to how comprehensive the legal protection in place is, whether it addresses both direct and indirect discrimination, whether it includes provisions concerning positive action, the breadth of social grounds covered and the exceptions to the prohibition of discrimination that are recognised, among other things.[27]

[22] A Stone Sweet, 'The Birth and Development of Abstract Review in Western Europe: Constitutional Courts and Policy-making in Western Europe' (1990) 19(1) *Policy Studies Journal* 81; Shapiro and Stone Sweet (n 15) 410.

[23] R Cichowski and A Stone Sweet, 'Participation, Representative Democracy and the Courts' in B E Cain, RJ Dalton and S Scarrow (eds), *Democracy Transformed? Expanding Political Opportunities in Advanced Industrial Democracies* (Oxford, Oxford University Press, 2003).

[24] C Guarnieri, 'Courts and marginalized groups: Perspectives from Continental Europe' (2007) 5(2) *International Journal of Constitutional Law* 187, 199.

[25] Shapiro and Stone Sweet (n 15) 417.

[26] LFM Besselink, 'The Protection of Fundamental Rights post-Lisbon—The Interaction between the EU Charter of Fundamental Rights, the European Convention on Human Rights (ECHR) and National Constitutions', available at www.fide2012.eu/index.php?doc_id=94, accessed 4 July 2013.

[27] M Bell, *Anti-Discrimination Law and the European Union* (Oxford, Oxford University Press, 2002), see Chapter 6.

The above-mentioned trend of judicial activism has emerged in tandem with a more proactive and favourable approach of judiciaries in some cases, in regard to the rights and interests of minorities and marginalised groups. Guarnieri describes the emergence of progressive associations of judges in countries like Spain, Italy, France and Portugal, among others, which organise at the European level. Influenced by socialist and leftist policies, these associations have a professed mission to protect fundamental rights, advance rule of law, and defend fundamental rights, including those of minorities, immigrants and those who are most deprived. The defence of immigrants' rights in particular, has become one of the main foci of judicial activism, especially among the judiciary's left-leaning contingents, in countries like France, Italy and Germany.[28] Some argue that expansive interpretations of rights by high courts are the result of strong inter-institutional competition and cooperation in the multi-level European system that leads judges to embrace the increasingly powerful fundamental rights idiom.[29]

Instances of judicial activism in various countries though should not leave the impression that higher and constitutional courts are reliable defenders of rights claimed by minorities, as studies on South-East European countries show.[30] In fact, constitutional courts are not always attentive to, and ready to stand on the side of, minorities, particularly if judiciaries lack autonomy and the judges who sit on them lack tenure.[31] In conditions of political and social dependence, judges are inclined to refrain from challenging State policy and tend to go along with the views and sentiments of the majority. For example, the constitutional courts of Central and East Europe that were established after the transition to democracy have rarely defended the rights of minorities. The readiness of constitutional or supreme courts to endorse minority-related claims, and the extent to which they do so, vary across countries and possibly across issues or over time.[32]

While national constitutions and higher or constitutional courts define the primary normative and judicial structures for legal action, a strong impetus for bolstering the legal norms and protection of minorities and vulnerable groups has come from the international and supranational arenas. To be sure, neither the EU law nor the ECHR contain minority rights, and they never made an explicit commitment to protect minority rights, which are not identical to human rights. The distinction between human rights as

[28] Guarnieri (n 24) 200–01; see also C Joppke and E Marzal, 'The New Constitutionalism and Immigrant Rights: The Case of the French Conseil Constitutionnel' (2004) 43 *European Journal of Political Research* 823.

[29] De S-O-l'E Lasser (n 1).

[30] D Anagnostou and Y Grozev, 'Human Rights Litigation and Restrictive State Implementation of Strasbourg Court Judgments: The Case of Ethnic Minorities from Southeast Europe' (2010) 16 *European Public Law* 401.

[31] Guarnieri (n 24) 210.

[32] W Sadurski, *Rights Before Courts* (Dordrecht, Springer, 2008) 59–61.

basic individual entitlements for all, and minority rights as special rights recognised for the exclusive benefit of a group is all too well known.[33] Yet, individuals belonging to minorities have claimed a significant degree of protection through appeal to human rights.[34] For example, in the frame of the ECHR, individuals belonging to minorities cannot be excluded from running for or holding political office because of unjustified language requirements. Yet, there is no right to use a minority language in the activities of elected bodies, unless there are a substantial number of speakers who make it necessary to provide for its use.[35]

Over the past 20 years, the ECtHR has increasingly applied and interpreted Convention principles to address broader rights claims and demands of minorities in the frame of individual petitions. And minority communities have increasingly employed individual litigation to address broader collective concerns, such as political participation, religious freedom and cultural pluralism, which are framed in reference to Convention rights. The ECHR and the Strasbourg Court have evolved into a unique adjudicatory mechanism based on the right of individuals to bring complaints against states once they exhaust domestic remedies. Several changes in the rules of the Court since the 1980s have bolstered the standing of individual applicants and opened up the judicial review process to intervention by third parties.[36] Along with the accession of nearly 20 new states from Central-East, South-East Europe and the former Soviet Union, as well as the adoption of Protocol 11, which rendered acceptance for individual petition mandatory for all states, they expanded and broadened access to the Strasbourg Court. All these changes paved the way for an unprecedented rise in litigation levels, including on the part of various kinds of minorities and vulnerable groups.[37]

Convention rules of standing restrict access for collective and organisational actors in the ECtHR. Article 34 ECHR in particular, gives the right to file a petition to 'any person, non-governmental organisation or group of individuals claiming to be the victim of a violation' of one of the

[33] G Pentassuglia, 'Minority Rights, Human Rights: A Review of Basic Concepts, Entitlements and Implementation Procedures under International Law' in *Mechanisms for the Implementation of Minority Rights* (Strasbourg, Council of Europe Publishing, 2004).

[34] P Thornberry and M Amor Martin Estebanez, *Minority Rights in Europe* (Strasbourg, Council of Europe Publishing, 2004) 14.

[35] Fernand de Varennes, 'Using the ECtHR to Protect the Rights of Minorities' in *Mechanisms for the Implementation of Minority Rights* (n 33) 101–02.

[36] See E Bates, The Evolution of the European Convention on Human Rights: From Its Inception to the Creation of a Permanent Court of Human Rights (Oxford, Oxford University Press, 2010) 403–04, and especially chapter 3 of the book. See also L Bartholomeusz, 'The Amicus Curiae before International Courts and Tribunals' (2005) 5 *Non-State Actors and International Law* 209, 234.

[37] See D Anagnostou, *The European Court of Human Rights: Implementing Strasbourg's Judgments on Domestic Policy* (Edinburgh, Edinburgh University Press, 2013), especially part II of the book.

Convention rights. However, groups and organisations can bring claims to the ECtHR only as long as they can show that they are victims in their own right of the law or practice that they challenge.[38] Unlike individuals and legal persons (trade unions, religious organisations, political parties, among others), minority groups cannot meet the so-called 'victimisation' requirement. They cannot show that they consist of identified persons, each of whom has authorised the lodging of an application in the Court, and has been affected by the violation claimed. As is rightly pointed out, unlike for legal persons, 'the modes of membership of [minority] groups are not legally organised and are therefore neither identifiable nor verifiable for the purpose of ascertaining whether the mode of affiliation is destructive of freedom or discriminatory'.[39]

Despite such constraints in standing for collective actors, individual litigation in the ECtHR has often addressed broader collective or structural issues pertaining to minorities, by benefiting from support by minority associations and by NGOs. Most notably, in its case law over the past 10 years, the ECtHR has incrementally expanded the nature and scope of protection against discrimination, largely in response to strategic litigation by civil society actors. Besides assisting and supporting individual victims to bring cases before the Strasbourg Court, such actors have persisted in documenting the widespread and often structural nature of racism and discrimination, for example in the instances of ill treatment of Roma by the police and racial segregation in the education system.[40]

Until relatively recently, the Court was disinclined or unwilling in its case law to move beyond a narrow conception of discrimination that dwells upon difference in treatment between analogously placed persons or situations. On top of a weak and auxiliary provision prohibiting discrimination (Article 14 ECHR),[41] the ECtHR maintained a very high standard of proof 'beyond reasonable doubt', rendering it extremely difficult to ascertain discriminatory treatment. In the broader European and EU context, where anti-discrimination norms have proliferated in the past decade or so, and in the context of cases originating in strategic litigation, a new approach has been emerging in the ECtHR's case law in cases concerning individuals who

[38] G Gilbert, 'The Burgeoning Minority Jurisprudence of the ECtHR (2002) 24 *Human Rights Quarterly* 736, 739–40.

[39] On this issue in regard to legal persons, see *Chassagnou and others v France* App nos 25088/94, 28331/95 and 28443/95 (ECtHR, 29 April 1999). See F Edel, *The Prohibition of Discrimination under the ECHR*, Human Rights files no 22 (Strasbourg, Council of Europe Publishing, 2010) 14–15.

[40] JA Goldston, 'The Struggle for Roma Rights: Arguments that Have Worked' (2010) 32 *Human Rights Quarterly* 311.

[41] It must be invoked jointly with another provision in the ambit of the ECHR. The adoption of Protocol 12 has now established a free-standing clause of anti-discrimination. It entered into force in 2005 with the ratification by 10 states, but to date, only 18 states have ratified it.

are homosexuals or members of vulnerable minorities such as the Roma.[42] This new approach exhibits concern over systematic and structural inequalities and for the first time acknowledges indirect discrimination.[43]

Fundamental rights of relevance to minorities and vulnerable groups have also developed in the frame of the EU. Since the 1960s and 1970s, the doctrine of direct effect of EU law established by the CJEU has allowed individuals to plead entitlements originating in the treaties before domestic courts. The doctrine of supremacy further requires national judges to ultimately refer and defer to EU law. Over time, these two principles formed the seedbed for a new set of rights to be invoked and enforced by individuals in national courts and in the CJEU. Such rights are linked not only to economic interests, but also to broader public interests that encompass environmental protection, anti-discrimination and gender equality. Originally viewing discriminations on grounds of nationality and unequal pay between men and women as barriers to the freedom of movement and the common market, the CJEU established justiciable rights prohibiting discrimination on the basis of nationality and gender.[44]

Over time, especially after the Amsterdam Treaty,[45] the CJEU elaborated the principle of equality and non-discrimination by extending it on other grounds, such as race/ethnicity, religion, sexual orientation and disability. In 2000 the EU adopted two directives against discrimination, which marked a turning point in the existing arsenal of legal instruments: the Racial Equality Directive (RED), which prohibits discrimination based on racial or ethnic origin in employment and occupation, social protection, education, and access to goods and services (including housing);[46] and the Framework Directive (FD), which prohibits direct and indirect discrimination based on religion or belief, disability, age or sexual orientation.[47]

[42] K Boyle, 'Article 14 Bites at Last' (2006) 5 *EHRAC Bulletin* 1. Available at http://ehracmos.memo.ru/files/bulletin-en-5.pdf, accessed 4 July 2013; see also R O'Connell, 'Cinderella Comes to the Ball: Article 14 and the Right to Non-discrimination in the ECHR' (2009) 29(2) *Legal Studies* 211, 224–25.

[43] This new approach gradually evolved from the late 1990s onwards. Through cases, such as *Assenov v Bulgaria* App no 24760/94 (ECtHR, 28 October 1998), *Velikova v Bulgaria* App no 41488/98 (ECtHR, 18 May 2000), *Anguelova v Bulgaria* App no 38361/97 (ECtHR, 13 June 2002) and *Nachova v Bulgaria* App nos 43577/98 and 43579/98 (ECtHR, 26 February 2004), the ECtHR established violation of Article 14 on procedural grounds (for lack of an effective investigation) and then on substantive grounds (that police violence was racially motivated). See also O'Connell (n 42) 228.

[44] See the special issues on EU gender equality law of *Feminist Legal Studies* (2002) 10 and the *European Law Journal* (2007) 13.

[45] The Amsterdam Treaty also committed the EU to take appropriate action to combat discrimination based on sex, racial or ethnic origin, religion or belief, disability, age or sexual discrimination (EC Treaty, Article 13).

[46] Council Directive 2000/43/EC of 29 June 2000 implementing the principle of equal treatment between persons irrespective of racial or ethnic origin.

[47] Council Directive 2000/78/EC of 27 November 2000 establishing a general framework for equal treatment in employment and occupation.

While they incorporated many of the principles developed by the CJEU over the years in regard to gender equality, the above directives were innovative in their emphasis on remedies and enforcement with a view to facilitating their practical use. In particular, the RED provides organisations with a legitimate interest the possibility to bring enforcement actions on behalf of or in support of complainants; it allows for shifting the burden of proof to the respondent state when facts establish prima facie discrimination; and finally, it obliges Member States to designate or establish specialised bodies for the promotion of equal treatment.[48] All together, the EU directives require more specific legislative protection than that conferred either by international instruments or by national constitutional guarantees. They have also established an autonomous body of anti-discrimination legislation out of scattered related provisions that existed in various sectors (ie labour, social security, etc) across most Member States.

The bulk of litigation comes to the Luxembourg Court through the preliminary reference procedure: national judges can ask the CJEU for a preliminary ruling when there is uncertainty concerning the proper interpretation of a national law or practice in relation to EU law.[49] Directing such a request is largely at the discretion of the domestic judges deliberating on a case or issue that raises a potential conflict with EU law. Apart from sex equality, litigation invoking the EU anti-discrimination directives has so far been limited at the CJEU, despite the efforts of several legal and experts' networks to promote strategic litigation. Until recently, there had not been more than a handful of cases on discrimination on the basis of religion, disability and sexual orientation under the FD.[50] In the case of vulnerable ethnic minorities, it has been argued that marginalised individuals from such minorities may lack the resources and information to seek remedies against discrimination via national and EU courts.[51] In the field of social policy, victims of discrimination can also have recourse, often with the support of an NGO, to the European Social Charter which is now effectively enforced through the collective complaints system before the European Social Rights Committee (ESRC) of the Council of Europe (CoE).

Besides taking recourse to European courts and quasi-judicial bodies, directly or indirectly, individuals and other social actors invoke and settle rights claims emanating from supranational and international legal sources

[48] Bell, Anti-Discrimination Law and the EU (n 27).

[49] S Douglas-Scott, 'The European Union and Human Rights after the Treaty of Lisbon' (2011) 11 *Human Rights Law Review* 645, 647.

[50] G de Búrca, 'Stumbling into Experimentalism: The EU Anti-Discrimination Regime' in C Sabel and J Zeitlin (eds), *Experimentalist Governance in the EU* (Oxford, Oxford University Press, 2010) 215–31.

[51] M Dawson and E Muir, 'Individual, Institutional and Collective Vigilance in Protecting Fundamental Rights in the EU: Lessons from the Roma' (2011) 48 *Common Market Law Review* 751.

in front of domestic courts. In the light of the principles of supremacy and direct effect, national judges are obliged to follow EU law and the case law of the CJEU and to remove or amend national law or policies that conflict with the former. In fact, most of the legal claims related to EU law are settled in domestic courts. However, there has been limited empirical and comparative research that demonstrates the extent and ways in which EU law influences domestic legal mobilisation patterns, as well as the approach of national judges more broadly, on questions related to minorities and vulnerable groups.

By expanding the scope of legal protection and extending to situations of indirect discrimination, the anti-discrimination directives described above are arguably likely to increase litigation and augment the role of courts, yet it is still too early to verify this.[52] Drawing on impressionistic evidence, others though argue that the retrospective as opposed to preventive nature of the directives, the introduction of new tools and concepts that are thoroughly unfamiliar to judges in lower courts, entrenched national legal cultures, as well as the inability to engage in class action in Europe, all constrain their legal mobilisation in national courts. Therefore, the ability of the directives to provide individual remedies and especially to redress the structural causes of inequality is questioned and remains to be seen.[53] While admitting that in principle the transposition of EU anti-discrimination directives enhances opportunities for litigation and activism, some scholars see this as being heavily dependent on the domestic capacity of civil society.[54]

Through their incorporation into domestic law, regional and international human rights can also be claimed in front of national courts, especially in countries that lack equivalent domestic legislation. For example, the International Convention on the Elimination of Racial Discrimination (ICERD) may be invoked by individuals in front of national courts. The incorporation of the ECHR in the domestic legal and constitutional order of nearly all contracting states also enables individuals to invoke it before domestic courts, which are obliged to enforce it. Research shows that the Convention has over time gained increasing traction and acceptance among national judges, especially among higher courts, which have emulated and engaged in a kind of rights review based on the principle of proportionality characteristic of common law systems and the Strasbourg Court.[55]

52 R Evans Case and TE Givens, 'Re-engineering Legal Opportunity Structures in the European Union? The Starting Line Group and the Politics of the Racial Equality Directive' (2010) 48(2) *Journal of Common Market Studies* 222.

53 V Guiraudon, 'Equality in the Making: Implementing European Non-discrimination Law' (2009) 13 *Citizenship Studies* 527.

54 Ibid 527–49; see also V Amireaux and V Guiraudon, 'Discrimination in Comparative Perspective' (2010) 53 *American Behavioral Scientist* 1691–714.

55 H Keller and A Stone Sweet (eds), *A Europe of Rights—The Reception of the ECHR in National Legal Systems* (Cambridge, Cambridge University Press, 2008).

National judicial interpretations overall closely attend to the Convention and the case law of the Strasbourg Court.[56] In exploring the attitudes of higher and constitutional court judges in France, Germany and Spain, Krisch unravels how they constantly seek to balance between Convention norms and national constitutional prerogatives, instead of asserting the latter over the former. Over time, the openness and flexibility characterising judicial attitudes has contributed to closely allying national approaches with Convention norms while also empowering and consolidating the authority of domestic judges.[57]

Concerning marginalised groups, it has been argued that while courts have been at the forefront in the expansion of migrants' rights domestically, the norms from which they draw emanate from domestic, rather than European or international, legal sources.[58] This, however, goes against substantial literature demonstrating the extensive infiltration of ECHR norms and case law domestically, as well as the dense processes of inter-judicial interaction and dialogue taking place in the context of European integration.[59] By taking these processes into account, constitutional courts must be seen to act more like conduits rather than shields: they often 'import', transmit and translate European and international norms into 'national constitutional paths', overcoming domestic political constraints and consolidating their authority. This 'conduit model' of constitutional courts arguably depicts accurately the approach of the Estonian constitutional court in its case law on minority language rights in the late 1990s.[60] The question whether legal sources of rights expansions are domestic or emanate beyond the State therefore appears out of place in light of the open, dense and pluralist interactions and influences among national, supranational and international judiciaries in Europe. Instead, close attention must be paid specifically to the extent and ways in which supranational and international norms influence constitutional and national judicial approaches to the rights of minorities and marginalised groups.

In addition to the legally binding and judicially enforced frames at the national, supranational and international level, the protection of the rights of minorities also comprises a variety of 'soft' law norms and related monitoring mechanisms. In the 1990s, the Council of Europe responded to ethnic tensions, primarily but not only in post-communist

[56] D Anagnostou, 'Politics, Courts and Society in the Domestic Implementation and Practice of the ECtHR's Case Law' in Anagnostou (n 37).

[57] N Krisch, 'The Open Architecture of European Human Rights Law' (2007) LSE Law, Society and Economy Working Papers 11.

[58] Joppke and Marzal (n 28).

[59] See for example the volume edited by G Martinico and O Pollicino, *The National Judicial Treatment of the ECHR and EU Laws* (Groningen, Europa Law Publishing, 2010).

[60] N Maveety and A Grosskopf, '"Constrained" Constitutional Courts as Conduits for Democratic Consolidation' (2004) 38 *Law and Society Review* 463.

Central, East and South-East Europe (CESE), by adopting two treaties: the European Charter for Regional and Minority Languages (ECRML) and the Framework Convention for the Protection of National Minorities (FCPNM or Framework Convention), both of which entered into force in 1998. The Framework Convention, adopted after an additional protocol to the ECHR on minority rights was rejected by states, has as its goal the 'protection of the rights of *individuals belonging to* a minority' who 'may exercise their rights individually and in community with others'.[61]

Both the FCPNM and the ECRML are 'soft' law instruments containing programme-type provisions that the contracting states vow to pursue; neither creates enforceable rights for minorities.[62] The principles and rights contained in the FCPNM may be invoked to legitimate minority claims before domestic or European courts, but national authorities are not obliged to directly apply these principles before their administrative and judicial authorities.[63] Nonetheless, the proliferation of 'soft' law standards and monitoring mechanisms of minority protection at the European level possibly influenced minorities to develop international strategies of action and to frame their demands and grievances in the language of rights.

II. MOBILISING LAW AND RIGHTS IN THE MULTI-LEVEL EUROPEAN SYSTEM: ANALYTICAL AND SCHOLARLY PERSPECTIVES

Having provided an overview of the multi-level legal and judicial system in Europe by relating it to the issues concerning minorities and marginalised social groups, we now turn to exploring the factors that influence and shape legal mobilisation. In the socio-legal (and largely Anglo-American) scholarly tradition, law and rights are predominantly understood as resources that are mobilised by individual and collective actors.[64] Being subject to multiple and changing interpretations, legal norms influence political opportunities by enabling or constraining the goals, actions and strategies of social actors. Legal mobilisation and litigation are often part of the repertoire of actions employed by social movement organisations, largely in tandem with public campaigns or broader political strategies.[65] In so far as legal action is one

[61] Emphasis added. Framework Convention for the Protection of National Minorities. See commentary and paragraphs 31 and 37 of the Framework Convention.

[62] F Benoit-Rohmer and H Hardeman, *The Minority Question in Europe: Towards the Creation of a Coherent European Regime* (Brussels, Centre for European Policy Studies, 1994).

[63] R Hofmann, 'The Framework Convention for the Protection of National Minorities: an Introduction' in M Weller (ed), *The Rights of Minorities in Europe* (Oxford, Oxford University Press, 2005) 5.

[64] For a classic analysis of rights in this tradition, see Scheingold (n 7).

[65] P Burstein, 'Legal Mobilization as a Social Movement Tactic: The Struggle for Equal Employment Opportunity' (1991) 96 *American Journal of Sociology* 1201, 1204.

among a wider array of strategies, it is evidently shaped by the broader political environment, and the openness or closure of alternative forms of action, such as lobbying Parliament, or joining forces with allies to pressure the government.[66] Formal but also informal domestic institutions and structures may offer to social actors various access points for influencing policy and pursuing demands, in comparison to which legal and judicial venues may appear propitious or conversely ineffective.

The multi-level legal system in Europe necessitates a reconceptualisation of legal opportunity structures (LOS) shaping litigation both at the national level and at the supranational and international levels. Conceptualised by analogy to the political opportunity structure (POS) approaches in the study of social movements, mainly in reference to national systems, LOS refers to a variety of conditions and characteristics that function as incentives or as constraints, prompting individuals or groups to resort to courts, or conversely discouraging them from doing so. It encompasses both structural features of a legal system (rules and institutions) but also contingent factors, such as alliances with political parties, other social groups and supporters, which are more transient and shifting.[67] At a minimum, the opportunity to litigate requires the existence of a judicially enforceable right of sufficient clarity, along with a court with authoritative jurisdiction over the respective domain or issue.[68] The extent to which rules and rights become more formalised and judicially enforceable is especially important, particularly in attracting litigation in a supranational or international court.[69]

Andersen identifies three main dimensions of LOS: access to formal institutional structure, availability of allies, and the configuration of power with respect to relevant issues/challengers.[70] In the first place, legal rules of standing that define who has access to courts influence the decision of individuals or social activists who hope to litigate and mobilise the law in court.[71] Restrictive rules of standing can limit the ability of individuals or groups to go to court, while the nature of the claims raised may also affect whether a litigant has standing.[72] Rules of access and standing also influence individual and group perceptions about how opportune and/or effective it is to litigate in supranational and international courts.[73] In regard to these courts, judicial institutions and rules that maintain the gate-keeping

[66] C Hilson, 'New Social Movements: the Role of Legal Opportunity' (2002) 9 *Journal of European Public Policy* 238–55.

[67] Ibid 242.

[68] Conant (n 3) 79.

[69] Cichowski (n 19) 10.

[70] EA Andersen, *Out of the Closets and Into the Courts—Legal Opportunity Structure and Gay Rights Litigation* (Ann Arbor, University of Michigan Press, 2006) 7.

[71] Ibid 9; see also Cichowski (n 3) 8.

[72] Andersen (n 70) 205.

[73] RA Cichowski, 'Courts, Rights and Democratic Participation' (2006) 39(1) *Comparative Political Studies* 50, 56.

role of states in access and enforceability are likely to limit the willingness to engage in legal action.[74] Last but not least, the ability and willingness to litigate and to access the judicial system is also influenced substantially by the costs involved in going to court, and the availability of legal aid to assist litigators with paying the legal fees and other expenses.[75]

In principle, the existence of enforceable legal norms, and the rules defining standing in and access to supranational and international courts are similar for prospective litigants across states. In practice though, they are often critically mediated and therefore differentially shaped by the national legal and judicial system where a litigant is situated. In regard to the ECtHR for example, the requirement for exhausting domestic remedies presupposes that an applicant has been able to access and go through the national legal and judicial system before being eligible to petition the Strasbourg Court. Concerning individual access to the CJEU, requesting a preliminary reference from Luxembourg varies across (and even within) states. It is arguably defined by legal culture and variable judicial attitudes prevailing across Member States, as well as in different parts of a national court system, which may also be influenced by inter-court dynamics and antagonisms, as studies have shown.[76] Other domestic factors and influences may be at play, but we lack country-based and comparative case studies that explore how domestic legal, judicial, institutional and social factors variably influence and distinctly shape patterns of legal mobilisation in the supranational and international arenas.

Apart from formal access, legal opportunities in national, supranational or international courts are shaped by judicial precedent and the extent to which a court is receptive or at least sympathetic to a particular set of claims raised before it. The scope and content of norms and most importantly of how these have been interpreted by judges in existing case law (judicial precedent) decisively shape the LOS: they influence the kinds of claims that can be raised and their persuasiveness.[77] Judicial precedent though is not curved in stone as is well known. In reviewing cases before them, international and EU judges may address a dispute in ways that expand the scope and meaning of treaty rights to new issues and situations.[78] Courts like the one in Strasbourg have devised principles, such as the Convention as

[74] R Keohane, A Moravscik and A-M Slaughter, 'Legalized Dispute Resolution: Interstate and Transnational' (2000) 54 *International Organization* 457.

[75] G De Fazio, 'Legal Opportunity Structure and Social Movement Strategy in Northern Ireland and Southern United States' (2012) 53 *International Journal of Comparative Sociology* 3, 6.

[76] C Kilpatrick, 'Gender Equality: A Fundamental Dialogue' in S Sciarra (ed), *Labour Law in the Courts—National Judges and the ECJ* (Oxford, Hart Publishing, 2001) 31–130; see also K Alter, *The European Court's Political Power: Selected Essays* (Oxford, Oxford University Press, 2009).

[77] De Fazio (n 75) 7; Andersen (n 70) 11–13.

[78] Cichowski (n 18) 6.

a 'living instrument' and its evolutive interpretation, which enable them to rethink and reformulate their interpretations in the light of social change. Therefore the receptivity of judges, but also of jurists more generally, to a legal claim may shift incrementally or through innovative rulings, influencing the decision of those who contemplate legal action.

The resulting jurisprudential standards can create or foreclose opportunities for social actors who seek to press their demands through courts.[79] If they are receptive, they can prompt further legal mobilisation in relation to particular kinds of claims, or they may foreclose opportunities for litigation if they do not vindicate an initial set of claims. How ready or open a particular court is to adopting a novel approach, and therefore how open or closed legal opportunities to press such an approach are, can in part be glimpsed on the basis of how uniform or conversely divided judges are (within a single court system or among different judiciaries) on an issue or right claim. Apparent divisions among judges signal a space of unsettled and ongoing contestation over how particular rights claims are to be understood, and they are likely to stimulate further litigation.[80] As noted, moments of judicial receptiveness to particular legal claims 'influence both the legal battles in which a social movement organisation becomes involved and the organisations' potential for success'.[81]

Domestic legal interpretations in regard to different rights claims, as well as the approach of national judges vis-à-vis international, EU and ECHR norms, vary across states, contributing to fragmentation of the LOS in the multi-level European system. With the existence of multiple sources of rights in Europe, national judges and constitutional frames can no longer maintain a monopoly in the domain of rights adjudication. Such multiplicity is likely to foster differences among judges sitting in a court, or within a national legal system. In domestic courts, a central issue of discord is the extent to which national judicial interpretations must conform to international norms. The extent to which they do so, or are disinclined to do so, critically influences the willingness to resort to an international court like the ECtHR, or whether an EU litigation strategy is pursued.

Another perspective on legal action is provided by resource mobilisation approaches. According to these, the ability of prospective litigants to exploit legal opportunities is highly dependent on the availability of resources, especially when they engage in a legal battle in a sustained and strategic fashion.[82] Resource mobilisation is determined as much by the

[79] Andersen (n 70) 13.
[80] Ibid 7–10.
[81] LB Edelman, G Leachman and D McAdam, 'On Law, Organizations and Social Movements' (2010) 6 *Annual Review of Law and Social Science* 653, 662; see also Keohane, Moravscik and Slaughter (n 74) 482.
[82] Galanter (n 13).

existence of legal aid schemes and other sources of financial support as by the presence of civil society organisations and other actors willing to mobilise social support, as well as lawyers and other experts behind a litigation strategy. Resources encompass the existence of legal support structures such as rights advocacy organisations, willing and able lawyers, as well as support from NGOs and government agencies.[83] For instance, independent equality agencies with a mandate to engage in litigation, such as the UK Equal Opportunities Commission (EOC), are considered to strengthen legal support structures. The EOC has been behind a wave of strategic litigation of national and EC anti-discrimination law.[84]

Resources and support structures for legal mobilisation in national, international or supranational judicial venues also vary across states, and they are at least in part linked to civil society development and capacity. For example, Harlow and Rawlings attribute pressure group activity in the UK in the 1970s and 1980s through national courts and in the ECtHR to the spread of new social movement organisations with origins in the 1960s. Their legal strategies were prompted by broadened access to lawyers and legal aid, in a context where a number of social groups were excluded from policy making. In response to such exclusion, support was rallied for a counter-strategy based on civil rights and legal action to challenge the centralised policies of the Tory government.[85] The availability of legal aid and socio-legal structures of support based on synergies between the legal profession and social activists also varies greatly across states in Europe, and is likely to differentially influence the possibilities for legal mobilisation in domestic, supranational and international courts.[86]

In the multi-level EU system, assessing legal support structures must also take into account the existence and density of transnational networks of lawyers, activists and civil society organisations at the European level, as well as the availability of international and private sources of funding. Support for national or transnational legal action may be provided by European-level interest groups and civil society, as well as by international organisations, such as bodies of the Council of Europe, the European Commission or the UN Refugee Agency, among others.

In sum, the preceding analysis suggests that a variety of domestic legal-judicial structures (such as rules of standing), and national differences in patterns of political support and availability of resources (financial, legal

[83] Epp, *The Rights Revolution* (n 1).

[84] Alter and Vargas (n 4) 455.

[85] C Harlow and R Rawlings, *Pressure Through Law* (London, Routledge, 1992) 293–94; see also M Rask Madsen, 'France, the UK, and the "Boomerang" of the Internationalisation of Human Rights (1945–2000)' in S Halliday and P Schmidt (eds), *Human Rights Brought Home: Socio-legal Perspectives on Human Rights in the National Context* (Oxford, Hart Publishing, 2004).

[86] Alter and Vargas (n 4) 469–71.

expertise and advice), are likely to mediate and shape European legal action. They refract the extent to which an international or supranational court augments or conversely mitigates the opportunities for litigation and legal mobilisation.[87] It follows that the EU and ECHR law and courts do not necessarily empower citizens with more rights and opportunities, enabling them to outflank restrictive national norms, as much of the scholarship to date claims. Instead, the interaction and relationship between the European and national legal-judicial systems is more complex and the outcome is not always in the direction of empowering citizens and augmenting legal opportunities to mobilise.[88] Opportunities and resources for claiming national constitutional, EU or ECHR rights before domestic courts, or for having recourse to European courts to do so, are far more contingent and varying than has so far been suggested in existing studies.

While theories attributing rights mobilisation to legal opportunities and support structures rely on factors external to social actors, some scholars shift attention to the internal characteristics of social actors, underscoring the role of social agency rather than that of structure. A group may arguably opt for litigation even when it has access to government policy makers, or even when its claims are likely to be unfavourably received by judges. In such cases, the priorities and values of an organisation and/or the characteristics of an interest group can influence its strategy options and therefore the resources that it is likely to raise and develop.[89] For example, how broad or narrow a group's mandate is can influence the kind of strategy (legal, political or other) that it is likely to pursue. Vanhala alternatively underscores the importance of framing processes, the extent to which these define the members of a group primarily as rights holders and the courts as an appropriate venue within which to pursue policy. For example, the spread of a new self-understanding that invokes equality among citizens and sees disability as requiring reasonable accommodation arguably determined the choice of legal strategies before the question of opportunities or resources was even raised.[90]

III. PURPOSE AND OVERVIEW OF THE VOLUME

Existing scholarship on Europe and European integration reviewed in the previous section has begun to explore how EU law is enforced at the

[87] Börzel (n 2) 132.

[88] Ibid. For a critical view on this point, see also A Vauchez, 'Democratic Empowerment through Euro-law?' (2008) 7 *European Political Science* 444.

[89] L Vanhala, 'Anti-discrimination Policy Actors and Their Use of Litigation Strategies: the Influence of Identity Politics' (2009) 16 *Journal of European Public Policy* 738–54.

[90] Ibid 744–46.

domestic or EU level through litigation.[91] Yet, we still lack country-based or comparative studies that explore:

(a) how rights litigation and legal mobilisation at the domestic level develops in tandem with a multiplicity of norms and judicial venues beyond the State,
(b) how rights litigation and legal mobilisation at the supranational and international level is thoroughly mediated and distinctly shaped by legal, judicial, social and political factors at the national level, and
(c) how litigation and legal action are connected to and influence broader social goals and the political strategies of social movement actors at the national and European level.

In drawing from existing scholarship on European integration, most of the chapters in this volume bring into sharp focus the close interdependence between the national, supranational and international legal and judicial structures. They start with the assumption that this conjunction between the different levels indelibly shapes the contours and distinctive features of the socio-legal field in the European system, as well as the opportunities and constraints for legal mobilisation within it.

The contributions contained in this volume at least partially shift attention to the social processes and the political context that shape whether and how individual and collective actors use the law and courts to advance their claims at the national and European level. What factors prompt individual and organisational actors to resort to legal processes and the courts? How does the multi-level context shape the availability of and access to various kinds of rights as norms that can be claimed by individuals and minority actors? Do the legally binding human rights frames and a variety of 'soft' law instruments of minority rights influence how social actors frame their demands as legal entitlements, and their decision to pursue litigation? Why do individuals have recourse to European courts, what factors enable them to do so, and what are the consequences for social reform and the rights that they enjoy in domestic policy and practice?

From this multi-level and partly bottom-up perspective, this volume seeks to explore the uncharted terrain of legal mobilisation in pursuit of collective and social reform goals. It seeks to map the diverse perspectives and levels of analysis employed by different disciplines such as law, sociology and political science to study the relationship between law, rights and social mobilisation in Europe. Its aims are both analytical and empirical. While the subject of a flourishing scholarship over the past couple of decades in the US, there has been relatively little research in European comparative

[91] See the special issue on 'Courts, Democracy, and Governance' (2006) 39 *Comparative Political Studies*.

legal and political analysis of whether and the extent to which citizens actually pursue their interests and seek to influence political processes through the legal and judicial system. This is a glaring gap in social science and legal scholarship. Ample evidence suggests a growing trend of rights litigation, accompanied by mobilisation by social movement actors and NGOs, and partly supported by a variety of equality bodies, both at the national and at the European level. Yet, we still have little knowledge and country- and area-specific documentation of this flourishing activity, as well as of its consequences for political participation, social reform and democracy in Europe.

For this reason, the main purpose of this volume is to be exploratory, engaging in a mapping exercise, albeit one that is far from comprehensive or exhaustive. Therefore, the case studies and comparative studies contained in it have been selected with a view to bringing to light distinct aspects and manifestations of legal mobilisation on behalf of minorities and vulnerable groups, as well as the factors that shape it. The aim is to identify themes and questions that can form the basis for a research agenda on legal mobilisation of rights on behalf of minorities and marginalised groups in the multi-level European system. This volume does not examine gender equality, a field that has seen the most extensive legal mobilisation in Europe, but that has also received the greatest attention by scholars elsewhere, in a substantial number of studies.[92]

Apart from this introductory chapter, this volume comprises three substantive parts. The first part focuses on rights and legal mobilisation on behalf of historical minorities and immigrants at the national level. Chapter 2 by Bruno de Witte explores the puzzle of 'rights without litigation' that characterises the use of minority languages, which have received increasing recognition across European countries over the past 25 years. Through a comparative study of six West European countries, de Witte seeks to identify the conditions and factors that account for the fact that legal action in courts has been absent or played only a limited role in the pursuit and realisation of minority language rights. Three sets of factors emerge as salient in this analysis: the dominance of the political process in deliberating and determining the scope of minority language rights; the distinctive nature of these rights, which are premised more on duties as opposed to individual entitlements; and the 'soft' law or programmatic nature of European norms concerning minority language rights along with the quasi-judicial fashion of monitoring state compliance with these.

Focusing on the case of Spain, though, the chapter by Xabier Arzoz partly contradicts the 'rights without litigation' paradigm in regard to the

[92] See special issue on 'Gender Equality, Legal Mobilization, and Feminism in a Multilevel European System' (2013) 28 *Canadian Journal of Law and Society*.

language rights of Basque speakers in the region of Navarre, where they are a minority. Legal mobilisation around minority language rights (MLR) took place in domestic courts after 1997 in response to a restrictive policy change initiated by the regional government, which provided for a narrower scope of rights than the constitution allowed for. Further encouraged by the ratification of the European Charter for Minority Languages, legal action was a component of the political strategy of minority activists to promote language rights and to resist their curtailment by national and regional authorities. Notably, in the context of regional decentralisation, litigation in courts has largely taken place to redress conflicts between different institutions and levels of government holding different positions on the issue. Judicial decisions, even if highly limited in regard to pronouncing substantive rights, influenced a change in the political climate, paving the way for moderate, but nonetheless significant, reform.

Sceptical about views that attribute the 'rights revolution' to EU integration and broader European-level developments, the third contribution to this part by Liora Israël fully shifts attention to the local and national context. It traces the social practices and commitments that lawyers and jurists increasingly developed through their close interactions and association with the activists and movements from the left since the late 1960s and the 1970s. Israël's analysis argues that the legalisation of immigration and the legal mobilisation on behalf of immigrants in France must be seen as an outcome of such processes of interaction and the new kinds of legal practices and cause lawyering that they gestated.

The second part of the volume focuses on European courts as complementary (to national) spaces for invoking human rights and fundamental rights protection. It explores the factors that prompt litigation in the ECtHR and the CJEU on behalf of vulnerable individuals and minorities, the actors involved in legal mobilisation, as well as the transnational networks that form around it. The contributions also reflect on the effects that court decisions have on the rights and politics of the groups involved. The chapter by Mark Dawson, Elise Muir and Monica Claes provides a detailed anatomy of the multi-level rights review system of the EU. It explores the opportunities that this multi-level system creates for various forms of legal proceedings at the national and the EU level, which can be initiated by individuals, groups and institutions in the area of equality law. The chapter by Evangelia Psychogiopoulou explores and compares litigation in the Strasbourg and Luxembourg Courts to claim rights protection on behalf of asylum seekers, by focusing on the case of Greece. Litigation has also been aimed at redressing key policy issues related to the European system of asylum management and the extent to which EU Member States abide by fundamental rights principles in dealing with asylum seekers.

The third part of the volume places emphasis on the role of NGOs and transnational human rights networks, the importance of which has grown in particular areas of rights claims. The contribution by Dia Anagnostou explores legal mobilisation on behalf of victims of state abuses under a state of emergency and armed conflict, in the Strasbourg Court. It probes into why the ECtHR's case law has over time evolved in the direction of giving greater weight to the rights claims of individuals while exercising greater scrutiny of state actions and assigning more substantial positive obligations on states. Anagnostou shows that advancements in European human rights law related to rights claims in contexts of armed conflict have largely been the result of a particular kind of legal activism that has developed and expanded over the past 20 years. It has emerged out of transnational collaborations and synergies forged between lawyers with human rights NGOs, who engaged in systematic and strategic litigation, targeting points of ambivalence or potential receptivity manifested in the earlier case law coming out of the Strasbourg Court.

The effects and influence that processes of legal mobilisation exert on the ECtHR's case law are also the focus of Loveday Hodson's chapter. It explores the level and nature of NGO involvement in cases related to LGBT rights and analyses the impact of this involvement in shaping the Court's jurisprudence. The analysis raises questions about the impact that gay rights activists have had on the nature and direction of the Court's jurisprudence, the effectiveness of Strasbourg litigation strategies as a means of securing gay rights, as well as about the accountability of NGOs as social movement actors.

Part I

Law, Rights and the Politics of Minorities in National Context

2

Linguistic Minorities in Western Europe: Expansion of Rights Without (Much) Litigation?

BRUNO DE WITTE

THIS CHAPTER SEEKS to map the development of linguistic minority rights in West European countries during the last twenty years or so. Although there is only a limited degree of legal convergence among those countries, there are nevertheless—or so it will be argued in this chapter—two general features that distinguish the issue area of language rights from others discussed in this volume. In the first place, the growing recognition and entrenchment of the language rights of members of historical minorities in Western Europe has taken place mainly through the domestic political process, with little or no role for the courts. Secondly, the impact of 'Europe' on this evolution has been significant but rarely decisive. It has not involved the usual channels of legal Europeanisation formed by EU law and the European Convention on Human Rights (ECHR or Convention), but rather the alternative, and softer, mechanisms set in place under two other conventions of the Council of Europe, namely the Framework Convention on National Minorities and the Charter on Regional and Minority Languages.

For both of these reasons, the issue area of the language rights of historical minorities is rather different from other areas discussed in this volume, such as the rights of immigrants or homosexuals, where the role of litigation has been more prominent, and where EU law and the ECHR occupy a more central position. This difference in the salience of litigation for various types of vulnerable groups calls for a differentiated account of the respective roles of political and legal-judicial mobilisation in the formulation and implementation of new rights. It also calls for recognition of the fact that European-level protection of rights takes place in more ways than by means of the ECHR and the EU, however important the latter two legal regimes may be.

This chapter is structured as follows. In the remainder of this introduction, the chapter's subject matter will be defined. In Section II, I propose an overall view of the evolution of language rights protection in West European countries during the past quarter of a century. In Section III, I will highlight the distinctive form that Europeanisation has taken in this policy area. In Sections IV to VIII, I will explore in somewhat more depth five West European countries, namely Italy, France, Belgium, the UK and Switzerland. Whereas these case studies confirm, broadly speaking, the two distinctive characteristics mentioned above, they also serve to qualify those overall claims of the chapter by showing considerable cross-national differences: in some countries (such as Italy), the courts have played a significant additional role, whereas they have been totally absent from the scene in other countries (such as the UK); in some countries (such as the UK), the impact of European legal norms and institutional mechanisms is noticeable, whereas in other countries (for example, France) the national institutions have effectively shielded their domestic arena from such influences.

This chapter adopts a comparative approach which is limited to 'Western Europe'. This term will be defined here as the countries of the EU-15 prior to the 2004 enlargement, with the exception of Greece and Spain (the latter country being the object of a separate contribution in this book), and with the addition of Switzerland. The choice is based on the hypothesis that this part of the continent is sufficiently distinct from the rest of Europe in respect of the language rights of minorities, for two cumulative reasons: (i) in contrast with the countries of Central and Eastern Europe that have undergone a complete constitutional transformation after 1990, implying in many cases—given the linguistic composition of those countries—the inclusion in the new constitutions of minority language rights whose interpretation has been shaped by powerful constitutional courts, West European countries have been marked by basic *constitutional stability* during the last 25 years; (ii) whereas Central, East and South-East European countries have been exposed to external pressure to comply with Europe-wide minority protection standards as part of the political conditionality related to their accession (past or future) to the EU, for West European countries the adoption of Europe-wide minority protection standards has been a matter of free choice and of *political expediency*. So, the choice of limiting this chapter to Western Europe is based on pragmatic reasons but also on the assumption that this part of the continent is, in terms of the legal regulation of linguistic diversity, sufficiently homogeneous, and sufficiently different from the rest of Europe.

The issue area dealt with in this chapter is the protection of *linguistic rights* claimed on behalf of *historical minorities*. In Western Europe, the primary marker of the historical (or 'autochthonous') minorities was and is language. Traditional *religious* minorities also exist throughout Western Europe, but they have not been politically or legally salient in recent times, except in Northern Ireland. The recent revival of interest in 'law and religion' has been fuelled mainly by the religious diversity created, in Western Europe, by the emergence of the so-called *new* minorities. Whereas this chapter deals with the historical minorities and not with the new minorities, I do not claim that there is an absolutely clear dividing line between those two categories, nor that there are always good reasons for a differential legal treatment of the two kinds of groups.[1] But in terms of the actual legal evolution, their situation could not be more different: the new European-level legal instruments enacted in the 1990s were exclusively intended for historical minorities. Furthermore, at the national level, the expansion of the language rights of 'home-based' minorities stands in stark contrast with the lack of recognition of special language rights for persons belonging to immigrant communities; indeed, those persons are increasingly subject, throughout Western Europe, to linguistic *duties* rather than *rights*. As a final introductory point, I will briefly explain what I mean by the term 'language rights'.

The core linguistic right is the right to speak one's language, or, more precisely, the language of one's choice. The core right is, or can be, accompanied by a series of ancillary rights without which the right to speak a language becomes less valuable for its beneficiaries, such as: the right to be understood by others when speaking that language (for example, by public authorities), the right to a translation or an interpretation from other languages (for example, in the course of a meeting or trial at which those other languages are spoken), the right to compel others to speak one's language, and the right to learn the language.

In terms of the legal recognition of those rights, a crucial distinction is often made between the *private* and the *official* use of the language. It is traditionally considered that states are free to decide whether, and to what extent, they allow the use of a plurality of languages for official purposes, in public administration and the courts, in the public service media and in public educational institutions. States can either opt for a system of rather strict linguistic uniformity (as do France and Germany) or give wide official recognition to regional and minority languages (as do Spain, Italy and the United Kingdom). However, the *private* use of language is not within the control of the State. As the UN Human Rights Committee held in its *Ballantyne* opinion of 5 May 1993, 'a State may choose one or more official

[1] For a systematic discussion of this question, see R Medda-Windischer, *Old and New Minorities: Reconciling Diversity and Cohesion* (Baden-Baden, Nomos, 2009), and several contributions in K Henrard (ed), *Double Standards Pertaining to Minority Protection* (Leiden, Brill, 2010).

languages, but it may not exclude, outside the spheres of public life, the freedom to express oneself in a language of one's choice'.[2]

I. THE OVERALL EVOLUTION AT THE NATIONAL LEVEL: INCREASED LEGAL RECOGNITION AND PROTECTION OF LINGUISTIC DIVERSITY

From the 1970s until now, we have witnessed throughout Western Europe a stream of constitutional and legislative changes giving greater recognition to the multilingual character of countries with regional and minority languages.[3] The most spectacular case, no doubt, is that of Spain, which will not figure further in this chapter as it forms the subject of a separate contribution by Xabier Arzoz.

Already prior to the 1970s, there were long-established regimes of official plurilingualism in Belgium and Switzerland, where the main principles of language law were set out in the early part of the twentieth century, but their language legislation has been further developed and diversified in recent decades. In Switzerland, in particular, the global revision of the Constitution in 1998 involved a codification and strengthening of the country's constitutional commitment to linguistic diversity. This was followed, more recently, by the new federal law on national languages of 2007. In Italy, specific language regimes had gradually been put in place for the largest territorial minorities in the border areas (mainly South Tyrol and Val d'Aosta); they were complemented in 1999 by a general law on the protection of all 'historical linguistic minorities' in Italy. In the United Kingdom, the Welsh Language Act 1993, the Gaelic Language (Scotland) Act 2005 and the Welsh Language Measure 2011 have strengthened the legal protection of those regional languages.

In Finland, existing language rights for the country's minorities were further strengthened by the adoption, in 2003, of the Language Act 423/2003 (dealing with the conditions for the official use of Finnish and Swedish in the various parts of the country) and the Sami Language Act 1086/2003,

[2] Human Rights Committee, 47th session, Communications Nos 359/1989 and 385/1989, *John Ballantyne and Elizabeth Davidson, and Gordon McIntyre v Canada*, views adopted on 31 March 1993, para 11.4.

[3] For a more extensive comparative law panorama than the one that is offered here, see S Mancini and B de Witte, 'Language Rights as Cultural Rights: A European Perspective' in F Francioni and M Scheinin (eds), *Cultural Human Rights* (Leiden, Martinus Nijhoff, 2008) 247–84, at 251–70; and X Arzoz, 'Language Rights as Legal Norms' (2009) 15(4) *European Public Law* 541–74, at 556 ff. An important recent comparative study, including both European and non-European case studies, is that of G Poggeschi, *I diritti linguistici: un'analisi comparata* (Rome, Carocci, 2010). See also, with a narrower geographical focus: Véronique Bertile, *Langues régionales ou minoritaires et Constitution: France, Espagne et Italie* (Brussels, Bruylant, 2008).

which is modelled on the former in providing for the official use of the Sami language(s) in the northern part of the country. In Germany, the regulation of language use is a matter for the *Länder.* The East German *Länder* of Brandenburg and Sachsen adopted laws, during the 1990s, for the protection of the Sorbian language, including a right for citizens to use that language in dealing with the public administration in traditional Sorbian areas. The *Land* Schleswig-Holstein enacted in 2004 a Law for the Promotion of Frisian in the Public Domain which makes Frisian the second official language in a small part of the Schleswig-Holstein territory. Whereas France has preserved the clearly dominant position of the national language, even there meaningful legislative reforms occurred, which have strengthened the formal status and practical use of some minority languages, in particular of Corsican. In 2008 the Constitution was modified so as to include a clause affirming that the regional languages form part of France's cultural heritage—a largely symbolic gesture rather than one having concrete legal consequences, but which is nevertheless indicative of an ideological shift.

This Europe-wide trend is all the more significant when compared with the evolution of the legal regime of immigration-based linguistic diversity in those same countries. The dominant view in most European countries was, and still is, that no special language rights should be granted to the members of the 'new' minorities created through immigration, even if many of them, having acquired the citizenship of their host state, can no longer be treated as 'foreigners'. When special migration-related language norms are adopted, they more often tend to impose linguistic conditions or duties, rather than rights. Proficiency, or at least adequate knowledge, of the national language is a traditional condition for the naturalisation of foreigners, and it has tended to be imposed with more rigour in recent years. Recently, a number of countries have also started to develop civic integration programmes involving duties for migrants to follow training courses in the language of the host country. Even access to public benefits is sometimes made dependent on participation in these language immersion programmes.[4] The most far-reaching linguistic requirements are those introduced in countries such as Germany, Austria and the Netherlands where the right for non-EU migrants to enter the country for family reunification purposes is made dependent on showing a basic knowledge of the national language. This requirement is often very difficult to meet and may

[4] For a comparative and theoretical approach to the latter question see G Hogan-Brun, C Mar-Molinero and P Stevenson (eds), *Discourses on Language and Integration: Critical Perspectives on Language Testing Regimes in Europe* (Amsterdam, John Benjamins Publishers Co, 2009).

act as a major barrier to migration.[5] We are indeed far removed from a 'language rights' perspective in such situations.

Returning now to the historical minorities, the enactment of new constitutional and legislative norms granting language rights or other forms of support to minority languages does not, of course, automatically translate into a change in the language choices by individuals. The legal reforms mentioned above may be more or less effective in achieving their stated aim of enlarging effective linguistic choice and promoting the survival and development of minority or regional languages. In fact, there may be good reasons to be sceptical about the extent to which legal reform leads to effective social change in this area,[6] but this is not an issue that will be addressed in the context of this chapter. Its main task is, rather, to map the nature of the political and legal mobilisation that has produced those policy changes, or (in some cases) has managed to prevent other changes. In this respect, the prevailing picture is that processes of *political* mobilisation of regional and ethno-linguistic interests have been more consistently used. They have also been more effective than processes of *legal* mobilisation in the narrow sense of that term, namely the recourse to litigation before domestic and international courts. This seems to contrast rather sharply with other issue areas such as gender equality and immigrant rights and also, though perhaps less sharply, with the evolution of the language rights of historical minorities in the Central and Eastern parts of Europe. This characteristic is complemented by the very distinctive and largely unanticipated role played in this issue area by the *quasi-judicial* monitoring bodies set up by the Council of Europe, namely the Advisory Committee under the Framework Convention on the Protection of National Minorities, and the Expert Committee under the European Charter of Regional and Minority Languages. The nature of their role will be addressed in general terms in the next section of this chapter.

[5] The question may arise whether such far-reaching language requirements are compatible with constitutional and European guarantees of the right to family life (which includes a qualified right to family unity). See for example the judgment of the German Supreme Administrative Court, which rejected a challenge against the German language requirement for family reunification: judgment of the Bundesverwaltungsgericht of 30 March 2010, with a critical comment by R Marx, 'Sprachnachweis und Ehegattennachzug' (2010) *Zeitschrift für Ausländerrecht* 15–21 and 27–35.

[6] By way of illustration, see the comparative study of nine countries by V Cardi, 'Regional or Minority Language Use before Judicial Authorities: Provisions and Facts' (2007) 6 *Journal on Ethnopolitics and Minority Issues in Europe* 2, showing that regional and minority languages are seldom used before judicial authorities despite the existence of legislation allowing for their use.

II. THE EUROPEANISATION OF LANGUAGE RIGHTS: THE COUNCIL OF EUROPE CONVENTIONS

The regulation of language use, and the legal status of historical linguistic minorities specifically, have been the object of major European standard setting during the last quarter of a century, but these standard-setting initiatives have not taken place, for the main part, within the two arenas in which most other transnational rights were developed, namely the EU and the ECHR.

The role of the EU in this policy domain has been very limited. Although various norms and mechanisms of minority protection have gradually become part of EU law, in particular with the adoption in 2000 of the EU directive to combat racial or ethnic discrimination,[7] they have not, so far, had much impact on linguistic rights. Among the main linguistic rights granted by EU law,[8] we can mention the right of EU citizens to make use of existing minority language regimes on the same footing as the nationals of their host country, the right of EU citizens to communicate with the EU institutions in either one of the 23 official languages of the EU, and more recently, the right of EU citizens to various modes of language assistance when involved in criminal proceedings in EU countries other than their own.[9] But, since EU citizens are normally not considered to be part of a linguistic minority, their language rights can hardly be considered as linguistic minority rights.

The ECHR, through the case law of the European Court of Human Rights (ECtHR), plays a growing role in the protection of minorities, including of Europe's historical minorities.[10] However, few of those judgments deal with

[7] See, on the development of forms of minority protection in EU law, B de Witte and E Horváth, 'The Many Faces of Minority Policy in the European Union' in K Henrard and R Dunbar (eds), *Synergies in Minority Protection—European and International Law Perspectives* (Cambridge, Cambridge University Press, 2008) 365–84; O De Schutter, 'Recognition of the Rights of Minorities and the EU's Equal Opportunities Agenda' (2010) 11 *European Anti-Discrimination Law Review* 23–34.

[8] See, on the various dimensions of EU language law, X Arzoz (ed), *Respecting Linguistic Diversity in the European Union* (Amsterdam, John Benjamins Publishing Co, 2008), in particular the chapters by Hilpold, Nic Shuibhne, Arzoz and de Witte.

[9] Directive 2010/64 of the European Parliament and of the Council of 20 October 2010 on the right to interpretation and translation in criminal proceedings [2010] OJ L 280/1. The Member States have been given an unusually long period for transposing this directive into their national law, namely until 27 October 2013.

[10] For discussions of the Strasbourg Court's minority-related case law and its domestic impact, see D Anagnostou, 'Does European Human Rights Law Matter? Implementation and Domestic Impact of Strasbourg Court Judgments on Minority-related Policies' (2010) 14(5) *The International Journal of Human Rights* 721–43; K Henrard, 'A Patchwork of "Successful" and "Missed" Synergies in the Jurisprudence of the ECHR' in K Henrard and R Dunbar (eds), *Synergies in Minority Protection—European and International Law Perspectives* (Cambridge, Cambridge University Press, 2008) 314–64; J Ringelheim, *Diversité culturelle et droits de l'homme. La protection des minorités par la Convention européenne des droits de l'homme* (Brussels, Bruylant, 2006); G Pentassuglia, 'The Strasbourg Court and Minority Groups: Shooting in the Dark or a New Interpretive Ethos?' (2012) 19 *International Journal on Minority and Group Rights* 1–23.

language rights, and those few (such as the recent judgments in *Oršuš v Croatia*[11] and *Şükran Aydin and others v Turkey*[12]) mainly stem from Central, East and South-East Europe, whereas the Convention's case law has not had any impact, so far, on the language laws of Western European countries. In particular, the European Convention organs have always steered clear of interfering with national laws dealing with language use in parliaments, by administrative authorities and by courts, and in public schools. This traditional attitude (which we will encounter when dealing with the case of Belgium, below) was illustrated in a case against France, in which the applicant's claim that she should be allowed to speak Tahitian in the regional assembly of French Polynesia was declared inadmissible for being outside the material scope of the Convention.[13]

Contrasting with this rather low-key role of the EU and of the ECHR, we have seen, during the past decade mainly, the emergence of an important role for two directly language-related Council of Europe instruments, namely the Framework Convention on National Minorities and the Charter for Regional or Minority Languages. Both these conventions entered into force in 1998 and contain binding obligations for the states parties. Neither of the two is as yet so universally accepted as the ECHR, but the number of states parties is rising. At the latest count (as of May 2013), 25 states had ratified the Charter for Regional or Minority Languages. The Framework Convention is much closer to becoming a genuine pan-European standard. It has now been ratified by 39 states and the only ones missing, apart from some mini-states, are Turkey and four EU states: Belgium, France, Greece and Luxembourg.

The two conventions deserve to be treated together, within the context of this chapter, for two reasons: their legal mode of operation is very similar, and their content overlaps in that both instruments offer protection for minority languages and their speakers.

Let us consider their legal mode of operation first. In contrast with the ECHR, the provisions of these two treaties do not seem easily capable of direct effect in the national legal orders of the states parties (and therefore not suitable for launching domestic litigation strategies).[14] Their international supervision mechanisms do not lead to binding judicial decisions.

[11] *Oršuš v Croatia* App no 15766/03 (ECtHR, 16 March 2010).

[12] *Şükran Aydin and others v Turkey* App no 49197/06 and others (ECtHR, 22 January 2013).

[13] *Birk-Levy v France* App no 39426/06 (ECtHR, decision on admissibility of 6 October 2010).

[14] But see the nuanced analysis of this question by F Palermo, 'Domestic Enforcement and Direct Effect of the Framework Convention for the Protection of National Minorities' in A Verstichel, A Alen, B de Witte and P Lemmens (eds), *The Framework Convention for the Protection of National Minorities: a Useful Pan-European Instrument?* (Antwerp, Intersentia, 2008) 187–214.

Instead, the states who have ratified those conventions must 'merely' submit periodical state reports on their application to the committees of experts that were set up under each of the two conventions. However, the dynamic approach adopted by these expert committees in fulfilling their monitoring tasks is quite remarkable, and perhaps even unprecedented in international monitoring practice. On the occasion of the submission of a state report, they visit the country concerned and meet with spokesmen of minority groups, they take account of 'shadow reports' and other submissions by NGOs in addition to the official state reports. In their own, often very long and detailed, reports they do not hesitate to make statements as to whether the states have adequately complied with their obligations, whilst expressing detailed views on how to improve the situation. Their reports are followed by recommendations, directed to the states concerned, which are adopted by the Committee of Ministers of the Council of Europe and, so far, this intergovernmental committee has followed very closely the views of the experts. Pressure is thus exerted on the states to adopt best practices as formulated by the expert bodies.[15]

In terms of its content, the European Charter for Regional or Minority Languages is the more directly relevant of the two instruments, since it focuses directly and exclusively on the role of public authorities in relation to the use of languages. Article 1 of the Charter defines its scope of application as 'the languages that are traditionally used within a given territory of a State by nationals of that state who form a group numerically smaller than the rest of the population of that State' and adds that 'it does not include ... the languages of migrants'. In the Charter system, no principled distinction is made between 'regional' and 'minority' languages, although the former category seems broader than the latter. Anyway, both these categories are defined in territorial terms, that is, with reference to particular geographical areas in which those languages are spoken by a sizeable group of people.

The Charter's main characteristic is its *à la carte* approach. Not only are state parties free to indicate which regional and minority languages they choose to protect under the terms of the Charter, but they also have considerable discretion in picking and choosing from among the many, rather

[15] These various reports and recommendations can be found on the web pages of the Framework Convention and of the Charter of Languages, within the Council of Europe's website. For accounts of the monitoring practice developed under the two Conventions, see R Dunbar, 'The Committee of Experts of the European Charter for Regional or Minority Languages (the CECL)' in G de Beco (ed), *Human Rights Monitoring Mechanisms of the Council of Europe* (London, Routledge, 2011) 150–70; and G de Beco and E Lantschner, 'The Advisory Committee on the Framework Convention for the Protection of National Minorities (the ACFSC)' in ibid, 100–26. See also, for a more detailed study of the role of the two committees, E Lantschner, *Soft Jurisprudence im Minderheitenrecht. Standardsetzung und Konfliktbearbeitung durch Kontrollmechanismen bi- und multilateraler Instrumente* (Baden-Baden, Nomos, 2009).

detailed, substantive provisions of the Charter. The Charter is therefore a very flexible instrument, requiring the contracting states to undertake only those obligations they are positively willing to undertake, with the expectation that states will prove willing to gradually expand the nature and reach of their commitments. As part of the *à la carte* approach, the states are entitled to distinguish between minority languages, giving more far-reaching protection to some than to others, as long as those distinctions are justified by reasons of the size or geographical concentration of the groups. However, once states have agreed to undertake commitments for the promotion of a given language in a given field (be it education, the media or public administration), then the Committee of Experts will closely check their compliance with those commitments.[16] This is the reason why, despite the cautious formulation of this Charter, which studiously avoids the use of the term 'rights', its content may nevertheless give rise to genuine individual rights in those countries in which it has been transposed into domestic laws that contain clear commitments for public authorities—and the states concerned may be called to task for their failure to respect those commitments.

The Framework Convention on National Minorities, for its part, overlaps with the Charter to the extent that language rights are an important part of the overall package of minority rights which it contains. Its Article 10(2) contains a very cautious and qualified *obligation* for states to allow the use of minority languages in relation to administrative authorities. Article 12(1) contains a more straightforward *right* for every person belonging to a national minority to learn his or her minority language. These clauses, and some others of lesser importance, form the focus of an intensive dialogue between the governments and the Framework Convention's Advisory Committee, whereby the experts who form part of the committee (like those of its twin committee under the Charter) push governments to give a more generous interpretation to their obligations under the Framework Convention.

In sum, it can be said that both these conventions form an important site for the gradual development of a common European understanding of the legal protection of regional and minority languages. In fact, the decision to ratify these two instruments prompted a number of European countries to adopt new laws on the protection of minority languages, so that one could witness a mini-wave of new minority protection legislation in the late 1990s.[17] However, the limits of the two Council of Europe conventions

[16] See for example the report of the Committee of Experts on Germany, of 25 May 2011, ECRML (2011) 2, which amounts to 102 pages of detailed analysis and recommendations addressed to the German government.

[17] In addition to the already mentioned Italian law of 1999, one may add the Slovak language law of 1999, and the Swedish Law on national minorities of 1999, which was immediately followed by two specific laws providing for the use of the Finnish and the Sami languages.

should be kept in mind. One limit is the fact, mentioned above, that several countries have so far consciously refrained from ratifying one or both of these conventions; in particular, Belgium, France, Greece and Turkey have not ratified either of them. Another limit is that both conventions are primarily addressed to the historical minorities of Europe. They do not address the question of whether language rights should also be granted to the members of the new immigrant minorities of Western Europe—despite some efforts by the Advisory Committee of the Framework Convention to encourage states to broaden their minority protection standards so as to encompass also, at least in some respects, the community languages spoken by those 'new' minorities.[18] The third, and most obvious limit, is that although these two instruments contain binding legal *obligations*, those obligations are translated into effective legal *rights* for speakers of minority languages if the states are willing to 'play the game'. In the absence of judicial enforcement of the conventions at the European level, compliance remains, in the end, a matter of political expediency. Still, there is no doubt that the duty to report and explain their minority policies to the European expert committees is 'shaming' the states into making more efforts than they would otherwise make in the absence of the conventions. The committees do not hesitate to indicate whether they consider states to have 'fulfilled', 'generally fulfilled', 'partially fulfilled' or 'not fulfilled' their obligations in respect of each of their minority languages.[19]

Having traced in this and the preceding section of the chapter the general framework of evolution of minority language rights in Europe, we will now look in somewhat more detail at five countries of Western Europe in order to examine, in each case, the role of political as opposed to judicial mobilisation, and the impact of European-level standards.

III. ITALY

The Italian Constitution, as adopted in 1947, contains a prominently placed provision (Article 6) which states that 'the Republic protects linguistic minorities with appropriate measures', but it took a very long time before such appropriate measures were adopted in respect of all of the country's linguistic minorities, due to the very uneven nature of political mobilisation on their behalf. On the one hand, very elaborate regimes of

[18] On this aspect of the monitoring practice of the Advisory Committee, see A Verstichel, 'Personal Scope of Application: An Open, Inclusive and Dynamic Approach—The FCNM as a Living Instrument' in Verstichel, Alen, de Witte and Lemmens (eds) (n 14) 127–57; and J Ringelheim, 'Minority Rights in a Time of Multiculturalism—The Evolving Scope of the Framework Convention on the Protection of National Minorities' (2010) 10 *Human Rights Law Review* 99.

[19] See Dunbar (n 15) 165.

minority protection were adopted, and entrenched through constitutional laws, for the regions of South Tyrol (protecting the German and Ladin languages there) and Val d'Aosta (protecting the use of French in public life).[20] On the other hand though, it took several decades of patient political lobbying before the Italian Parliament adopted in 1999, more than 50 years after the constitutional mandate was formulated, a general law on the protection of historical linguistic minorities.[21] It applies to a listed number of small communities speaking the following languages: Albanian, Catalan, Croat, Franco-Provençal, French, Friulian, German, Greek, Ladin, Occitan, Sardinian and Slovenian.[22] The legislator chose not to include the Romani language, based on the argument that this language, unlike the others, is not rooted in a particular part of the country.

In principle, the general Law of 1999 does not prevent a more far-reaching accommodation of regional languages by means of other, more specific, laws as is the case most obviously with the sophisticated regime of protection of the rights of German and Ladin speakers in South Tyrol. The Italian Parliament also adopted a specific law in 2001 that considerably strengthened the language rights of the Slovene minority based in one part of the region Friuli-Venezia Giulia.[23] However, when the *regional* parliament of Friuli-Venezia Giulia adopted a law giving additional protection to the speakers of the Friulian language, that law was challenged by the government. As a result, those parts of it that contrasted with the 1999 law were declared unconstitutional by the Constitutional Court in a judgment of 2009.[24] The Court seems to have adopted the view that language regulation is a matter for the *national* legislator, which the regional and local authorities may *complement* but without adding extra rights that would affect the dominant status of the Italian language. For example, the

[20] Some of those linguistic regimes have been fine-tuned through litigation, and in particular through a number of judgments of the Constitutional Court which has generally adopted—unlike its French counterpart—a minority-friendly approach. On the other hand, some limited elements of the South Tyrol minority protection regime have been successfully contested by the invocation of EU law norms of free movement before local courts and the European Court of Justice in Luxembourg. See, on this point, GN Toggenburg, 'Regional Autonomies Providing Minority Rights and the Law of European Integration: Experiences from South Tyrol' in J Woelk, F Palermo and J Marko (eds), *Tolerance through Law. Self-Governance and Group Rights in South Tyrol* (Leiden, Martinus Nijhoff, 2008) 177–200.

[21] The evolution of the debate, and the various bills presented in the course of the years by members of the Italian Parliament (rather than by the governments) can be traced in the annual comments by P Carrozza, 'Minoranze linguistiche' in S Cassese (ed), *Annuario delle autonomie locali* (Edizioni delle Autonomie) from 1981 through to 1996.

[22] Note that, in the case of French, German and Ladin, the Law of 1999 applies only to the small communities residing *outside* Val d'Aosta and South Tyrol, respectively.

[23] For a detailed analysis of those various layers of Italian language legislation, see V Piergigli, *Lingue minoritari e identità culturali* (Milan, A Giuffrè, 2001); see also P Hilpold, 'Minderheitenschutz in Italien: völkerrechtliche und verfassungsrechtliche Grundlagen' in P Hilpold (ed), *Minderheitenschutz in Italien* (Vienna, Braumüller, 2009) 3–35.

[24] Judgment of 18 May 2009 in case no 159/2009.

Law of 1999 allows for the teaching of the minority language in public schools on the basis of a demand expressed by a sufficient number of parents, whereas the regional law provided for the teaching of Friulian *unless* parents objected in sufficient numbers to its inclusion in the curriculum; this provision was struck down by the Court. The Constitutional Court's judgment was criticised by legal authors who point out that the regulation of languages is not listed by the Constitution among the policy competences of the central state. There are therefore no good reasons to prevent regional legislatures such as those of Friuli or Sardinia from going further than the minimum standard of protection laid down in the 1999 Law.[25]

The 1999 Law itself was not the result of a litigation strategy but rather of a patient strategy of political mobilisation, which was eventually successful at a time when the Parliament had a centre-left majority. This legislation also coincided with the ratification by Italy of the European Charter on Regional and Minority Languages and of the Framework Convention on National Minorities. The 1999 law may thus be seen, in part, as a deliberate effort to put Italy's legal house in order when signing up to European instruments which Italy could hardly afford to reject in the light of its Constitution's traditional commitment to the protection of linguistic minorities.

The 1999 Law is a framework document which requires implementation by the national administrative authorities and, above all, by the regions and localities where these often very small minorities reside. It does not use the 'language of rights' and it seems very difficult to envisage that individual litigation could lead to legal changes on the ground. The implementation efforts by the administrative authorities at all levels seem not to be very effective, or when active steps are being taken (as in the case of Friulian mentioned above), they are thwarted by the national government with the help of the Constitutional Court. This is where Italy's engagement with the Council of Europe instruments becomes meaningful. One small example, among many, may serve as an illustration of the mild pressure exercised by the dynamic monitoring mechanism established in Strasbourg. Article 9 of the Framework Convention states, in very vague terms, that minorities should have adequate access to the media. However, the Law 482/99 contains a rather more robust commitment to *increase* transmission time for minority language programmes on public radio and television. The lack of effective implementation of this commitment was criticised by the

[25] R Toniatti, 'Pluralismo sostenibile e interesse nazionale all'identità linguistica posti a fondamento di un nuovo modello di riparto delle competenze legislative tra Stato e Regioni' (2009) 5 *Le Regioni* 1121; and E Stradella, 'La tutela delle minoranze linguistiche storiche tra Stato e Regioni davanti alla Corte costituzionale' (2009) 5 *Le Regioni* 1150.

Advisory Committee in its opinion on Italy of February 2005.[26] This criticism does not have any immediate domestic legal effects, but it 'shames' Italy into improving the situation in view of its next report to the Advisory Committee. Thus, the vague language of the European instruments is fleshed out by their monitoring bodies on the basis of more concrete commitments which states have made in their own domestic legislation and which are then 'turned against them' by the external expert body.

IV. FRANCE

More than in any other country of Western Europe, the expansion of minority protection in France in the course of the last quarter of a century—an expansion which is real, although modest in comparison with other countries—has been entirely due to successful political mobilisation, occasionally supported by minority nationalist violence as in the case of Corsica. The role of courts and of international bodies has been negligible.

As regards the role of the courts, we can even find some evidence of the opposite phenomenon, namely of judicial counter-mobilisation, that is, successful litigation aimed at stopping government plans that appeared likely to weaken the unitary and/or unilingual character of the French State. Traditionally, minority advocacy groups have found more political support with the socialist party than with the parties of the centre-right. So, each time a socialist government came to power, in 1981, in 1988 and in 1997, new plans were made to give greater recognition to the country's regional minorities and their languages. In more than one case, though, such plans were thwarted by the intervention of judicial bodies which enforced traditional Jacobin-republican ideology.

For example when, in 1991, the then socialist government, supported by its majority in Parliament, decided to adopt a new Special Statute for Corsica extending the island's existing autonomy, a number of opposition deputies challenged the bill before the Conseil constitutionnel.[27] The Conseil reduced much of the statute's symbolic appeal by declaring its Article 1 to be unconstitutional in so far as it referred to the 'Corsican people, component part of the French people'; the reference to a Corsican people, so the constitutional judges held, was contrary to the principle of the indivisibility of the French people as embodied in Article 1 of the

[26] Advisory Committee on the Framework Convention for the Protection of National Minorities, Second Opinion on Italy adopted on 24 February 2005, paras 89–91 and para 154 (first recommendation).

[27] Until its recent reform, the Conseil constitutionnel could not review the constitutionality of existing statutes but only of bills of statutes that have been adopted by Parliament but not yet officially promulgated. There was thus a short 'window for challenge' which in practice could only be used by the opposition parties in the Parliament.

French Constitution.[28] In the same decision, the Conseil also held that the *mandatory* teaching of the Corsican language in schools was similarly unconstitutional. Since, at that time, no constitutional provision protected the use of the French language (a constitutional amendment to that effect was enacted only in 1992, in the wake of the Maastricht Treaty), the Conseil invoked a violation of the principle of equality, which is a rather disputable basis for the rejection of the limited mandatory teaching of any given language. Indeed, in other countries, and in the new European instruments, it is exactly the other way round: the principle of equality is the basis for a *duty* to provide some degree of minority language education.[29]

A similar story unfolded in 1999. The socialist government had signed the European Charter for Regional or Minority Languages in May 1999, thus boosting the hopes of regional language activists that accession to the Charter mechanism would lead the French State to devote more resources to the regional languages and recognise enforceable rights to their users. Those hopes were smothered when right-wing opposition MPs challenged the proposed ratification law before the Conseil constitutionnel, which declared, on rather tenuous grounds, that ratification of the Charter for Regional or Minority Languages would be contrary to the Constitution.[30] Thus, the signing of the Charter was never followed by ratification, although some commentators have drawn new hope from the recent constitutional amendment proclaiming regional languages to be part of the country's cultural heritage. The Framework Convention on National Minorities, which is a rather more radical instrument than the Charter for Languages, was not even signed by France, after the Conseil d'Etat (acting in its capacity of legal advisor to the government) opined that its ratification would also be contrary to the Constitution.

Thus, the potential impact of the new European minority instruments adopted in the 1990s was not felt because France did not ratify either the Framework Convention or the Charter of Languages. Mobilisation of judicial and international resources has thus been pretty unsuccessful in the case of France. The courts have, on the contrary, been successfully mobilised by the defenders of French unity and uniformity to stop at least some of

[28] On the place of the Special Statute of 1991 in the evolution of France's policy on Corsican autonomy, see F Daftary, 'Experimenting with Territorial Administrative Autonomy in Corsica: Exception or Pilot Region?' (2008) 15 *International Journal on Minority and Group Rights* 273, at 288–90.

[29] For an (approving) comment of the Conseil constitutionnel's decision, see L Favoreu, 'La décision "Statut de la Corse" du 9 mai 1991' (1991) *Revue française de droit constitutionnel* 305.

[30] Among the many commentaries of this salient decision, see F Mélin-Soucramanien, 'La République contre Babel—A propos de la décision du Conseil constitutionnel no. 99-412 DC du 15 juin 1999' (1999) *Revue du droit public* 985–1000, and P Fraisseix, 'La France, les langues régionales et la Charte européenne des langues régionales et minoritaires' (2001) 1 *Revue française de droit administratif* 59.

the reforms designed to enhance the legal status of France's regional communities and languages. It remains to be seen what will be the impact of the recent constitutional amendment, which gives formal recognition to the existence of regional languages. So far, it seems to have a merely symbolic function. In a decision of 2011, the Conseil constitutionnel, true to its role, stated that this constitutional provision did not form a *right* which could be invoked by individuals to challenge the constitutionality of the existing (and modest) legislative arrangements for the teaching of regional languages.[31]

V. BELGIUM

The peaceful coexistence of Belgium's historical language communities—namely, the Dutch-speaking Flemings, the French-speaking Walloons and the small German-speaking community in the east of the country—has been framed by complex legal arrangements which combine federal solutions, consociational arrangements, and, to some extent, also the protection of the individual linguistic rights of the members of those communities.[32] Elements of this complex package deal, which was gradually revamped and constitutionally entrenched in the period 1960–80, have been contested before the domestic courts and at the international level. Remarkably enough, members of the 'real' minority, namely the German-speakers, have never resorted to judicial or international mobilisation for the advancement of their rights and interests. The political process has produced, in their regard, a legal regime which offers excellent protection for their regional and cultural identity; to a large extent, they have been free-riders of the federal reforms which were primarily aimed at solving the Flemish–Walloon conflict. Contestations of the Belgian language regime have, rather, emerged from the side of those who considered themselves to be the victims of the system of territoriality that was enacted by the language legislation of the early 1960s. That system resulted in the formation of large areas with a single official language, namely the Dutch-language area in the north and the French-language area in the south, whereas only a small central area around Brussels is officially bilingual. This created linguistic minorities on

[31] Conseil constitutionnel, Decision no 2011-130 QPC of 20 May 2011, *Mme Cécile L et autres.* See, for some earlier and rather sceptical commentaries on the new constitutional provision: C Lavialle, 'Du nominalisme juridique. Le nouvel article 75-1 de la Constitution du 4 octobre 1958' [2008] *Revue française de droit administratif* 1110; L Malo, 'Les langues régionales dans la Constitution française: à nouvelles donnes, nouvelle réponse?' [2011] *Revue française de droit constitutionnel* 69.

[32] For a detailed study of the origins and later development of Belgian language legislation, see J Clement, *Taalvrijheid, bestuurstaal en minderheidsrechten. Het Belgisch model* (Morstel, Intersentia, 2003); and N Bonbled and S Weerts, 'La liberté linguistique' in M Verdussen and N Bonbled (eds), *Les droits constitutionnels en Belgique*, vol 2 (Brussels, Bruylant, 2011) 1097–147.

both sides of the internal 'language borders'. The claims of members of those minorities to use their own language in dealing with public authorities and in public education were denied for the sake of the overall 'linguistic peace' in the country.

The language areas regime, and the resulting curtailment of minority language use in those areas, was established in its present form in the early 1960s. At that time, there was no constitutional review of formal legislation in Belgium, so that the only available arena for judicial challenge was situated abroad, namely in Strasbourg. The famous *Belgian Linguistics* judgment of 1968 was one of the first important judgments of the ECtHR. It was brought by French-speaking persons living on Flemish territory. Although the Court found a breach of the Convention on some minor points, the main features of the Belgian language legislation were upheld by the Court and the litigants were effectively defeated. The Court adopted interpretations of the right to non-discrimination, of freedom of expression and of the right to education, which basically permitted states to impose the exclusive use of one official language in the administration, the judiciary and the public school system.[33]

Further cases, in which the applicants contested more limited aspects of the Belgian official language regime were brought before the Convention organs in Strasbourg during the 1980s. In the case of *Clerfayt, Legros and others v Belgium*, the applicants, who were local councillors in the six *communes à facilités*,[34] complained about the fact that they were not allowed to speak French in the local council as a result of the system of territorial unilingualism. The latter allowed for the exceptional use of French only by the *citizens* but not also by the elected *officials* of the locality when performing their official duties. The applicants argued that this violated their political rights as protected by Article 3 of Protocol No 1 to the Convention. The European Commission of Human Rights rejected their claim on the simple ground that Article 3 only applied to legislative organs and not to local councils,[35] and the case did not reach the Court. One of the applicants in this case, who had also been elected in the Flemish regional parliament on a French minority party list, managed to take another claim up to the level

[33] This judgment of 1968 is still considered as one of the '*grands arrêts*' of the Strasbourg Court, especially for its early formulation of the Court's non-discrimination test. The case was recently revisited in the light of later developments in human rights law and theory by J Ringelheim (n 10) 278–93.

[34] The *communes à facilités* are six local communities close to Brussels (in fact, suburbs of Brussels) which form part of the Dutch language area but in which, in derogation from the normal rules, residents may choose to use French in their dealings with local authorities. On these exceptions to the territoriality principle, see W Swenden, 'Personality versus Territoriality: Belgium and the Framework Convention for the Protection of National Minorities' [2002/3] *European Yearbook of Minority Issues* 331–56.

[35] *Clerfayt, Legros and others v Belgium* App no 10650/83 (ECommHR, decision of 17 May 1985).

of the Court in *Mathieu-Mohin and Clerfayt v Belgium*.[36] This claim was similarly unsuccessful.[37]

After this episode, the ECHR system became unattractive for litigants seeking to contest the Belgian language regime. However, a new 'European' battlefront was opened in the 1990s with the adoption and subsequent entry into force of the Charter of Regional and Minority Languages and the Framework Convention on National Minorities. In particular, the question of whether Belgium should sign and ratify the Framework Convention became the object of heated debates. The main divisive issue was whether French-speakers resident in the Flemish part of Belgium might claim the status of 'national minority' under the Framework Convention and the accompanying language rights accorded to minorities, thus leading to the creation of a new quasi-bilingual area around Brussels, to be carved out from the unilingual Dutch-language region. The discussion was rather open-ended and inconclusive due to the fact that the authors of the Convention have avoided including a definition of minority, thereby leaving it to each ratifying state to adopt its own interpretation of that concept.[38]

Despite this discretion left to it on how to define national minorities, Belgium refrained from signing and ratifying the Convention due to the opposition of all the Flemish parties in the government and Parliament. Thereupon, a number of French-speaking politicians (headed, once again, by Georges Clerfayt, a repeat-player in European challenges of the Belgian regime), managed to take this debate to the European level by convincing the Parliamentary Assembly of the Council of Europe to prepare a report and to debate the issue. In October 2001 the Parliamentary Assembly's Committee on Legal Affairs and Human Rights asked the Venice Commission for a legal opinion.[39] At its 8–9 March 2002 session, the Venice Commission adopted an opinion with the innocuously worded title 'Possible groups of persons to which the Framework Convention for the Protection of National Minorities could be applied in Belgium'.[40] One of the main issues considered in the opinion was whether, under the

[36] *Mathieu-Mohin and Clerfayt v Belgium* App no 9267/81 (ECtHR, 2 March 1987), Series A no 113.

[37] See Ringelheim (n 10) 298–305.

[38] On this question of the lack of definition of the term 'minority', see Verstichel (n 18) 127–57.

[39] The European Commission for Democracy through Law, better known as the 'Venice Commission', is a committee of independent experts that assists the Council of Europe bodies through providing legal expertise, in particular by identifying best practices and formulating advisory opinions in matters of constitutional law. It has mainly been active in relation to proposed constitutional and judicial reforms in the countries of Central and Eastern Europe. For a recent example in relation to language law, see its Opinion on the Draft Law of languages in Ukraine, March 2011, CDL-AD (2011) 008.

[40] CDL-AD (2002) 1. The opinion can be found on the Commission's website www.venice.coe.int. See the related comment by Simona Granata-Menghini, 'The Application of the Framework Convention for the Protection of National Minorities in Belgium—The Opinion

Framework Convention, a particular language group (such as the French-speaking population in Belgium) could be a co-dominant group at the national level, but at the same time constitute a minority when considered within the context of a particular region of that country, namely Flanders. The Commission held that, in a federal state such as Belgium, the existence of a minority group must be assessed both at State and at sub-State levels. It found that French-speakers in the Dutch-language region, and also Dutch-speakers in the French-language region, were to be considered as minorities in the sense of the Framework Convention. The Parliamentary Assembly's *rapporteur*, Nabholz Haidegger, followed the interpretation adopted by the Venice Commission and this view was also laid down in the Assembly's resolution on the question.[41] The resolution has no legal binding value and did not have any immediate impact on Belgian language policy. The initiative of the Council of Europe's parliamentary body may, in fact, have been counterproductive, since it hardened the resolve of the Flemish parties to prevent Belgium's ratification of the Framework Convention. That Convention is still un-ratified today, as is the Charter of Languages, which leaves Belgium among the few 'conscientious objectors' among European states.[42]

Whereas European law has not made much difference, so far, to Belgian language legislation, litigation at the *national* level has occasionally been very intense, although it has mostly related to secondary aspects of the language regime. One should note that since the 1960s when the essential features of the current language regime were put in place, the general constitutional landscape has changed in the sense that Belgium now has a Constitutional Court with the power to review the constitutionality of federal and regional legislation, including therefore new language legislation. A number of constitutional judgments about the regulation of language use have been handed down in recent years, although their capacity to disrupt the legislative framework is limited by the fact that the Court is composed of equal numbers of Dutch- and French-speakers, a rule which is itself an element of the Belgian consociational model enshrined in the Constitution. This can be illustrated by one of the most prominent of those cases, involving a Flemish law imposing a duty on the prospective tenants of 'social' (ie public) housing to either speak Dutch or declare their willingness to learn

of the European Commission for Democracy through Law' [2002/3] *European Yearbook of Minority Issues* 359.

[41] Parliamentary Assembly of the Council of Europe, Resolution 1301(2002) 1, *Protection of Minorities in Belgium*, 26 September 2002.

[42] For a thorough discussion of the political and legal dimensions of the Belgian (non-)ratification debate, see J Velaers, 'Het Kaderverdrag tot bescherming van de nationale minderheden: een "non possumus" voor Vlaanderen?' in A Alen and S Sottiaux (eds), *Taaleisen juridisch getoetst* (Dordrecht, Kluwer Mechelen, 2009) 103–58.

the language. The Constitutional Court decided that, since the law did not actually limit those persons' freedom to *use* the language of their choice (a right which is protected by the Constitution), and since it did not impose any direct sanctions for the failure to learn Dutch, the law was not in breach of the Constitution.[43]

VI. UNITED KINGDOM

In the UK, the legal system had been rather slow in responding positively to the linguistic diversity that traditionally existed in the country. This situation has changed quite markedly during the last quarter of a century. The greater recognition of the status and official use of minority languages is only partially related to the devolution of powers to Scotland and to Wales that took place in 1998. Indeed, some important legislative reforms strengthening the position of the Welsh language were adopted by the UK Parliament at Westminster in pre-devolution times. The main legislative milestones were the Education Reform Act of 1988, which introduced Welsh as a compulsory subject throughout the Welsh public education system, and the Welsh Language Act 1993, which provided for a major expansion of the administrative and judicial use of the language. The combined effect of those Acts has been to turn Wales into an officially bilingual region. Those laws were enacted on the initiative of the Conservative Party despite the fact that this party had little electoral support in Wales, and little ideological sympathy for language minority claims. Their enactment tends to be explained by the combination of an active grassroots campaign conducted, for many years, by the Welsh Language Society (a non-governmental pressure group), the growth of political nationalism represented by the Plaid Cymru Party, and the benevolent attitude of the Welsh Office, a decentralised body of the UK government located since 1964 in Cardiff, which tended to promote 'Welsh causes' at central government level.[44]

After devolution, the policy for the protection of minority languages continued unabated. The Scottish Parliament adopted in 2005 the Gaelic Language (Scotland) Act which followed the model of the Welsh Language Act, though in a much more modest way, as the language itself has become much more marginal than Welsh.[45] In Wales the devolved government

[43] Belgian Constitutional Court, judgment of 10 July 2008, no 101/2008. See a comment by N Bernard, 'L'arrêt Wooncode de la Cour constitutionnelle du 10 juillet 2008: quand l'arbre (linguistique) cache la forêt' (2008) *Journal des Tribunaux* 689–98.

[44] For an account of the political conditions under which Welsh language legislation came about under Conservative governments in the UK, see A Thomas, 'Language Policy and Nationalism in Wales: A Comparative Analysis' (1997) 3 *Nations and Nationalism* 323–44.

[45] A comparison between both Acts is offered by R Dunbar, 'The Gaelic Language (Scotland) Act 2005' (2005) 9 *Edinburgh Law Review* 466–79.

took a number of new initiatives, culminating recently in the adoption of a new legislative act, the Welsh Language Measure 2011. In Northern Ireland, the legal status of Irish, and its effective use in public education and public administration, has been much strengthened in the course of the implementation of the 'Good Friday' Agreement of 1998 between the UK and Ireland.[46] Here, we see an interesting coincidence in time between the settlement of the Northern Irish conflict (including its language rights dimension) and the entry into force of the Council of Europe conventions; the UK's ratification of those conventions may have been prioritised, in part at least, because of the negotiations surrounding the Northern Ireland peace agreement.

A typical characteristic of all UK language legislation is the careful avoidance of terms that could imply speakers of minority languages having individual *rights* that can be enforced in court. Rather, those statutes formulate extensive and detailed *duties* for the public authorities to adopt measures (mainly the so-called 'language schemes') that will facilitate the effective use of the minority language in schools and in public services. This approach is not necessarily less effective in achieving the protection objective; indeed, it may be argued that the Welsh legislation has been quite successful in reversing the secular decline in knowledge and usage of the language. But it virtually eliminates the potential for legal mobilisation and litigation before the courts if a government service, or a local authority or school board, proves less than willing to comply with the official language policy.[47] In this respect, the UK language planning model, which was also adopted by Ireland when its Parliament enacted the Irish Official Languages Act of 2003, is quite different from the model adopted in many continental countries which recognise constitutional *rights* to use the minority language, even though these rights are sometimes qualified by numerical or territorial criteria.

On the other hand, we may note that the European Charter of Regional and Minority Languages is playing a rather important role in the public debate on minority languages in the UK. When ratifying the Charter in the late 1990s, or shortly afterwards, the UK decided to bring no less than seven languages within its scope: Irish, Scottish Gaelic, Welsh, Scots, Ulster

[46] For a detailed study of the recent evolution of language legislation in Northern Ireland, see J Muller, *Language and Conflict in Northern Ireland and Canada—A Silent War* (Hampshire, Palgrave, 2010).

[47] See on this point the detailed analysis by R Dunbar, 'Language Legislation and Language Rights in the United Kingdom' [2002/3] *European Yearbook of Minority Issues* 95–126. For a critical examination of the willingness of public authorities to actively engage in the promotion of the minority language, comparing Northern Ireland, the Basque Country and Wales, see CH Williams, 'Governance without Conviction' in S Pertot, T Priestly and C Williams (eds), *Rights, Promotion and Integration Issues for Minority Languages in Europe* (Hampshire, Palgrave, 2009) 89–122.

Scots, Manx Gaelic and Cornish, including therefore, in the latter case, a virtually extinct language. However, the UK government was careful to specify that it would not accord the same status to each language or the same benefits to the speakers of each language, but it would establish a hierarchy of protection in accordance with the number of speakers and the territorial patterns of settlement.[48] States are free to resort to such picking and choosing, due to the Charter's *à la carte* system. However, once states have decided to undertake commitments for the promotion of a given language in a given field, be it in education, in the media or in public administration, they open themselves up to the monitoring by the Council of Europe's Committee of Experts. The United Kingdom's experience is very typical in this respect. Although the UK was very cautious in accepting commitments upon ratification, avoiding any that would call into question the legal status quo of the late 1990s, the Committee of Experts nevertheless expressed detailed criticism of various aspects of the UK language regime in its opinions. In its subsequent reporting, the UK has sought to respond to those concerns in a constructive spirit. Despite the non-binding nature of the observations by the Strasbourg body, it has effectively acted as an external check on domestic language policies. Minority pressure groups have also used the opportunities offered by the mechanism to express their views to the Committee and to mobilise its support for their cause, even though, for now, the concrete impact of the Charter is not very significant.[49]

VII. SWITZERLAND

The total revision of the Swiss Constitution, approved in 1998 after long years of discussion, codified existing unwritten principles and constitutional conventions relating to federalism, consociationalism and linguistic diversity, and strengthened some of those existing features of the 'Swiss model'. In relation to linguistic diversity, the constitutional text now contains a combination of fundamental rights and institutional principles aimed at

[48] See the United Kingdom's second periodical report on its application of the Charter, 1 July 2005, MIN-Lang/PR (2005) 5. The fact that the number of speakers is not the only consideration is shown by the low priority given to Scots, which is spoken by many people but whose political and cultural status is weak.

[49] For a critical evaluation of the role of the Charter so far, see W McLeod, 'A New Multilingual United Kingdom? The Impact of the European Charter for Regional or Minority Languages' in Pertot et al (eds) (n 47) 44–59.

preserving the plurilingual character of Switzerland, with the following four main building blocks:[50]

(i) Four national languages (German, French, Italian and Romansh) are recognised in Article 4 of the Constitution, despite the fact that very unequal numbers of people speak those languages.[51] Three of these languages are recognised as official languages at the federal level, with a more limited right to use Romansh in dealing with federal authorities (Article 70, paragraph 1).

(ii) The cantons have the competence to determine their own official languages, but must take into account the traditional territoriality principle, whereby the existing geographical pattern of language use must be preserved as far as possible. They also have a duty to protect the linguistic minorities traditionally based in the canton (Article 70, paragraph 2).

(iii) The freedom to use the language of one's choice is recognised as a fundamental right (Article 18).

(iv) Whereas the cantons have a general competence for cultural affairs, the Federation is given a specific duty to complement and support cantonal action for the protection of linguistic diversity, with particular reference to the plurilingual cantons and to the cantons Ticino (where most Italian speakers live) and Graubünden (where most Romansh speakers live) (Article 70, paragraphs 4 and 5, in conjunction with Article 69).

Some of the elements of the current ethno-linguistic balance in Switzerland derive from older judgments of the Federal Court (Tribunal fédéral), which generally sought to strengthen the principle of linguistic territoriality to the detriment of the 'local' minorities who happen to be on the wrong side of the linguistic border. This insistence on the territoriality principle has operated, depending on the local situation, either in favour of the dominant language group (the German-speakers), or in favour of the smaller language groups (the French-, Italian- and Romansh-speakers). The adoption of the new constitutional provisions was, however, not at all court driven. It was rather the result of a very careful and drawn-out process of political delib-

[50] For a comprehensive analysis of the evolution of Swiss language law, see D Richter, *Sprachenordnung und Minderheitenschutz im schweizerischen Bundesstaat* (Berlin, Springer, 2005), and a more recent synthetic account in English by the same author: D Richter, 'The Model Character of Swiss Language Law' in AL Kjaer and S Adamo (eds), *Linguistic Diversity and European Democracy* (Aldershot, Ashgate, 2011) 189–204.

[51] At the census of 2000, 63.7% of the resident population indicated German as their main language, as against 20.4% French, 6.7% Italian and a mere 0.5% Romansh. 9% of the resident population (mostly foreigners) spoke other languages (figures of the Bundesamt für Statistik, www.bfs.admin.ch).

eration in which there was no place for judicial activism, nor for direct interference by international bodies. The deliberation process continued, after the adoption of the new Constitution, leading to a legislative restatement of federal language legislation in 2007.[52] Today, some 10 years after the adoption of the new Constitution, it seems that the Swiss regime of cultural coexistence remains solid, despite occasional internal skirmishes and despite some occasional mild criticism from the side of the Council of Europe bodies, particularly as regards the critical state of the Romansh language.[53]

As regards the European standards, it is worth noting that Switzerland—unlike Belgium with its similarly delicate and cumbersome cultural accommodation regime—did not refrain from entering into European obligations as regards the protection of minorities and regional languages. Indeed, it became a party to the Charter of Regional Languages (in December 1997) and to the Framework Convention (in February 1999) around the same time as the new Constitution was adopted, which shows the government's confidence that Swiss language legislation would live up to the new European minimum standard. Upon ratifying the Framework Convention, the Swiss government submitted the following Declaration: 'Switzerland declares that in Switzerland national minorities in the sense of the Framework Convention are groups of individuals numerically inferior to the rest of the population of the country or of a canton, whose members are Swiss nationals …'. Thus, while it was careful to exclude the large foreign population from the benefit of the Convention,[54] Switzerland did accept the inclusion of local minorities ('within a canton'), which is precisely the issue which—as we saw—makes Belgium hesitate in ratifying the Convention. The Swiss government has reported extensively to the two treaty bodies. Most recently, in December 2009, it submitted its fourth periodical report on the application of the Charter of Regional and Minority Languages, in the form of a detailed document of 99 pages, which received a rather positive appraisal from the Committee of Experts.[55]

[52] Loi fédérale sur les langues nationales et la compréhension entre les communautés linguistiques/Bundesgesetz über die Landessprachen und die Verständigung zwischen den Sprachengemeinschaften, of 5 October 2007.

[53] See the Report of the Committee of Experts on the Charter for Languages, *Application of the Charter in Switzerland—3rd monitoring cycle*, ECRML (2008) 2 of 12 March 2008. It contains a long series of recriminations about the federal government's lack of efforts to effectively implement the constitutional mandate to protect the Romansh language.

[54] Similarly, the Charter of Regional Languages was declared by Switzerland to apply only to Italian and Romansh, to the exclusion of both French and the immigrant languages.

[55] Application of the Charter in Switzerland, 4th monitoring cycle, Report of the Committee of Experts of 8 December 2010, ECRML (2010) 8.

VIII. CONCLUSION: NATIONAL VARIATIONS ON A COMMON THEME OF 'RIGHTS WITHOUT LITIGATION'

Each European country has followed its own political and legal trajectory in dealing with linguistic diversity. Despite this idiosyncrasy, there have been 'horizontal' influences between countries (for example, between the UK and Ireland, or between Nordic countries), and there has been a clear trend towards greater recognition of minority languages throughout Western Europe, leading to more 'linguistic democracy'. Minority language speakers increasingly have had the opportunity to lead their lives while using their own language, not only in the private but also in the public sphere, just like the speakers of the majority language; and rights to language education contribute to preserve knowledge of the minority languages for future generations.

Whereas litigation and court cases have played a certain role in some of the countries considered, they have rarely shaped the legal regime of linguistic diversity in a decisive way. Moreover, where courts have intervened, they have not necessarily protected the weaker party, namely the speakers of the minority language, but occasionally (particularly in France) they have sought to safeguard the dominance of the majority language in the face of timid political reforms proposing greater recognition of linguistic diversity. So, the trajectory of greater recognition for language rights has been mainly steered by *political mobilisation rather than litigation*, and one may assume that the very success of political mobilisation has made legal mobilisation unnecessary in some countries. Where federalism or regional devolution have decentralised the power to regulate languages, regions have used that power to advance the status of the regional language, as has happened most clearly in the autonomous communities of Spain but also in Wales and even in Germany. However, national governments and parliaments have, on the whole, not been unsympathetic either towards minority languages. Minority languages have gradually been accepted—even in France, with the recent constitutional amendment—as part of the country's cultural heritage and overall identity.

These domestically driven developments have been affected, since 1990, by important Europe-wide legal developments. Whereas the EU and the ECHR have not had much influence on the protection of linguistic minorities in Western Europe, the elaboration in the 1990s of new European minority protection instruments, which were primarily intended to prevent conflict in Central and Eastern Europe, has had an unanticipated knock-on effect in Western Europe by entrenching 'best practices' which all European countries (or at least those that have ratified the Council of Europe instruments) are expected to follow. The monitoring practice under the twin conventions of the Council of Europe has produced a hybrid kind of actor, namely the expert committees examining state reports. The non-judicial nature of those committees blends easily with the 'rights without litigation' approach which dominates domestic language legislation: those committees seem to be situated halfway between law and politics. Their opinions are couched in terms of (non-)compliance with legal obligations and, although they do not consider themselves as political actors, their activity feeds into the domestic political scene, by giving intellectual support and occasions for mobilisation to minority language activists.

3

Legal Mobilisation at the Subnational Level: The Case of Language Rights in the Spanish Autonomous Community of Navarre

XABIER ARZOZ

MOBILISATION OF LANGUAGE rights in Spain shows two basic dynamics of conflict: the affirmation of language rights by the periphery against the centre (within the more general conflict between centralism and autonomy) on the one hand; and the affirmation of language rights within bilingual communities on the other hand. These two conflicts both run in parallel with, but also intersect, each other, shaping the context and conditions for social and legal mobilisation around language rights in Spanish regions.

The actors in the inter-community conflict are the national and subnational institutions (mainly the central and regional governments and the Spanish Ombudsman). National institutions contest subnational language policies and subnational governments attack national legislation when they consider it intrusive to their competencies in the field of culture and language. These actors play out their legal struggles mainly on the constitutional level and within the jurisdiction of the Constitutional Court.[1] The conflict over minority language rights is bound up with the logic of the Spanish system, which I have defined elsewhere as 'a multinational quasi federal system in a unitary state'.[2] There is of course still space for political

[1] Recent struggles include Judgments 31/2010 on the linguistic provisions of the Statute of Autonomy of Catalonia of 2006 and 165/2013 on the suppression of linguistic requirements within the public employment of the Balearic Islands.

[2] X Arzoz, 'Die geschichtlichen Autonomien der Basken, Galizier und Katalanen als Beispiel eines multinationalen "Quasi-Föderalismus" im Einheitsstaat' in C Pan and BS Pfeil (eds), *Zur Entstehung des modernen Minderheitenschutzes in Europa* (Berlin, Springer, 2006) 387. See also J Martínez, 'Der präföderale Staat: Das Beispiel Spaniens' in I Härtel (ed), *Handbuch Föderalismus*, Band IV (Berlin, Springer, 2012) 819.

actors and language rights activists striving after more rights, principally at the national (federal) and the EU level.

The actors in the intra-community conflict are various activists' groups and subnational authorities. Dissatisfied groups regard subnational language policy as providing too little protection of the minority language, while others, in contrast, see such policy as leaning too much on the side of minority rights. On the one hand, minority language activists argue that their language is endangered, that the need for more communal language rights is a question of survival and that they are victims of past repression (during Franco's dictatorship) and ongoing injustice. They argue that, even though three decades have passed since the Constitution of 1978, their constitutionally entrenched language rights are still being impinged upon. On the other hand, adversaries of subnational language policy contest communal language rights and duties. They invoke liberal principles and individual rights, as well as constitutional safeguards, in order to promote the use of Castilian only with the authorities and to consolidate Castilian-speaking education all over the country.

This chapter investigates the extent and nature of language rights mobilisation at the subnational level in Spain, in particular in Navarre. The language issue is one of the enduring dividing lines in the society of Navarre.[3] About one-third of the population favours the promotion of a minority language policy, another third opposes it and the remaining third is neither in favour of nor opposed to it. Due to these intra-regional divisions, Navarre is one of the two officially bilingual autonomous communities in Spain that have the least advanced schemes of language protection and promotion (the other one is Valencia). Minority language activists are confronted with a regional political elite, supported by a democratic majority, which is reluctant to grant the full set of language rights that are recognised by law. This reluctance is not accidental, but it is an inherent aspect of a political discourse that combines liberal principles with conservative regionalism. It projects regional values as the 'quintessence' of the Spanish nation, at the same time rejecting the existence of linguistic and cultural bonds with the adjoining Basque Country (in the case of Navarre) and Catalonia (in the case of Valencia).

In view of such political opposition to minority language rights in Navarre, social actors and civil society seek legal remedies in the courts for the non-compliance of the regional government with the scope of language rights that is provided for in the Constitution. The devolution of power to

[3] Cf X Erize Etxegarai, *Nafarroako euskararen historia soziolinguistikoa (1863–1936)* (Pamplona, Gobierno de Navarra, 1997); *Vascohablantes y castellanohablantes en la historia del euskera de Navarra* (Pamplona, Gobierno de Navarra, 1999); 'El discurso contrario a la "normalización" de la lengua vasca en Navarra (1997–2002)' (2001) 46 *Revista Internacional de Estudios Vascos* 661.

subnational authorities has not attenuated but has frozen linguistic conflicts in the region. For two decades now, a Conservative party has been in government in Navarre, which subscribes to a strong regionalist discourse. It rallies support by defending a separate identity of Navarre from the culturally and linguistically close neighbours, the Basque Autonomous Community. In 1997 the government of Navarre initiated a revision of its language policy. This revision was regressive in nature and prompted significant legal and judicial mobilisation on behalf of the minority of Basque-speakers in the region. More than 30 lawsuits were brought by individuals, associations and municipalities. They were decided by the courts in the period 1999–2009, and many of them reached the Supreme Court.

This chapter proceeds as follows. The first section presents the legal framework that shapes minority legal mobilisation around language rights in Navarre. National (constitutional) and subnational (legislative) norms are largely configured and interpreted under the influence of the corresponding international and European norms. The second section provides an overview of legal mobilisation around minority language rights in Navarre in the period 1997–2009. The third section analyses how courts have responded to the legal challenges brought by individuals and social actors and the impact that these legal challenges have had on the development of language policy.

I. THE LEGAL FRAMEWORK

A. The Constitutional Level: the Spanish Linguistic Model

Spain is a decentralised state divided into 17 autonomous communities with legislative and executive competencies shared between the two levels of government. Since 1978, the protection of minority languages has been constitutionally enshrined in Spain. Article 3(3) of the Constitution of 1978 declares that 'the richness of the linguistic modalities of Spain, is a cultural patrimony which will be the object of special respect and protection'. In the decentralised Spanish state, the linguistic model and the territorial model are intrinsically linked.

The constitutional linguistic model has two basic components. The first is unilingualism at the national (federal) level: Castilian is the official language of Spain. Its recognition indicates that the characteristics of the traditional unitary state are largely preserved and that the panoply of State institutions continues to operate only in one language. The second component of Spain's linguistic model is formal bilingualism at the subnational level. Regional or minority languages have been given official status (they are designated as 'co-official languages') within their geographical areas, in addition to the official language of the state. As a result of this, six officially

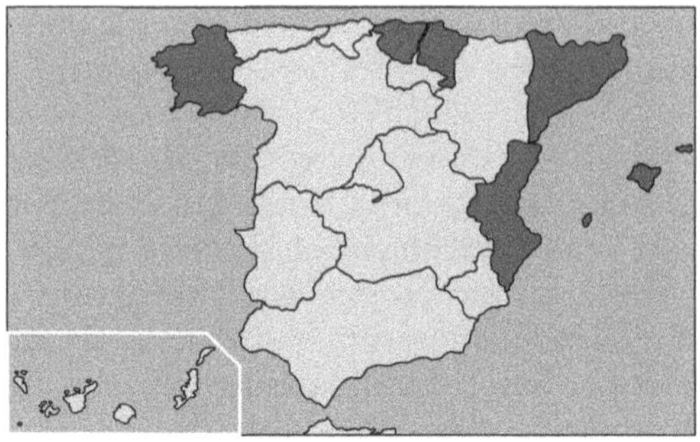

Figure 1: Territorial autonomy and officially bilingual autonomous communities in Spain

bilingual territories have emerged in the Autonomous Communities of the Basque Country, Balearic Islands, Catalonia, Galicia, Navarre and Valencia.[4] In the rest of the country, Castilian is the only official language (see Figure 1). Minority languages that are spoken in other autonomous communities are only protected through an approach that is not based on rights. Aragonese and Catalan (in Aragon), Asturian (in Asturias) and Galician and Leonese (in Castile and León) are not considered official and their speakers do no generally enjoy linguistic rights.[5] In some cases, the authorities of autonomous communities may facilitate the use of minority languages in specific social settings.[6]

In Spain, there is no federal legislation on the use of co-official languages. Unlike in Canada, where federal interventions in provincial jurisdictions have been aimed at improving the situation of official-language minorities (eg French-speaking minority in Alberta and in New Brunswick and English-speaking minority in Québec), in Spain interventions by central institutions (Spanish Ombudsman, central State's legal services, etc) have always been for the protection of Castilian-speakers.

Instead, the legal protection of co-official languages is an issue that is generally devolved to the relevant bilingual autonomous communities. The power to legislate on the co-official status is a competence of so-called horizontal character. Public authorities at any level of government (national,

[4] These comprise the bilingualism of Castilian-Basque, Castilian-Catalan/Valencian or Castilian-Galician.

[5] See X Arzoz, 'Linguistic Minorities in Spain' in D Richter et al (eds), *Language Rights Revisited—The Challenge of Global Migration and Communication* (Berlin, Berliner WissenschaftsVerlag-Wolf Legal Publishers, 2012) 271.

[6] See X Arzoz, 'Lenguas y modalidades lingüísticas en la Constitución Española: ¿dos regímenes jurídicos diferenciados?' in A Milian Massana (ed), *El plurilingüisme a la Constitució española* (Barcelona, Institut d'Estudis Autonòmics, 2009) 61; JM Pérez Fernández, 'La tutela de las lenguas regionales o minoritarias estatutarias y su encaje en el modelo constitucional español: ¿un tertium genus en el reconocimiento de los derechos lingüísticos?' (2008) 89 *Revista Española de Derecho Constitucional* 157.

subnational and local) in a bilingual autonomous community are obliged to comply with the language legislation in accordance with their respective powers and duties. The co-official status of the minority language has territorial character.[7] The national government cannot hamper or restrict the power of regional authorities to legislate on minority language rights.[8]

The decentralisation of authority has created a legal and institutional framework in which regional or minority languages and cultures can flourish. However, their potential to do so is a highly conditional one. It depends on the extent to which local-regional authorities and speakers share the view about the intrinsic value of their vernacular language. If such a common understanding breaks down, then the significance of institutional arrangements is reduced to an empty framework of protection. Autonomous authorities have tended to water down their constitutional and legal obligations. This is what has happened in two Spanish autonomous communities, in Navarre[9] and in Valencia.[10] In a situation defined by political reluctance or resistance to protect minority languages, legal mobilisation has been crucial to challenge language policy decisions at the subnational level in Navarre.

B. The Subnational Level: From Official Status to the Linguistic Zoning Approach

The Spanish Constitution recognised the official status of minority languages in their respective territories, in addition to Castilian. It would be up to the statute of each autonomous community to define the official status of the minority language in its territory. The autonomy statute of Navarre (1982) established that Basque would be the official language only in the Basque-speaking areas. In this way, it curtailed the territorial scope of the constitutional provisions granting official status to minority languages. In this restrictive frame, the Basque Language Act, passed by the Parliament of Navarre in 1986, established a rigid and exclusionist scheme based

[7] Constitutional Court, Judgments 82/1986, 214/1989 and 56/1990.

[8] J Vernet, E Pons, A Pou, JR Solé and AM Pla, *Dret Lingüístic* (Valls, Cossetània, 2003) 97–101.

[9] X Arzoz, 'La convivencia lingüística en Navarra' (2004) 69(II) *Revista Vasca de Administración Pública* 35; X Arzoz, 'Estatuto jurídico del euskera en Navarra' in JM Pérez Fernández (ed), *Estudios sobre el estatuto jurídico de las lenguas en España* (Barcelona, Atelier, 2006) 387.

[10] A Guia Conca, *La llengua negociada* (Valencia, Edicions 3 i 4, 2001); MA Pradilla, *El laberint valencià. Apuntes per a una sociolingüística del conflicto* (Benicarlo, Onada, 2004); J Ochoa Monzó, 'Estatuto jurídico del valenciano' in Pérez Fernández (ed) (n 9) 349; M Doppelbauer, *València im Sprachenstreit. Sprachlicher Sezessionismus als sozialpsychologisches Phänomen* (Vienna, Braumüller, 2006); M Teodoro i Peris, 'La llengua a l'Estatut valencià. Comentaris a les disposicions lingüistiques del nou Estatut valencià' (2008) 49 *Revista de Llengua i Dret* 125.

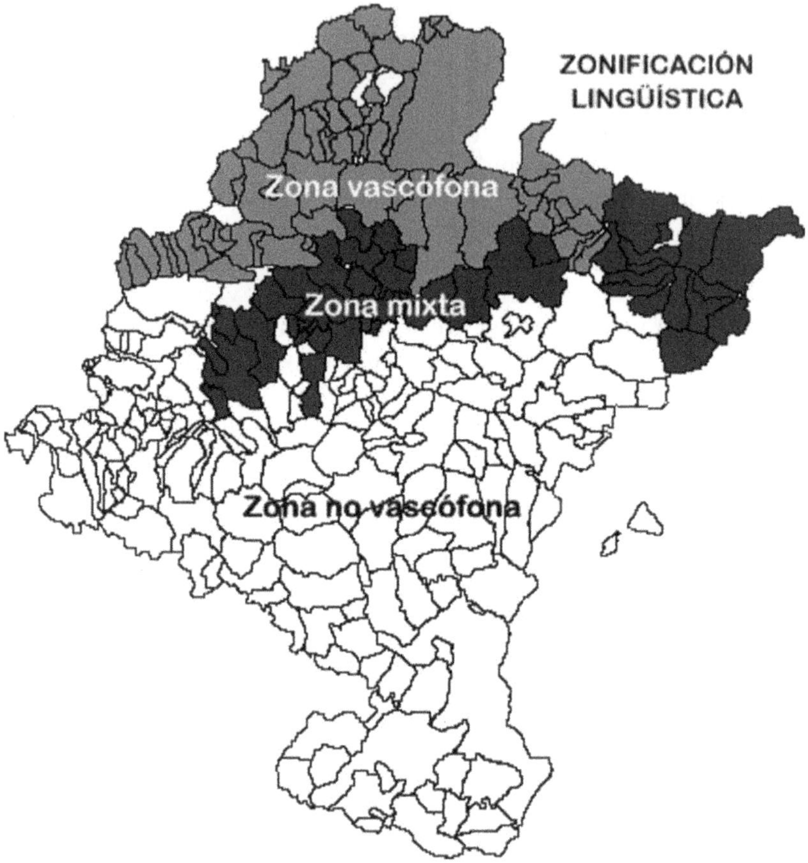

Figure 2: Linguistic zoning in Navarre 1986–2010

on linguistic zoning: the northern part of the autonomous community is identified as 'Basque-speaking', the central part as 'mixed' and the southern part as 'non-Basque-speaking' (see Figure 2).

This linguistic zoning is highly controversial among activists actively committed to the preservation of the Basque language in Navarre. It confines the official status of Basque to the narrowest possible territory, leaving the most populated areas of the community outside of the official status. Only 9.8 per cent of the whole population of Navarre lives in the Basque-speaking area, which is basically a rural area comprising various Pyrenean valleys.[11] The most populated area is the so-called 'mixed' zone: 53.9 per

[11] 50% of the whole population of the 'Basque-speaking' zone understands, speaks and writes the Basque language, 27% understands, speaks and writes it with difficulty, and 23% has no command of it.

cent of the whole population of Navarre lives there, and it is the territorial area of the autonomous community, in which the main part of the regional administration is located.[12] Basque has traditionally been spoken in the 'mixed' zone.

The frontiers dividing the linguistic zones are not time-honoured borders between self-consciously defined cultures of Basque- and Castilian-speakers. Basque- and Castilian-speaking Navarrese share the same culture. The linguistic zoning can be regarded as an attempt to eradicate or restrict bilingualism and the alternative ethno-cultural identity of Navarre's Basque-speakers. Terms such as 'borderlands', 'hybrid cultures', 'mixed communities'—to which the expression 'mixed zone' from the linguistic zoning of Navarre can also be added—convey 'an a priori (nationalist) impulse to fix members of such communities with authentic and lasting identities that have been at most temporarily disrupted by accidents of mixing'.[13]

For areas other than the 'Basque-speaking' zone, the Basque Language Act does not clearly formulate in legal terms citizens' rights and authorities' duties. Instead, it intentionally leaves wide discretion to the authorities of the day to determine the content of their obligations. The Act avoids recognising expressly official status for the Basque language in the 'mixed' zone, even though it allows for some official uses of the language. As a consequence, there is no legal certainty about the status of Basque in the 'mixed' zone. For some, this is tantamount to denying it official status in the 'mixed' zone, while for others, it provides for limited recognition by partly permitting its official use.

Although approved in 1986 by an absolute majority in the Parliament of Navarre,[14] the Basque Language Act of Navarre was strongly rejected by two rival sets of political actors, for different reasons: the Basque nationalist parties, that is, the forces most committed to the defence of the language; and a regionalist Conservative party (Navarre's People Party, UPN) opposed to the very idea of language promotion and the extension of minority language rights to the entire area of the autonomous community. The Basque Language Act was meant to be a political compromise, yet it did not appease the two mentioned political rivals.

The Basque Language Act requires subordinate legislation to provide clarification and additional measures of implementation. Although the

[12] 10% of the population of the 'mixed' zone understands, speaks, reads and writes Basque, 11% understands, speaks, reads and writes with difficulty, and 79% has no command of the language. These are official data provided by a study conducted under the auspices of the regional government. Cf Government of Navarre, *Estudio sociolingüístico sobre el vascuence en Navarra 2003* (Pamplona, Gobierno de Navarra, 2004).

[13] PM Judson, Guardians of the Nation—Activists on the Language Frontiers of Imperial Austria (Cambridge, MA, Harvard University Press, 2006) 21.

[14] In certain issues such as language, the passing of laws of the Parliament of Navarre requires an absolute majority in a final vote on the whole of the draft.

Language Act must be passed in the regional Parliament by absolute majority, the approval of subordinate legislation and its implementation are matters left to the subnational government. Notably, no subordinate legislation was passed from 1986 to 1994. This partly changed over the following 10 years when four decrees were passed. The first Decree—Decree 70/1994—was withdrawn due to opposition within the governing party. A second, slightly amended Decree in the same year—Decree 135/1994—established a minimum legal framework for the protection and promotion of the Basque language, including in the so-called 'mixed' zone. In any case, Decree 135/1994 was not an expression of a strong minority language policy. Nevertheless, in 1997 the regionalist Conservative party (UPN) initiated a regressive revision of the language policy,[15] prompting a wave of legal mobilisation on behalf of the minority language rights, which is analysed in Section II.

One of the consequences of the linguistic zoning is the restriction of minority language rights in the educational system of Navarre. In the Basque-speaking and in the 'mixed' zones, individuals have the right to choose Basque, Castilian or both as the language of instruction. In the 'non-Basque-speaking' zone, however, Castilian is the only language of instruction in public schools. To be sure, the Basque Language Act vaguely foresees the teaching of the Basque language in the 'non-Basque-speaking' zone, and its support with public subsidies when there is sufficient demand. Yet, subnational legislation failed to pursue in practice the possibility of public or private schools teaching in Basque in the 'non-Basque-speaking' zone. In this zone, many parents who wished to provide their children with education in Basque, organised private schools on a cooperative basis (so-called *ikastolas*). Even though these schools have not had the legally required authorisation to operate, this did not prevent them from receiving public subsidies now and then from the subnational government, like other private schools.

The establishment of the private Basque language schools has attracted a great deal of attention and social support, inside and outside of the autonomous community. Social mobilisation prompted the subnational government to change its policy on this issue. In 2000 it started to recognise these schools because they had already consolidated themselves or because they had become too popular among the electorate. Basque schools in the

[15] I Agirreazkuenaga, 'Dictamen jurídico emitido a requerimiento del Alcalde del Ayuntamiento de Lekunberri (en representación de otras Administraciones e instituciones) sobre la legalidad del Decreto Foral 372/2000, de 11 de diciembre, por el que se regula el uso del vascuence en las Administraciones públicas de Navarra (BON de 5 de enero de 2001)' (2001) 59 *Revista Vasca de Administración Pública* 432; I Agirreazkuenaga, *Diversidad y convivencia lingüística* (Diputación Foral de Gipuzkoa, 2003) 350; Arzoz, 'La convivencia lingüística en Navarra' (n 9) and Arzoz, 'Estatuto jurídico del euskera en Navarra' (n 9).

towns of Tafalla and Sanguesa were definitively authorised.[16] In 2002 the subnational government developed a scheme to help those private schools that had not yet been granted authorisation. It extended such authorisation to four more schools in 2006[17] and provided them with financial assistance in 2007.[18] However, additional financial aid was restricted. It was explicitly granted only to the same four private schools, while additional aid was limited to three years and it could not exceed a given amount.

C. The International Framework: the European Charter for Regional or Minority Languages

It is well known that the European Convention on Human Rights (ECHR) does not provide special rights for speakers of minority languages. The prohibition of discrimination as set out by Article 14 of the Convention does not extend to state restrictions in language rights. Therefore, individuals have not been able to raise claims aimed at correcting, improving or implementing minority language rights in the European Court of Human Rights (ECtHR) with any prospects for success.

The main international instrument for improving or protecting the legal status of speakers of minority languages is the European Charter for Regional or Minority Languages (the Charter). It is an international treaty adopted under the auspices of the Council of Europe to make up for the ECHR shortcomings in regard to the rights of minorities to enjoy their own culture, to use their own language, and to establish their own schools. The Charter constructs a comprehensive framework that should match as closely as possible the needs and interests of each minority language, as well as those of the groups who use such a language. On 5 November 1992, Spain signed the European Charter for Regional or Minority Languages, but did not ratify it until 2 February 2001.

The Charter can empower the less privileged linguistic minorities in Spain, such as the Basque-speakers in Navarre.[19] As an international treaty ratified by Spain, the Charter constitutes part of the internal legal order.

[16] Orders of Navarre's Minister for Education and Culture 77/2000 and 140/2000.

[17] 'Arangoiti ikastola' in Lumbier, 'Argia Ikastola' in Fontellas, 'Erentzun Ikastola' in Viana, and 'Ibaialde Ikastola' in Lodosa.

[18] Law no 7/2007 of 23 March 2007 (Official Bulletin of Navarre, no 40, 2 April 2007).

[19] For a general discussion on the scope and the impact of the Charter see JM Woehrling, *The European Charter for Regional or Minority Languages. A Critical Commentary* (Strasbourg, Council of Europe, 2005); X Arzoz, 'The Implementation of the European Charter for Regional or Minority Languages in Spain' in *The European Charter for Regional or Minority Languages: Legal Challenges and Opportunities* (Strasbourg, Council of Europe Publishing, 2008) 83; A López Basaguren, 'The Spanish Constitution: Problems in Applying the Charter' in *Minority Language Protection in Europe: Into a New Decade* (Strasbourg, Council of Europe, 2010) 117; Council of Europe, *Shaping Language Rights. Commentary*

It possesses a rank superior to that of domestic law and only inferior to the Constitution. Therefore, the Charter's obligations can be enforced by domestic courts, provided that the obligations are regarded by the courts to be self-executing. Article 10(2) of the Spanish Constitution recognises international treaties concluded by Spain in the field of human rights.[20] In 2005 the Spanish Constitutional Court expressly acknowledged that, by virtue of Article 10(2), the Charter will provide for interpretive criteria on the scope of protection of constitutional provisions concerning the status of minority languages.[21]

It must be recalled that Spain's Constitution limits itself to proclaiming basic principles but it says little on the scope and content of protection to be afforded to the non-Castilian languages spoken in Spain. The status and protection of minority languages are devolved to the relevant autonomous communities, which enjoy a wide discretion to adopt their linguistic legislation and to implement the constitutional principles. Therefore, as the aforementioned Constitutional Court ruling of 2005 indicates, the significance of the Charter is enormous in the Spanish legal order: the central government and the autonomous communities have to guarantee, at a minimum, the level of linguistic protection provided for in Part III of the Charter.

Equally importantly, the Charter has its own monitoring mechanism. States have to submit a report on the implementation of the Charter every three years, and a Committee of independent experts monitors the compliance of states with the Charter obligations. On the basis of the Committee's report, the Committee of Ministers of the Council of Europe makes recommendations to the states. Delegations of the Committee of Experts conduct country visits and hold interviews and meetings with authorities, cultural institutions and NGOs working in the field. Until now, there have been three monitoring cycles on the application of the Charter in Spain, and the Committee of Experts has given three reports on Spain.[22]

In the particular circumstances of Navarre, the Charter has also proved to be a useful instrument, at least politically, to counter domestic reluctance, political inertia and ideological constraints. In fact, the 2003–07 government agreement between the regionalist party (UPN) and the centrist party (CDN) stipulated that all obligations derived from the Basque Language Act and from the European Charter for Regional or Minority Languages

on the European Charter for Regional or Minority Languages in the Light of the Committee of Experts' Evaluation (Strasbourg, Council of Europe Publishing, 2012).

[20] Article 10(2) of the Spanish Constitution reads: 'The rules relating to the fundamental rights and liberties recognized by the Constitution shall be interpreted in conformity with the Universal Declaration of Human Rights and the international treaties and agreements thereon ratified by Spain'.

[21] Constitutional Court, Injunction 16/2005, para 5.

[22] The text of the Charter and the reports of the Committee of Experts can be downloaded at www.coe.int/minlang, accessed 1 November 2013.

must be complied with. The agreement also stated that it will promote education and language teaching in Basque in line with the principles of the Basque Language Act and the voluntary nature of Basque education. The 2007–11 government agreement renewed these commitments. This shows that even in a period characterised by a regressive and confrontational language policy, subnational authorities tried to gain credibility for their decisions by invoking full compliance with the European standards enshrined in the Charter.

II. MINORITY LANGUAGE LEGAL MOBILISATION IN NAVARRE: AN OVERVIEW

Studies on legal mobilisation mainly take into account public interest litigation, that is, legal challenges that are pursued by individuals and organisations. Private litigation may also have implications for public policy and consequences for the cause of linguistic diversity. Yet, litigants engaging in it primarily defend a private right or expectation (a licence, a subsidy, and so on).[23] But in the case of Spain, legal mobilisation has also taken place in the context of inter-institutional conflicts between different public actors and State institutions. For instance, the subnational government of Navarre has gone to court to challenge the decisions that certain public institutions (municipalities or the public university) adopted on the use of the Basque language in their territory, when these decisions are regarded as particularly favourable to the minority language (access to public employment, official names, road signs, etc).

Subnational language policy is contested by individuals and social groups mainly in ordinary courts, since they can only indirectly reach the Constitutional Court. The separation between ordinary and constitutional jurisdiction, also established in other European states (Germany, Italy, Poland, Czech Republic, Hungary, etc), is decisive for the scope and strategies of legal mobilisation in Spain. Private persons and most public entities have *locus standi* only with regard to administrative acts and subordinate legislation. On the other hand, *locus standi* to challenge pieces of legislation (either national or subnational legislation) before the Constitutional Court is restricted to specific institutions of the State (the national and subnational governments and Parliaments, as well as the Spanish Ombudsman).

Language activists in Navarre have moved from the traditional discourse of 'endangerment' of the Franco era, to a rights-based discourse in order to

[23] Certainly some public interest litigation can take place under the umbrella of private interests, for instance, when a non-governmental association asks for a broadcasting licence for the promotion of the Basque language and challenges the denial of it before the courts. But this would imply a closer examination of the nature and objectives of many lawsuits.

advance minority language rights. The discourse of 'endangerment' depicts minority languages as autonomous entities in need of being defended against attack from the incursion, both territorial and functional, of larger ones.[24] The shift in discourse to a rights-based approach has been prompted both by domestic and international law. The guarantees included in the Spanish Constitution and the European Charter for Regional or Minority Languages opened space for political and legal activism around language rights in Navarre. While some opportunities were created following decisions by the Constitutional Court on the Spanish language model, many more developed at the subnational level in the interplay between parliamentary legislation, social mobilisation and judicial decisions.

A. Targets and Grievances

Social actors opposed the language policy of Navarre's government before and after the change of language policy in 1997. But social and legal mobilisation for the defence of language rights mainly developed after the 1997 change. That year marked the beginning of a regressive shift in the language policy that had been in place until then. Legal mobilisation has primarily pertained to (a) the status of Basque language in the 'mixed' zone and (b) educational language rights in the 'non-Basque-speaking' zone. Nearly every language policy decision taken by the subnational government on these two issues from 1997 onwards was challenged in courts. Legal challenges targeted subordinate legislation (regulations), as well as decisions of public administration (administrative acts) on issues such as the installation of monolingual signage in public buildings and roads, or the publication of monolingual brochures, among other things.

The first conflict concerned the status of the Basque language in the Public University of Navarre. In Spain public universities have the power to pass their own institutional rules within the existing legal framework, as they enjoy a certain degree of autonomy recognised by the Constitution. In order for such rules to have legal effects though, the respective statute has to be approved by the subnational government, which has competence in, and provides the funding for, higher education. However, the subnational government can only amend a public university's statute if it believes it violates the law. The Statute of the Public University of Navarre, located in the capital city of Pamplona/Iruña, within the 'mixed' zone, committed itself to use both Castilian and Basque in its public communication, publications and signs. It also vowed to provide teaching in Basque in the future, if there was significant demand and a real social need. In pursuing these

[24] A Duchêne and M Heller (eds), *Discourses of Endangerment* (London, Continuum, 2007).

goals, it established a policy of recruiting Basque-speaking teaching and administrative staff. These provisions were consistent with the status of the Basque language in the 'mixed' zone as defined by the Basque Language Act of 1986. Since the Public University of Navarre is the only public university of the autonomous community, its services should address equally both Basque- and Castilian-speakers.

When the local government in Pamplona/Iruña rejected the above-mentioned provisions on the use of Basque, approved by the Public University of Navarre, the High Court of Navarre quashed the government's amendments as contradictory to the Basque Language Act.[25] However, the Court clearly stated that subnational institutions, the Parliament and the government of Navarre, had competence to regulate the status of Basque language in higher education. This was an explicit statement that the subnational government could not violate the law as it stood (the Basque Language Act of 1986). If the local government wished to circumvent the 1986 Act, it would have to ask the Parliament to pass a new Act. In fact, the local government drafted a law that sought to limit teaching in the Basque language only to those curricula that are established by the university, but which are not awarded with officially recognised degrees. The regional government gave up the draft after its legal services opined that such a law would in any case require an absolute majority in Parliament, which was probably lacking.

In 2000, the adoption of Decree 372/2000 to implement the Basque Language Act signalled a new language policy premised on two basic ideas. The first one was to halt the promotion of the Basque language, as it was assumed that its legal protection led to discrimination against individuals who do not speak it. The second idea behind Decree 372/2000 was to curtail the legal possibilities that had been timidly opened and implemented to support the Basque language in the 'mixed' zone, with the final objective of assimilating the linguistic status of the 'mixed' zone with that of the non-Basque-speaking zone. On the basis of Decree 372/2000, the subnational government subsequently approved in 2001 various acts: a decision of 5 February 2001 limiting the relevance of the knowledge of Basque for public employment in the regional administration, and two implementation plans for the Basque-speaking zone and for the 'mixed' zone. All these acts were adopted in the absence of significant consultation with public entities and civil society organisations.

The adoption of Decree 372/2000 triggered several legal challenges by municipalities and individuals in the courts, both on formal and substantive grounds. In response, the High Court of Navarre quashed the Decree

[25] High Court of Navarre, Judgment of 4 January 1999 (RJCA 1999\671). The representation of the government of Navarre gave up the appeal submitted against that Judgment before the Supreme Court: Supreme Court, Injunction of 25 October 2004 (JUR 2004\310712).

on formal grounds,[26] and the two implementation plans were also annulled in separate rulings. Subsequently, the Spanish Supreme Court confirmed the rulings.[27] These were important initial victories for the social actors involved in litigation.

The regional government immediately approved a new Decree, which included all the provisions of the annulled Decree 372/2000, but now complying fully with the formal requirements. The Consultative Council of the Basque Language, an organ created by law and consisting of representatives of different political, cultural, educational and civil society institutions and independent experts, had been hostile to the restrictive minority language policy of the regional government. When their opinion was not requested, 12 of its 20 members resigned and the Council remained inactive for the following three years. After the annulment of Decree 372/2000 by courts, the regional government reinstated the Consultative Council. It appointed to it new members who were favourable to its language policy, and who were not necessarily 'people of recognised prestige in the field of Basque language and culture' as required by law.[28] A new regulation established that the agreement of three of its members was enough for the Consultative Council to approve by majority an opinion, where this was legally required. The new consultative organ was no longer going to be an obstacle in the government's plans.

The new Decree 29/2003 was again challenged massively before the courts.[29] Now, the High Court of Navarre had no alternative but to review the legal content of the Decree. It quashed four paragraphs of the Decree, which clearly contradicted the Basque Language Act and the Spanish legislation on public servants, and this ruling was later confirmed by the Supreme Court.[30] Those paragraphs quashed by the courts had mandated

[26] High Court of Navarre, Judgments of 26 June (619/2002, 620/2002 and 621/2002), 28 June 2002 (641/2002), 5 July 2002 (671/2002), 18 July 2002 (700/2002) and 27 September 2002 (869/2002). The Decree had been approved without requesting the opinion of two consultative organs, including the Consultative Council of the Basque Language, as required by law.

[27] Supreme Court, Judgments of 5 June 2006 (RJ\2006\3094), 7 June 2006 (RJ 2006\3943), 28 May 2007 (RJ\2007\5395), 21 December 2007 (RJ\2007\8842), 6 February 2008 (RJ\2008\980), 20 February 2008 (RJ\2008\1245). With regard to the annulment of the implementation plans, cf Judgments of 7 June 2006 (RJ\2006\3444, 2006\3441, 2006\3443) and 27 June 2008 (RJ\2008\6123). With regard to the annulment of the decision of 5 February 2001 on the relevance of the knowledge of languages, cf Judgment of 28 May 2007 (RJ\2007\5395) and 1 July 2008 (RJ\2008\8032).

[28] Lawsuits brought against the government's appointment of the new members of the Consultative Council of the Basque Language were unsuccessful.

[29] The main rulings are Judgments of 20 May 2004 (587/2004), 25 June 2004 (624/2004), 5 July 2004 (698/2004), 30 July 2004 (804/2004), 30 September 2004 (919/2004 and 929/2004), and 16 December 2004 (1218/2004 and 1220/2004). In similar terms but with a more restricted declaration of invalidity: Judgments 633/2004 of 3 June 2004 and 932/2004 of 29 September 2004.

[30] Supreme Court, Judgments of 19 December 2008 (RJ\2009\246), 19 May 2009 (RJ\2009\5620), 7 July 2009 (RJ\2009\6927), 14 July 2009 (RJ\2010\568).

that communications from the regional administration to individuals and legal persons located in the Basque-speaking zone had to be written in Spanish, if the interested person had not asked expressly for the use of Basque, instead of being always bilingual; that civil servants in posts for which the knowledge of Basque is a legal requirement could only move to an equivalent post for which the knowledge of Basque is also required; and that in competitions for public sector employment, the marks assigned to the knowledge of Basque as a merit could not be more than those assigned to the knowledge of French, English and German, as working languages of the European Union.

In contrast, other legally questionable provisions of Decree 29/2003 were not quashed. Their controversial character lies in what silence implies. Article 16 of the Decree imposes that signs in public offices and all kinds of public statements in the 'mixed' zone must be in Castilian only. This went against the practice established in the previous two decades in the municipality of Pamplona, the Public University of Navarre and the regional administration itself. Nevertheless, the High Court of Navarre did not quash Article 16, assuming that this provision did not amount to a prohibition of also using Basque. In this regard, it overlooked policy documents and unofficial statements disclosing a clear intention on the part of the subnational government to remove all existing bilingual signs from the 'mixed' zone. The provision for an official Basque–Spanish translation service in regional administration[31] was also challenged in court on grounds that it implicitly sought to undermine the use of the Basque language by civil servants. The High Court of Navarre was not convinced by this claim despite the fact that Decree 29/2003 was silent on the duty of the public administration to answer in Basque to the citizens in the 'mixed' zone. Instead, the Court declared that it could not quash provisions on the basis of fears and suspicions, overlooking the fact that the silence of a regulation can be a way to undermine the law.[32]

B. Litigation

Public interest litigation on language policy in Navarre originated from individuals, trade unions, cultural organisations and municipalities. It must be noted that there are differences in the *locus standi* recognised to different kinds of litigants. In the first place, cultural associations have *locus standi* to challenge subordinate legislation before courts. One example is the Euskara Kultur Elkargoa, which was created in 1998 and has assumed

[31] Article 12(3) of Decree 29/2003.
[32] See above note 30.

an active role in legal mobilisation on behalf of Basque-speakers' language rights.[33] This association is located in Navarre and its statutory purpose includes all kinds of activities for the promotion of the Basque language and culture and its knowledge, use, development, transmission and dissemination.[34] Secondly, individuals also have *locus standi* to challenge subordinate legislation on the status of the Basque language, in so far as they live in the Basque-speaking zone and enjoy language rights awarded by the subnational language legislation.[35] This also applies to citizens living in the non-Basque-speaking zone, since the Basque Language Act recognises certain language rights to all citizens regardless of the linguistic zoning.[36] This judicial attitude of accepting legal challenges from individuals is consistent with the general flexible approach of the Spanish judiciary concerning *locus standi*.[37]

Trade unions of Basque nationalist ideology (LAB, ELA, STEE-EILAS, SORTZEN) have also challenged decisions concerning the conditions of recruitment for public employment, which they considered to be at odds with citizens' language rights.[38] However, they lack *locus standi* to challenge subordinate legislation (for instance, primary education regulations) as these matters are considered to go beyond the interests that trade unions represent.[39]

Municipalities such as Lekunberri, Lesaka, Aranguren and the Valley of Baztan have also challenged regional decisions on language policy in court. The Spanish legal order makes municipalities' *locus standi* dependent on a breach of law that impinges upon their competences. To be sure, the Supreme Court excludes language policy from the scope of municipal autonomy. This means, for example, that municipalities cannot rule extensively on the use and development of the Basque language at the local level, since this matter is conferred upon the authorities of the autonomous community.[40] The interpretation, which is not without objections, restricts

[33] High Court of Navarre, Judgment of 21 November 2005 (1054/2005).

[34] High Court of Navarre, Judgment of 16 December 2004 (1218/2004).

[35] High Court of Navarre, Judgments of 3 June 2004 (633/2004) and of 29 September 2004 (932/2004).

[36] High Court of Navarre, Judgments of 4 October 2004 (918/2004) and of 16 December 2004 (1220/2004).

[37] The courts have also accepted that a civil servant of the municipality of Pamplona who holds a post for which the knowledge of Basque is a requirement had *locus standi* to challenge Articles 18(3) and 22(1) of Decree 29/2003: cf High Court of Navarre, Judgment of 2 June 2004, confirmed by the Supreme Court's Judgment of 19 December 2008 (RJ\2009\246). An individual was also recognised to have *locus standi* to challenge a Spanish-only highway signage that ignores the dual, Basque and Spanish, official name of the municipality in which the highway is located: cf Supreme Court, Judgment of 23 December 2009 (RJ\2010\1344).

[38] High Court of Navarre, Judgments 123/2005 of 4 February 2005 and 215/2008 of 30 April 2008.

[39] High Court of Navarre, Judgment 41/2009 of 27 January 2009.

[40] Cf Supreme Court, Judgment of 3 June 2009 (RJ\2009\6445).

the municipalities' *locus standi* in this field. Nevertheless, the right of a municipality to choose a composite Spanish-Basque official name falls within its constitutionally entrenched local autonomy, in so far as legislation does not exclude it. In this case it was the regional government that lodged an application against the decision of a municipality located in the 'mixed' zone to adopt a composite Spanish-Basque official name.[41]

Often, legal challenges are initiated simultaneously by different litigators, jointly or separately. For instance, the central piece of the regressive legislation in the field of language rights promoted by the government of Navarre, Decree 29/2003, was challenged by Euskara Kultur Elkargoa, by a number of municipalities and by individuals.[42] Other legal persons also contested in court aspects of the same Decree. This strategy of parallel and, in some cases, joint litigation aims at increasing social mobilisation and at minimising the risk of being denied *locus standi*.

C. Europeanisation of Language Rights

The ratification of the European Charter for Regional or Minority Languages has influenced minority language mobilisation by providing legitimacy to minority rights claims.[43] Yet, its compliance has been a problematic and recurring issue in challenges against language policy decisions in regional courts.[44] At the same time, language rights activists have paid more and more attention to the monitoring cycles of the Charter: they comment on the state's report and even prepare their alternative reports in advance, with a view to influencing the content of the Committee of Experts' report.[45] The way language rights activists in Navarre have engaged in its monitoring mechanism deserves closer attention.

[41] High Court of Navarre, Judgment of 13 October 2006, confirmed by the Supreme Court, Judgment of 31 May 2011 (RJ\2011\4851), with regard to Estella-Lizarra.

[42] High Court of Navarre, Judgments 633/2004 of 3 June 2004, 918/2004 of 4 October 2004, 932/2004 of 29 September 2004, and 1218/2004 and 1220/2004, both of 16 December 2004.

[43] The ordinances on the use and the promotion of the Basque language approved recently by diverse municipalities of Navarre refer in their Preambles to the European Charter for the Protection of Regional or Minority Languages and in particular to two state obligations from Article 10 of the Charter, which are controversial in the 'mixed' zoning in the law and practice of the government of Navarre: 'to ensure that such of their officers as are in contact with the public use the regional or minority languages in their relations with persons applying to them in these languages' and 'to ensure that users of regional or minority languages may submit oral or written applications and receive a reply in these language'. Cf Ordinances of Zizur Mayor-Zizur Nagusia (Official Bulletin of Navarre, no 69, 4 June 2008), Orkoien (Official Bulletin of Navarre, no 132, 26 October 2009) and Puente La Reina-Gares (Official Bulletin of Navarre, no 66, 31 May 2010).

[44] Cf High Court of Navarre, Judgment 1054/2005 of 21 November 2005.

[45] On the monitoring mechanism by the Committee of Experts cf above Section I.C.

In the first monitoring cycle concerning the implementation of the Charter in Spain, the Charter's Committee of Experts visited Navarre and met with government officials and civil society. It is not surprising that the question of the status of the Basque language in the 'mixed' zone of Navarre was raised already in the first monitoring cycle: is the exclusion of this zone from the application of the Charter provisions compatible with the spirit, objectives and general principles of the Charter, or is it at odds with it? The Committee of Experts did not provide an answer, which probably lies beyond its mandate. Yet, it considered three kinds of arguments supporting an enhanced status for Basque in the 'mixed' zone of Navarre, such as the knowledge of Basque by the population, the number of pupils receiving Basque-medium education (30 per cent in the 'mixed' zone) and the importance of Pamplona/Iruña, capital city of Navarre. Pamplona/Iruña has the highest concentration of Basque-speakers in a single town, and it is the main urban and administrative centre of Navarre. According to the first Committee of Experts' report, these aspects have to be taken into account by the competent State authorities with a view to deciding the appropriate level of protection for the Basque language in the 'mixed' zone.

Evidently, the way in which the Spanish authorities balanced the various views and interests concerning the protection of the Basque language in the 'mixed' zone of Navarre was accepted by the Committee of Experts provisionally and it might be reviewed in subsequent reports.[46] In any case, the Committee of Ministers of the Council of Europe[47] took into account the observations of the Charter's Committee of Experts. It also explicitly recommended, 'as a matter of priority', that the authorities of Spain 'consider the possibility of applying an appropriate form of Part III protection to the Basque language within the "mixed zone" as defined by the legislation of Navarre'.

The attention that the Committee of Experts devoted to Navarre and to the status of the Basque language in the 'mixed' zone, in their first report on the implementation of the Charter in Spain, reflected the influence of and lobbying by the relevant minority language activists, both from Navarre and from the Basque Autonomous Community. Unfortunately, the Committee of Experts' second and third reports (2008 and 2011) have not reviewed the issue of the legal status of the Basque language in the 'mixed' zone. The Committee has merely assessed the efforts that have been made to follow the recommendation issued in the first monitoring round (to consider the possibility of applying an appropriate form of Part III protection

[46] Woehrling notes that the Committee of Experts has not yet had a proper discussion on the specification by contracting states of the territorial scope of Part III obligations. See Woehrling (n 19) 68.

[47] The Committee of Ministers and the Parliamentary Assembly are the main political institutions of the Council of Europe.

to the Basque language within the 'mixed' zone). The Committee of Experts also includes the information provided by the Navarre authorities under the relevant provisions in its reports. In this way, it monitors de facto the compliance of Navarre authorities with the Charter obligations also with respect to the 'mixed' zone.

III. THE IMPACT OF MINORITY LANGUAGE LEGAL MOBILISATION IN NAVARRE

A. Legal Mobilisation and Courts

The analysis in the previous section shows that legal mobilisation on behalf of language rights in the last 15 years has been above all a reaction to a severe curtailment of language rights since 1997. As such, legal mobilisation was an integral part of the broader social mobilisation against the restrictive language policy of the government of Navarre. All judicial decisions reviewed in this chapter were taken by regional courts, and they were fought out by the regional government until they reached the Supreme Court, which confirmed them. Regional courts have competence to review subordinate legislation and decisions taken by the regional and local authorities. Appeal to the Supreme Court is only available when a regional court judgment is claimed to violate national or EU law. The constitutional jurisdiction in turn is limited to reviewing complaints concerning infringement of fundamental rights.[48] Therefore, making a successful appeal to the Supreme Court is difficult as the substantive law in the field of language use is subnational law, while reaching the Constitutional Court is even more difficult. In fact, there is no case law from the Constitutional Court on minority language rights or on the status of the Basque language in Navarre.

Regional courts are constrained in judicial review by institutional factors: they are very dependent on the doctrine of the Supreme Court and the Constitutional Court and their decisions may be appealed to in the Supreme Court. In any case, they are probably not institutionally strong enough to promote policy change. Judges sitting in regional courts tend to change posts from one autonomous community to another, and they do not necessarily have a profound knowledge of the local society. They lack a bilingual background and often share the linguistic prejudices of the general public.

From the case law reviewed in this chapter, it can be deduced that, in general, judges sitting in the regional court have not responded favourably to language rights claims. All rulings of the High Court of Navarre

[48] In Spain, language rights are not fundamental rights, but certain fundamental rights have a linguistic dimension.

that challenged the position of the regional government can be explained by judges' sacred respect for the principle of legality. The clearest evidence of this is that the Supreme Court in Madrid has systematically confirmed all of them. The provisions annulled by the High Court of Navarre were fundamentally inconsistent with the law in force. In contrast, provisions that were ambiguous or intentionally silent on the official use of the Basque language in certain domains were not quashed because a majority of the judges sitting in the Court did not consider that they were circumventing language rights recognised by law. Sometimes, the same ruling that reversed a governmental decision paradoxically also hinted at ways in which the government could circumvent it.[49] Even the partial annulment of Decree 29/2003, considered the most spectacular success of legal mobilisation of the period, was far from a bold ruling. It was a compromise between different positions represented within the court: a proactive and a minimalist stance on language rights.[50]

The impact of the European Charter for Regional or Minority Languages on domestic legal mobilisation has not been translated into influence over the courts' jurisprudence on minority language rights. The High Court of Navarre has tended to minimise the domestic impact of the Charter on the implementation of language rights. Most of its judges hold the view that the relevant Charter provisions have been implemented sufficiently through subnational legislation, and even more extensively than provided for by the Charter.[51] Based on that assumption, regional courts do not check effectively the compatibility of language policy norms and decisions taken by regional authorities with the Charter: judicial review refers only to domestic legislation, mainly subnational legislation. In this respect, the ratification of the Charter has not contributed to expanding the scope of judicial review.

The relatively modest outcomes of minority language legal mobilisation can probably be explained, at least in part, by the legal nature of language rights. In earlier research I have argued that the tendency to conflate language rights and human rights is not only erroneous, but it also leads to a distorted image of the relationship between law and politics.[52] While human rights limit State behaviour, language rights are, more often than not, an issue devolved to the political process. The recognition of language

[49] High Court of Navarre, Judgment of 4 January 1999 (RJCA 1999\671). As mentioned above in the text, this ruling stated that if the government wanted to modify the status of the Basque language in the Public University of Navarre, it had to ask the Parliament of Navarre to pass new legislation.

[50] Two judges were against the invalidity of Article 15(1) and another judge advocated the invalidity of four further paragraphs: Articles 12(3), 15(2), and 16(1) and (2).

[51] High Court of Navarre, Judgments 932/2004 of 29 September 2004, 947/2004 of 1 October 2004, 1218/2004 of 16 December 2004, 371/2005 of 11 April 2005.

[52] X Arzoz, 'Language Rights as Legal Norms' (2009) 15 *European Public Law* 541; X Arzoz, 'Accommodating Linguistic Difference: Five Normative Models of Language Rights' (2010) 6 *European Constitutional Law Review* 102.

rights (as such or as part of minority rights) is based primarily on contingent historical reasons. It implies a number of decisions that must be adopted by each society, at various levels of decision making, and by the different branches of government. The issue cannot be decided upon consensus among states. Even if one accepts that the principle of equality obliges a government to provide public services in certain languages if there is a 'reasonable' number of speakers and if they are geographically concentrated, it is nevertheless up to each society to decide the specific balance between conflicting interests: democratic participation and substantive equality, on the one hand, and administrative efficacy, on the other.

The case law reviewed in this chapter shows that the contribution of the adjudicatory process to the recognition and promotion of language rights is rather limited. Ordinary courts can annul decisions or pieces of subordinate legislation that break the law on substantive or formal grounds. Yet, they have neither the competence nor the legitimacy to create or give shape to language rights or even engage in the deliberations that are required to that effect. In other words, legal mobilisation can be relatively successful as a defensive strategy against non-compliance with language rights already guaranteed in law, but it turns out to be rather unsuccessful as a means to promote a broader understanding of language rights.

Although the Charter's monitoring mechanism does not possess true or full jurisdictional character as the Committee of Experts' decisions are not binding upon states, language minority groups should be particularly attracted to the Charter. The Charter can give support to their claims of improving, correcting and implementing the overall legal position of minority language speakers within the domestic legal order. After all, the Charter may offer a crucial advantage when compared to the other international bodies that have the possibility to examine such or similar complaints. Unlike the ECHR, the Charter provides through its monitoring cycles a systematic and permanent assessment and improvement mechanism that could prove a more effective strategy than step-by-step litigation in supranational courts. The minority group associations have the opportunity to communicate directly with the Committee of Experts. They can provide to the Committee facts for the monitoring reports, and most importantly, they can open a conversation on reasonable and feasible means to comply with Charter obligations. In this way, they can influence the conclusions and recommendations of the final report.

B. Legal Mobilisation and Politics

The government of Navarre fought every adverse ruling given by regional courts up to the final judicial instance of the state. This means that, in most cases, it took around six years to get a definitive judgment and, consequentially, six years in each case for the regional government to conform to the rule of law. Unlike such lengthy legal battles, politics tends to be more dynamic, and elections are held every four years. Governments do not like to face continuous social and legal mobilisation and continuously adverse judicial decisions.

Legal mobilisation and judicial decisions may bestow legitimacy on a group's demands and raise the political and social profile of an issue. In my view though, the judicial decisions of regional courts do not contribute to policy change directly or indirectly: they contribute little to altering public opinion or to generating a more favourable attitude with regard to minority language rights. However, subnational governments are afraid of the political consequences of adverse judicial decisions, above all when elections are near: a series of unequivocally adverse judicial decisions may annoy certain voters from the centre. In Navarre, the population is traditionally divided into almost three equally strong social segments in its attitudes vis-à-vis the Basque language (favourable, non-favourable and indifferent). Language policy will always inevitably face a certain opposition. But both a strong language policy and a policy to marginalise the Basque language will equally be contested by a social majority, since the third of the population that neither favours nor opposes minority language promotion will still regard it as too extremist and peace disturbing.

From that perspective, one can assume that social and legal mobilisation on behalf of the Basque language did have a certain impact in the regional elections of 2007.[53] The adverse set of rulings of the High Court of Navarre analysed in this chapter brought not only a legal, but also a political defeat to the government of Navarre's language policy. Whether the reason for the subsequent reorientation of the language policy was the adverse rulings of the regional courts (the cause) or the increasing political alienation of certain small but crucial segments of Navarre's society (the effect) is open to discussion. As a matter of fact, in the regional elections of 2007 the governing parties retained the majority but lost their previous absolute majority in the Parliament of Navarre. A new force Nafarroa Bai ('Yes to Navarre'), overtly committed to a more activist language policy, emerged from those elections, gathering the support of nationalist and pro-Basque language voters. Governing with the parliamentary support of the socialist party, the regionalist party had to reorientate its policy. Already before the elections, in March 2007, a law to provide four Basque schools in the non-Basque-speaking zone with additional financial support was passed.[54]

[53] See PM Ayerdi Etxeberri, 'Actitudes políticas y resultados electorales de Navarra desde 1977' (2010) 7 *Iura Vasconiae: Revista de Derecho Histórico y Autonómico de Vasconia* 117.

[54] Law 7/2007, of 23 March 2007, concerning the financing of *ikastolas* from the non-Basque-speaking zone that had been subsidised previously by Law 26/2002, of 2 July 2002, related to the improvement of non-university education (Official Bulletin of Navarre, 2 April 2007).

After the 2007 elections, a number of positive developments were initiated, with the intention of appeasing the social unrest and avoiding the emergence of a parliamentary block against the government. In September 2007 a new organisation for the protection and promotion of the Basque language and the language rights of the citizens was created: Navarre's Institute for the Basque Language, or Euskarabidea. It is interesting to note that the Preamble of the law that created this body appeals to the European Charter for Regional or Minority Languages and its ratification by Spain. This shows that the Europeanisation of language rights gives new impulse to legal mobilisation.[55] A new regulation on the composition of the Consultative Council of the Basque Language was also adopted, in order to rebuild its declining prestige as a participatory and advisory body for language planning and policy of the regional government.[56]

In January 2009 the regional government made the first contacts and meetings since 2000 to coordinate language policy with the government of the Basque Country, the adjoining autonomous community that shares the same co-official language, with the aim of diffusing tensions. One of the explicitly agreed points with the authorities of the Basque Autonomous Community in July 2009 (this time with the new socialist government that came out of the elections in March) is that subsidies for cultural and linguistic activities in the territory of Navarre granted by the Basque government in the future will be filtered and co-decided by the government of Navarre. A new Decree was passed in 2009 to regulate the relevance of the knowledge of the Basque language in access to public employment in the regional administration.[57] Most importantly, the Decree defines a relatively broad list of public positions that entail contact with the public, and for which knowledge of Basque is assigned higher value. These positions include journalists, social workers, social educators, labour and training officials, library officials, tourism clerks, employees at the regional police of Navarre, fire brigade, forest rangers, clerks and administrative assistants, road guards, telephonists, caretakers and museum guards.

In September 2009 the socialist party (PSOE) and the centrist party (CDN) agreed to present a legal initiative to move four municipalities (Aranguren, Noain, Galar and Beriain) into the 'mixed zone'. While these four municipalities belong to the area of Pamplona/Iruña in terms of their socio-economic characteristics (housing, public transport, etc), they are assigned to the

[55] Decree 183/2007 of 10 September 2007 (Official Bulletin of Navarre, no 118, 21 September 2007). The new Decree that replaces it, Decree 133/2011 of 24 August 2011 (Official Bulletin of Navarre, no 172, 31 August 2011), even appeals to Article 22 of the Charter of Fundamental Rights of the European Union, which establishes: 'The Union shall respect cultural, religious and linguistic diversity'.

[56] Articles 23–27 of Decree 183/2007 of 10 September 2007.

[57] Decree 55/2009, of 15 June 2009, for the regulation of the treatment of the Basque language in the employments of the Administration of the Foral Community of Navarre and its agencies (Official Bulletin of Navarre, no 81, 3 July 2009).

'non-Basque' zone for linguistic and educational purposes.[58] The proposal for amending the Basque Language Act served as an excuse for the big partner in the government agreement, the regionalist party (UPN), to break its six-year-long government agreement with the centrist party (CDN).

The Basque Language Act (1986) was finally amended in 2010.[59] It allowed for the inclusion of four more municipalities in the 'mixed' zone. The Preamble of the amendment states that, in the 24 years since the adoption of the Act, social and urban development has created in the region of Pamplona/Iruña a conurbation with similar sociological and linguistic characteristics, where the demand for Basque-medium public education has grown enormously. Therefore, the amendment gave to four municipalities close to Pamplona/Iruña the option of joining the 'mixed' zone, subject to approval by the absolute majority of the respective town councils.[60] Three of those municipalities have already approved their incorporation into the 'mixed' zone (see Figure 3). Noain is the only municipality which has not

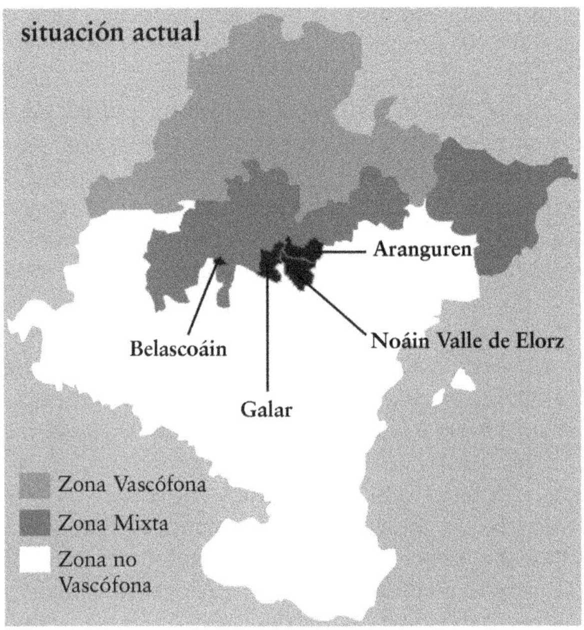

Figure 3: Linguistic zoning in Navarre after the 2010 amendment

[58] The Parliament of Navarre had already approved in June 2005 with 39 votes in favour, 2 votes against and 5 abstentions, a petition to the government of Navarre to review the borders of the 'mixed' zone in the area of Pamplona. Cf Bulletin of Sessions of the Parliament of Navarre no 49, Session no 42, of 9 June 2005, at 55.

[59] Law 2/2010, of 23 February 2010, amending Article 5(1)(a) and (b) of Law 18/1986, of 15 December 1986, on the Basque Language (Official Bulletin of Navarre, no 30, 8 March 2010).

[60] The four municipalities are Aranguren, Belascoáin, Galar and Noáin-Valle de Elorz. The joint number of inhabitants of Aranguren, Galar and Noáin-Valle de Elorz is about 16,000 and the three municipalities occupy jointly a territory of 133 km^2 close to the municipality of Pamplona. By contrast, Belascoáin is a small municipality (100 inhabitants) 20 km away from Pamplona.

joined the 'mixed' zone. Nevertheless, some elements of the official status of the Basque language have been implemented in Noain: Basque-medium education is available at pre-school and primary school and public signs are also in Basque.

Although the official rationale given for the amendment was the social and urban development of the area surrounding Pamplona, the political relevance of this change in the otherwise unreformed Basque Language Act of 1986 cannot be underestimated: the Preamble expressly mentions the demand for Basque-medium education and the need for adjusting the language legislation to the 'administrative and linguistic reality', which is tantamount to respecting the democratic principle. This development has been welcomed by the Committee of Experts of the European Charter for Regional or Minority Languages in its third report on the application of the Charter in Spain submitted to the Committee of Ministers of the Council of Europe.[61]

IV. CONCLUSION

Given the high polarisation among political parties in linguistic issues, the linguistic zoning scheme devised in Navarre in 1986 has remained in place unaltered for many years. Nevertheless, the regressive language policy initiated by the subnational authorities in the late 1990s mobilised language activists who had been campaigning unsuccessfully for decades in favour of a more permissive minority language policy in Navarre. They resorted to legal mobilisation and they even succeeded in annulling the main legal instruments of that language policy on substantive grounds.

The social and legal mobilisation on behalf of language rights and the series of adverse judicial decisions considerably eroded public support for the governing political party. This paved the way for a regrouping of the political forces in favour of a moderate but consistent language policy and opened up new political opportunities to address the demands of the majority of the citizens. A moderate pro-Basque language political coalition emerged in the elections of 2007. The governing party lost its absolute majority in regional Parliament and it was politically compelled to take appeasing measures, making relatively small but significant amendments to the language policy. The most interesting development was a limited revision of the borders of the linguistic zones after 24 years of standstill. Cross-party consensus on the need for that revision emerged as the main positive by-product of a decade of legal mobilisation. Nonetheless, there is a long way to go before language rights of Basque-speakers are fully accommodated in Navarre.

[61] European Charter for Regional or Minority Languages, Third report of the Committee of Experts in respect of Spain, para 331.

4

*Rights on the Left? Social Movements, Law and Lawyers after 1968 in France**

LIORA ISRAËL

AS IN THE United States and probably most European countries, the last half of the twentieth century in France has been 'in part, a story of law's role in movements for social change', to quote Austin Sarat and Stuart Scheingold.[1] This phenomenon is now at the centre of attention of numerous publications that explore the growing impact of law and the judiciary on French politics and society.[2] Nevertheless, few scholars address the question of the genesis of these new relations between law and politics.[3] In this chapter, I argue that the rise of a 'politics of rights' in France can best be understood in a micro-level sociological frame. Contrary to analyses that highlight the impulse given by EU laws, courts and European institutions more broadly,[4] I propose to shift attention to the endogenous dynamics taking place. This chapter argues that the politics of rights has primarily evolved from, and is embedded in, the social and legal practices of lawyers and activists, instead of being driven mainly by the judicially articulated norms and legal rules that emanate from European integration processes.

From this domestic and bottom-up perspective, the social and political context of the 1970s is crucial, and most notably, the dynamics of contention[5] involving lawyers as professionals and as citizens in the wake of the

* Translation from French to English by the author.

[1] A Sarat and S Scheingold, 'What Cause Lawyers Do *For*, and *To*, Social Movements' in A Sarat and S Scheingold (eds), *Cause Lawyers and Social Movements* (Stanford, Stanford University Press, 2006), 1.

[2] J Commaille and M Kaluszynski (eds), *La fonction politique de la justice* (Paris, La Découverte, 2007).

[3] A new approach has been recently developed to analyse as a social field European law: see notably A Vauchez and B de Witte (eds), *Lawyering Europe: European Law as a Transnational Social Field* (Oxford, Hart Publishing, 2013).

[4] M Lasser, *Judicial Transformations: The Rights Revolution in the Courts of Europe* (Oxford, Oxford University Press, 2009).

[5] D McAdam, S Tarrow and C Tilly, *Dynamics of Contention* (Cambridge, Cambridge University Press, 2001).

May 1968 events. It is not by chance that the French politics of rights grew in relation to issues advanced by the new social movements of the 1960s and 1970s. One of the most important issues was the development of legal advocacy in favour of immigrant workers, as I will show by examining the history of the GISTI (Information and Support Group for Immigrant Workers).

In this chapter, I explore the socio-historical conditions that made possible a new alliance between law and politics on the left of the political spectrum in France. The phenomenon of legal mobilisation with a view to social change is evidenced in the United States and in continental Europe. Yet, French and North American traditions differ markedly in respect of the political uses of law. In his seminal book *Politics of Rights*, Stuart Scheingold depicted how by the early 1970s America was still caught up in the 'myth of rights', namely, the assumption that the legal invocation and judicial realisation of rights is tantamount to actual social change, which had already been noted much earlier by Alexis de Tocqueville.[6] By contrast, during the 1960s, French legal tradition was still centred on law instead of rights. This made it difficult for political and social movements to consider the law as a useful tool in their political agenda, as law was seen first and foremost to be the realm of State action.

Focusing on the case of France, this chapter argues that the political events in May 1968, and the subsequent social movements in the early 1970s, were a fertile ground for the development of new forms of legal activism and consciousness. In order to understand this shift and the evolving dynamics between law, rights and social movements, it focuses on social actors and more precisely on lawyers. The approach employed in this study draws inspiration and analytical insights from the work of Stuart Scheingold and Austin Sarat on cause lawyering.[7] Lawyers—at least some of them—were responsible for mobilising law and rights increasingly as part of social movement activism. In this process, issues of legal aid, legal services and legal counselling are crucial to understanding the linkages that were created to render the legal system accessible to the deprived, marginalised and segregated segments of the population.

People rarely mobilise law and rights by themselves, especially when they lack various forms of capital—social, legal or educational. Their ability to do so often depends on the role of lawyers, who may constrain or, conversely, facilitate access to law. In this regard, the turmoil of the late 1960s and early 1970s in France transformed, for various reasons that I analyse and discuss below, the legal and political consciousness of an increasing

[6] S Scheingold, *The Politics of Rights—Lawyers, Public Policy and Political Change* (New Haven, Yale University Press, 1974).

[7] A Sarat and S Scheingold, *Cause Lawyering: Political Commitments and Professional Responsibilities* (Oxford, Oxford University Press, 1998).

number of lawyers. By doing so, it paved the way for substantial changes in the lawyering practices, organisational logics, and forms of mobilisation in the legal professions. Similar trends can be observed in other European countries during the same period, notably in Italy[8] and in the UK.[9]

Contrary to most studies that focus on popular legal consciousness,[10] this analysis specifically explores the legal consciousness of lawyers. Existing analyses of legal consciousness have tended to treat lawyers in a homogeneous fashion, as if all of them shared the same legal knowledge and representations. Yet, as political crises may reveal, there are many ways of lawyering that develop in relation to the political context. As Thomas Hilbink has argued in relation to civil rights movement activism:

> The experiences of lawyers in the Deep South demonstrated, at their most basic, that not all lawyering was the same. Lawyers were able to distinguish between mainstream practices and cause lawyering practices. Activists recognised distinctions between lawyering approaches that put lawyers in charge and those that helped the movement take the course activists wished.[11]

My aim in this analysis is to combine insights from the legal consciousness and the cause lawyering approaches to understand better the role of lawyers in the framing of legal mobilisation in France. By taking into account the structural role of historical events, this study places the emphasis on what Noga Morag-Levine has called 'cause lawyering organisations' (CLOs) to depict how jurists can organise themselves, not only as allies of social movements, but as collective actors for political purposes.[12] The first part of this chapter presents the 1968 events as an experience and an experiment for lawyers. The second part identifies the new forms of practice and organisation that developed among lawyers. The third part of the chapter explores in greater depth the example of the GISTI, an advocacy group (or CLO) on behalf of immigrants. GISTI pursued an ambitious line of action between political radicalism and legal technique. This chapter argues that through its victory in the courts, GISTI contributed to the legalisation of immigration policies, even if this was not always synonymous with the rise of immigrant rights. This analysis also depicts how law became progressively a legitimate

[8] M Malatesta, 'Défenses militantes. Avocats et et violence politique dans l'Italie des années 1970 et 1980' (2012) 3 *Le mouvement social* 85.

[9] P Gheda, 'Les droits de l'homme au service de la lutte politique. Les avocats dans le conflit nord-irlandais (1970–2000)' (2012) 3 *Le mouvement social* 49.

[10] P Ewick and SS Silbey, *The Common Place of Law. Stories from Everyday Life* (Chicago, University of Chicago Press, 1998).

[11] T Hilbink, 'The Profession, the Grassroots and the Elite: Cause Lawyering for Civil Rights and Freedom in the Direct Action Era' in Sarat and Scheingold (eds) (n 1) 78.

[12] N Morag-Levine, 'The Politics of Imported Rights: Transplantation and Transformation in an Israeli Environmental Cause-Lawyering Organization' in A Sarat and S Scheingold, *Cause Lawyering and the State in a Global Era* (Oxford, Oxford University Press, 2001) 334–53.

frame for collective action in the wake of new social movements, but at the same time a new type of constraint.

I. THE POLITICISATION OF LAW IN THE LATE 1960S

Law, albeit powerful, was historically considered as problematic on the left of the French political spectrum. If political trials have been important in the shaping of modern politics in France,[13] law was not in itself considered an instrument of changing politics and society. 'Political lawyers' in the French context played a major role in the development of liberal politics, as Lucien Karpik has shown.[14] Traditionally though, the use of the law was mostly defensive and even suspect for leftist parties and organisations, such as workers' unions. Nonetheless, this did not prevent leftist organisations from developing a legal approach, which, albeit highly critical, was open to the possibility of resorting to court as a political arena.[15]

The left's approach to law was intellectually linked to a class-based social analysis: it associated the legal system with the reigning ideological apparatus, which, according to the left, reflected and reproduced the domination of the bourgeoisie. This Marxist perspective on law survived in the third quarter of the twentieth century, when the Communist Party still represented up to 25 per cent of the popular vote in France. While more accepting of legalism in the sense of strict adherence to the law, the attitude of the Socialist Party, which was dominant on the left side of the spectrum, was still one that harboured suspicion. This ambivalent or negative attitude of the political forces on the left is crucial to understanding why legal mobilisation was not at the outset considered a useful tool of political action. Law had to be used, mostly to defend activists, but the aim was to change rather than to use the law.

A predominantly defensive use of the law also characterised the legal battles associated with the May 1968 events. As in many other countries, French students engaged in a large-scale mobilisation that combined political protest and cultural effervescence. Unlike in other countries, political protests were not limited to the student movement but they also extended to the working and middle classes.[16] While embodying dreams of freedom,

[13] E Claverie, 'Procès, affaire, cause. Voltaire et l'innovation critique' (1994) 7 *Politix*.

[14] Karpik shows that 'throughout the 19th century, lawyers in France were deeply involved in political action to pursue an overriding goal—to become recognized as spokesmen for the public'. See L Karpik, 'Lawyers and Politics in France, 1814–1950: The State, the Market, and the Public' (1988) 13 *Law & Social Inquiry* 707. See also L Karpik, *French Lawyers. A Study in Collective Action, 1274–1994* (Oxford, Clarendon Press, 2000).

[15] S Elbaz and L Israël, 'L'invention du droit comme arme politique dans le communisme français: l'Association Juridique Internationale' (2005) 85 *Vingtième siècle* 31.

[16] P Artières and M Zancarini-Fournel (eds), *68, Une histoire collective* (Paris, La Découverte, 2008); K Ross, *May '68 and its Afterlives* (Chicago, University of Chicago Press, 2002).

the year of 1968 was also marred, at least in France, by instances of harsh repression against the youth. In the last days of April 1968, a number of students in the Nanterre University were arrested. Following the first riots in the Latin Quarter in early May, the Sorbonne University was closed, and more students were arrested. Soon afterwards, the first students and rioters were put on trial, and seven students in Nanterre and Paris were fined and given suspended prison sentences from one to three months. One of the first counsels to defend the students in front of the Paris Court (which exceptionally opened on Sunday 5 May) was Henri Leclerc, member of the radical party PSU (Parti Socialiste Unifié), and defender of the main student union (UNEF).

The biggest demonstration of May 1968 took place on the 13th of the month in Paris. On the same day, the appeal of the first sentences against the rioters was also scheduled (exceptionally, as it normally took at least one month between those two stages of the judicial process). According to Henri Leclerc,[17] the leaders of the students waited for his phone call to launch the march. All of the students were finally released moments before the huge demonstration. In those momentous days of mid-May 1968, the judiciary apparently sent two opposite messages to the student rioters, one of disapproval, soon followed by one of lenience. In either case, regardless of which stance it decided to adopt, the judiciary was dependent on the decisions of the State authorities. In the end, the judiciary considered that lenience could ultimately be more effective than severity in calming down the protest. The government balanced between the will to appease[18] and the continuing use of repression.

In the course of a few weeks, several lawyers were suddenly required to defend an increasing number of students and/or activists. This led some of the lawyers to temporarily specialise on that type of defence. Most of them were close to the movement, as former defenders of political activists or even as young practising lawyers still close to the universities. In Paris, some of these lawyers created a movement called Groupement d'Action Judiciaire (Legal Action Group), that would later give birth to the Mouvement d'Action Judiciaire or MAJ (Legal Action Movement). The group initially focused on issues concerning the political repression of the youth and its legal dimensions. They denounced the use of courts for political purposes, and at the same time coordinated action in favour of the accused individuals, whom many of the lawyers belonging to Legal Action Group defended in courts.

From 1968 and until 1974, the repression against leftist students and activists did not subside. The Interior Minister, Raymon Marcellin, was obsessed with what he considered to be the 'leftist danger'. Regulations

[17] Interview with the author, Paris, March 2005.

[18] For instance, in May 1968, the Parliament voted for amnesty for those rioters who had already been condemned.

adopted in 1936 against pre-World War II fascist movements were re-enacted in June 1968 against leftist organisations. According to the new decree, being a member of those banned organisations alone could lead to a trial in front of the Cour de Sûreté de l'État, a special military court created at the end of the Algerian war. Cases brought before this court were far more severely treated than those reviewed by an ordinary court.[19] For example, it condemned activists to sentences of up to two years of imprisonment for handing out political leaflets. In such a context, lawyers rarely engaged in a political defence and instead invoked attenuating circumstances, while playing down the political involvement of their client. One exception was the trial of Alain Geismar, one of the most famous student leaders, in October 1970. At the end of the trial, Geismar asked his counsel, Henri Leclerc, to remain silent, and delivered a political speech. His last words to the magistrates were: 'If you want to judge the leaders of the Maoists, you will need to go to the factories, workers are waiting for you. The workers are our masters'.[20]

During the May 1968 events, law schools, although traditionally more conservative than other faculties, did not remain outside the movement. In Paris, a strike committee was formed, in parallel with the events in the nearby Sorbonne. The committee, which was called PAN (Panthéon-Assas-Nanterre—the three locations of the Paris Law Faculty), organised general meetings attended by professors, young lecturers and students. The symbolic significance of such meetings was heightened by the proposals that emerged from them. The most controversial proposal, which was shocking for distinguished law professors, was to abrogate the *agrégation*, a national competitive exam that gave access to the rank of full professor. The issue of academic recruitment was in fact the core of the controversy that unfolded in the Faculty of Law in Paris during May and June 1968. Grouped in working committees, the lawyers edited a pamphlet entitled *The Critical University*, which focused on issues such as relations between the university and society, the reform of teaching methods, or legal curricula.

This period of reflection in law faculties, more reformist than revolutionary, did not have many consequences since, in November 1968, a new law completely reorganised French universities. But a more important legacy of this period was the great division of the Paris Law Faculty into two universities: Paris I, more liberal, multi-disciplinary and oriented towards public law, and Paris II-Assas, more conservative, with professors more often specialised in private law. This division has strongly marked the political and professional

[19] See M Rajsfus *Mai 68. Sous le pavés, la répression (Mai 1968–1974)* (Paris, Cherche Midi, 1998).

[20] *Pourquoi nous combattons, Déclaration d'Alain Geismar à son procès (20, 21, 22 Octobre 1970)* (Paris, Maspero, 1970).

identities of those law schools to the present day. It clearly reflected the politicisation of law as an intellectual discipline, which was soon to be mirrored also in the development of new forms of legal practice.

II. INNOVATIVE PRACTICES AND LEGAL MOBILISATION

Practising lawyers and law students experienced the events in their own ways. Even if the legal field was less affected by riots and strikes than other social sectors, lawyers did develop a new sensibility and new ways of thinking, practising and organising. Despite their marginalisation in the legal profession, lawyers sympathetic to the events of 1968 exerted influence on the legal field as a whole by opening new debates in the profession.[21] Three domains of legal mobilisation can be identified in the late 1960s and early 1970s: new forms of collective action among lawyers, renovation of existing legal practices, and collaboration with social movements. All of these can be considered as steps towards better inclusion of lawyers in social movements, but also as new forms of social legitimisation of the law in contested terrains.

A. New Forms of Collective Action Among Lawyers

Defence lawyers who had witnessed the repression their clients had endured compellingly denounced the callousness of the police and the justice system towards the rioters.[22] The group began to meet informally in cafés and then more regularly, every two weeks from June 1968. Jean-Jacques de Felice, known for his anti-colonial stance, took the lead. Initially called GAJ, this group gathered dozens, maybe as many as a few hundred, lawyers, as well as several magistrates, social workers and law teachers. They oriented their actions in two directions. In the first place, they assumed the defence of students, including on disciplinary matters in universities. They also defended foreigners who were expelled from France because of their political commitment during the events, as well as workers on strike. Secondly, they progressively developed a new understanding about the potential uses of the law even as they maintained their opposition to the oppressive nature of the legal system. Those lawyers were truly conscious about the

[21] The impact of the events on the right, including on rightist lawyers, is beyond the scope of my study here. Marc-Olivier Déplaude's study on French doctors shows how the reaction to 1968 gave rise to a new conservative conception of medical training. See M-O Déplaude 'Une mobilisation contre-révolutionnaire: la refondation du Syndicat autonome des enseignants de médecine en mai 1968 et sa lutte pour la "sélection"' (2009) 73 *Sociétés contemporaines* 21.

[22] UNEF-SNE Sup, *Le Livre Noir des Journées de Mai* (Paris, Seuil, 1968).

limitations of their legal realm of action, as one can read in this text written by a member of the GAJ (probably at the end of 1968) about the events of May: 'we cannot count on courts as substitutes to revolution, but we can exploit their contradictions'.[23]

The GAJ changed its name to MAJ in 1969 and developed relations with workers' unions and political parties.[24] It took on to the analysis and mobilisation of new labour laws enacted after the strikes, notably those establishing new union rights. At the same time, the MAJ participated in the creation of collectives called Défense Active and Défense Collective, oriented respectively towards anarchists and activists. A presentation by Défense Collective stressed the fact that 'the lawyer, with his knowledge of law and the courts, must help to destroy this instrument of domination'.[25] Until the decline of their organisation in the second half of the 1970s, lawyers linked with the MAJ were characterised first by their orientation towards social movements and their willingness to help them in dealing with law, and secondly by their theoretical and often reflexive stance. This intellectual perspective was clearly noticeable in the participation of many lawyers of the MAJ in the journal *Actes—Cahiers d'Action Juridique*, created in 1973. The journal had as its goal to 'develop a steady articulation between a critical, a theoretical and a practical analysis of institutional protests'.[26]

B. Unions in the Legal Field

Among the earliest organisations of lawyers, even before the establishment of GAJ, was the Syndicat de la Magistrature (Magistrates' Union, or SM), created in February 1968, and formally founded in June of the same year. Subsequently, the Syndicat des Avocats de France (French Attorneys' Union, or SAF) was set up in 1972, also as a direct consequence of the events of May 1968.[27] The professional organisation Union Professionnelle des Magistrats also later transformed itself into a union, the Union Syndicale des Magistrats (Syndicalist Union of Magistrates, or USM).

One must understand the profound meaning of the word 'union' chosen by the various organisations, in connection with the social unrest of the late 1960s: it reflected a breach of the self-image of those professionals, who had always represented themselves in terms of public interest, as

[23] Typescript, 8 pages, probably May–June 1968. Archives Jean-Jacques de Felice, BDIC Nanterre.

[24] It changed its name when it discovered that a group dedicated to the defence of consumers already used the name.

[25] Platform for 'Défense collective' (1972) *Les Temps Modernes* 310 bis, 378.

[26] Editorial (1973–1974) 1 *Actes* 3.

[27] Interview of the author with one of its founders Claude Michel, Paris, April 2006.

fulfilling a public duty, and as members of the bourgeoisie. The recruitment of those professionals changed dramatically during the period under study. Magistrates in particular had recently seen the creation of a new school devoted to their training.[28] This school imbued a new collective spirit among them, which was crucial to understanding the context from which the SM emerged.[29] Indeed, the choice of the term 'union' can be interpreted in two ways. First, it was a way to desanctify legal professionals by giving them a name associated with the labour force. The lawyers and judges who joined those organisations expressed the will to defend their professional interests, along the lines followed by workers' unions, which had gained substantial benefits after the general strike in the country in May 1968. But, far from being only an interest group, lawyers' unions also wanted to address the public and to urge the political authorities to publicise debates concerning the legal domain. A central objective was to use their professional expertise in the service of the public, and to scrutinise or question public policies in domains such as civil liberties, prison and detention conditions, or access to law and justice.

The controversial position adopted by the lawyers engaged in those new union-type organisations was rendered visible by the disciplinary procedures instituted against some of them. In reference to Andrew Abbott's analysis of the profession being defined by its frontier,[30] disciplinary procedures regarding the normative definition of legitimate practice have to be considered seriously. Notably, the public exposure of lawyers was often criticised for being 'too political'. It also triggered heated debates concerning the extent to which it was legitimate for lawyers or for judges to intervene in the political sphere. In this respect, the Magistrates' Union called into question the traditional vision of the judiciary and its relationship with the authorities. In 1974, a magistrate, Hubert Dujardin, was brought before the Conseil Supérieure de la Magistrature (the judges' disciplinary court) for having allowed a journalist to observe what happened in his office. In 1975, Judge Patrice de Charrette in Béthune indicted a plant manager for murder after the death of a worker. The Minister of Justice, Jean Lecanuet, criticised the decision of the magistrate and accused the union of promoting a 'class justice'. The former Minister of Justice, Jean Foyer published an article in the right-wing daily newspaper *Le Figaro*, entitled 'Judges against justice', in which he wrote that 'while it appears to be a professional syndicate, this Union is actually a subversive leftist organisation'. The outcomes

[28] JP Mounier, 'Du corps judiciaire à la crise de la magistrature' (1986) 64 *Actes de la Recherche en Sciences Sociales* 20.

[29] A Boigeol, 'La formation des magistrats: de l'apprentissage sur le tas à l'école professionnelle' (1989) 76–77 *Actes de la Recherche en Sciences Sociales* 49.

[30] A Abott, *The System of Professions. An Essay on the Division of Expert Labor* (Chicago, University of Chicago Press, 1988).

of the affair were two-fold. First, Patrice de Charrette became the symbol of the new judges, who were named 'red judges' in *Paris Match*, a popular magazine. In addition, the Magistrates' Union sued Jean Foyer and *Le Figaro* for defamation. This action led to the conviction of the former Minister of Justice. On appeal, however, he was acquitted on grounds of bona fides.[31]

The mid-1970s were a time of high media exposure for the SM. Their engagement with several high-profile scandals inaugurated a new political and public visibility of their profession. A 1976 case represented a turning point. Following the attempted removal of a deputy prosecutor, Etienne Ceccaldi, who was investigating a case of illegal agreements between oil companies in Marseilles, a special gathering of 250 judges who were members of the SM decided to call a strike. Being illegal for magistrates—because of the requirement of impartiality—strikes did not belong to the repertoire of actions of the judiciary. Nevertheless, 330 judges of the Magistrates' Union joined the strike.[32] While such actions were criticised for being politically motivated, conflicting with the judicial function, they gradually strengthened the position of the Syndicat. It allowed the organisation to take a position on issues that were far from politically neutral such as financial crime, the partiality of justice, the right of magistrates to strike, and relations between the justice system and the press. From a methodological point of view, disciplinary cases can be considered as a symptom of tensions arising at the boundaries between professional and political commitment. In this regard, it is possible to analyse such cases as moments of crystallisation of the identity of the Magistrates' Union, which provided opportunities to actively define, through the defence of colleagues, new modes of action in the public sphere.

Established by socialist and communist lawyers, in a profession where it was legitimate to be politically committed, as epitomised by the traditional figure of the 'political lawyer', the SAF intended to defend the independence and values of the legal profession, and at the same time the general project of a more democratic justice. The SAF mobilised in cooperation with other organisations, such as the SM, in high-profile cases, and it protested also against trial procedures that were followed in cases of flagrant misdemeanours. Labour law was a main area of specialisation, and a focus of the lawyers' union action. The defence of employees could reconcile the lawyers' professional role with their commitment to the labour struggles.[33] The rise of the SAF

[31] The decision is unpublished, but reference to it is made in a special issue of the journal of the union, *Justice*, for its 20th anniversary (1988).

[32] The judges who participated in the strike numbered 190 according to the Ministry of Justice.

[33] L Willemez, 'A Political-Professional Commitment? French Workers and Unions' Lawyers as Cause Lawyers' in A Sarat and SA Scheingold, *The Worlds Cause Lawyers Make. Structure and Agency in Legal Practice* (Stanford, Stanford University Press, 2005).

was, as in the case of the SM, embroiled in scandals, mostly concerning the bad relations of the SAF members with local Bars or the judiciary.

Legal professionals' unions were successful in enlisting and mobilising members within their profession. The SM had 12.3 per cent of judges in its ranks in 1978 (nearly 700),[34] while the SAF counted about 1,000 lawyers as its members. In 1978 the SAF had established sections in 62 local Bars,[35] and began to enter their executive boards, with the election of the first heads of the Bar belonging to the union.[36] The two unions embodied the possibility of a new political-professional commitment. But they existed alongside a burgeoning number of more radical organisations acting on behalf of particular struggles during the 1970s.

The MAJ, mentioned above, originally stood on the left wing of the SAF, often closer to the PSU, or even to Maoist or Third World movements. It represented a continuation of the role of some lawyers in the struggles for decolonisation, such as the Caribbean lawyer Marcel Manville, Jean-Jacques de Felice who was close to Kanak struggles,[37] or Georges Pinet, who defended Afar and Issas in Djibouti. The lawyers of MAJ were critical of the SAF, arguing that the latter did not call into question the role of law as such. Instead, they called for forms of action closer to the social movements of feminists, anti-war activists, or farmers. In the area of feminism, the lawyer Odile Dhavernas claimed that fighting in the field of law should be associated with a systematic explanation and demystification of the rule of law as well as of the functioning of justice for women.[38] Dhavernas highlighted the importance of access to law and justice, a theme which, more than any other, symbolised the way in which the legal activists sought to bring law to social movements.

Even if it was common for practising lawyers to display a political commitment, some cases raised the question of political defence and its limits. A case involving a German lawyer, Klaus Croissant, epitomised this issue. He was the lawyer of the German Rote Armee Fraktion, the most well-known left-wing terrorist organisation during the German 'years of lead'.[39] During the summer of 1977, the West German government indicted Klaus Croissant as a supporter and an alleged member of the Rote Armee Fraktion. Having fled Germany, Croissant was living in Paris, and the German government asked the French authorities to extradite him. This extradition request was

[34] A Devillé, 'L'entrée du syndicat de la magistrature dans le champ juridique en 1968' (1992) 22 *Droit et Société* 639.

[35] These represented roughly three-quarters of the French Bars.

[36] First in Bobigny in 1974 (Claude Michel), and then in 1979 in Lyon (Paul Bouchet).

[37] The main ethnic group in New Caledonia, a French territory located in the Southwest Pacific Ocean.

[38] O Dhavernas, *Droit des femmes, pouvoir des hommes* (Paris, Seuil, 1977).

[39] D Della Porta, *Social Movements, Political Violence, and the State. A comparative Analysis of Italy and Germany* (Cambridge, Cambridge University Press, 2006).

the occasion for the French Bars, the Human Rights League, the Lawyers' and Magistrates' Unions, and the Communist Lawyers' group to reassess the right to due process, even for terrorists, and to draw the line between legal defence at the bar and political advocacy. Despite the support by intellectuals such as Jean-Paul Sartre or Michel Foucault, Klaus Croissant was extradited to Germany at the end of the year, and 5,000 people marched against his deportation in November 1977 in Paris.

The case of Klaus Croissant drew attention to the issue of due process in cases related to terrorism, and raised the question about the role of the nascent European judicial cooperation. The European Convention on the Suppression of Terrorism had been enacted in Strasbourg on 17 January 1977, and the additional protocol to the European Convention on Human Rights (ECHR) on Mutual Assistance on Criminal Matters was about to be signed. At that time, both were seen as potential threats to the protection of civil liberties for human rights and legal advocacy groups. Germany and Italy were engaged in a fight against terrorism and enacted special laws, leading some French activist lawyers, notably in the journal *Actes*, to warn against increasing repression in Europe.

Elsewhere in Europe, for example in Northern Ireland, political struggles evolved from the 1970s, along a path that progressively envisaged law as a site of political and social action.[40] Such legal struggles were also evidenced in cases that eventually reached the European Court of Human Rights (ECtHR). The petition lodged by Croissant in the latter was unsuccessful, but another ECtHR judgment, related to the conflict in Northern Ireland, which was issued in 1978, declared that State treatment against Republican activists amounted to 'inhuman and degrading treatment' and was in breach of Article 3 of the ECHR.[41]

C. Transformation of Lawyering

Relations between legal professionals and social movements often develop as lawyers commit themselves to a cause. During the period of the 1970s, several French lawyers could clearly qualify as cause lawyers. Robert Badinter became famous as an advocate against the death penalty, especially when he defended the murderer of a child in 1976, and 'put on trial' the death penalty in general instead of defending his client in particular.[42] The client, Patrick Henry, was sentenced to life imprisonment. Gisele Halimi had been

[40] K McEvoy, 'Law, Struggle and Political Transformation in Northern Ireland' (2000) 27 *Journal of Law in Society* 542.

[41] *Ireland v the United Kingdom* App no 5310/71 (ECtHR, 18 January 1978). See also Gheda (n 9).

[42] R Badinter, *L'abolition* (Paris, Seuil, 2000).

the lawyer of members of the Algerian National Liberation Front during the Algerian war and one of the founders of the feminist movement La cause des femmes in 1971. In 1972 she defended a young woman who had become pregnant as a result of rape and had an abortion. The trial, massively covered by the media, marked a turning point towards the legalisation of abortion in 1974; the French expression 'Procès de Bobigny' is now directly associated with this struggle.[43] Robert Badinter or Gisele Halimi can be considered as cause lawyers in the most classical sense of the term compared to their US counterparts in the 1970s. At the same time, the orientation of other lawyers towards marginalised segments of the population, who were neglected by their colleagues, also led them to develop innovative practices.

The journal *Actes*, created in 1973 by young lawyers, was aimed at disseminating unpublished court decisions for political reasons, and making available legal tools. In their first issue, they published a case study concerning the question of the owner–tenant relationship:

> We present the case for the defence of tenants seeking compensation for what they feel they overpaid to their owner. This is not an article about doctrine, because we do not present cases from the point of view of Sirius. We believe that we must take sides. We hope that this issue helps the tenants by providing advice to overcome their problems and to advance the law in the direction indicated.[44]

This kind of publication sought to promote legal practice as a form of collective action. The establishment of legal firms constituted a further step in this direction. It began in 1971 with the reform of the legal profession, whose 'neo-capitalist' purpose was initially stigmatised by those lawyers committed to a social cause. Designed to benefit business lawyers, this reform offered new opportunities of association between colleagues. Access to justice could indeed benefit from the organisation of lawyers into a collective. Law firms were created, with the most famous one located in Paris, 52 Boulevard d'Ornano (and therefore called Cabinet d'Ornano).[45] By establishing its location in a deprived area of the capital, when all the legal firms were in the centre of Paris, that firm wanted to develop an innovative professional practice. As Leclerc explains:

> Our goal was to practice better our profession, to be more effective for all our customers, to better meet the demand of organisations, unions and associations, to offer to the poor a quality of services equal to what the powerful and wealthy people could expect from their lawyers. We also wanted to create other relations, non-hierarchical, between lawyers working together in equal ownership shares,

[43] G Halimi (with a foreword by S de Beauvoir), *Le procès de Bobigny: Choisir la cause des femmes* (Paris, Gallimard, 2006).

[44] 'Dossier de défense: les charges locatives' (1973–1974) 1 *Actes*.

[45] These can be seen as the equivalent of 'law collectives', which appeared in the USA in the same period.

with minimal differences in income, which would be linked to the activity and not to the input of customers. A sort of 'cooperative'.[46]

This new approach provoked a protest from the Paris Bar defending the traditional model of the profession. But the Cabinet d'Ornano also hosted a law shop, where people could get legal advice for a small fee without prior appointment. Law shops constituted a radical innovation that was opposed to the classic model of the legal profession. Lawyers, law professors, students, and even non-lawyers played a leading role in energising those new spaces for legal practice, which developed quickly in the early 1970s in Paris but also in Bordeaux, Montpellier, Grenoble or Strasbourg. The French law shops were rather similar to their counterparts in other countries, such as in the United States and Canada.

Concerning their ideological commitment, some law shops took a step further from that taken at Boulevard d'Ornano: they abandoned the lawyer–client relationship in favour of general discussions about law and legal problems brought by individuals. A book emerged from such an experience at the law store located in Paris at Place des Fêtes, a very deprived area of northern Paris, out of which certain principles of organisation emerged:

The law shop must have the resources to provide excellent legal information. That is why we do not reject legal specialisation. But the discussion should not be limited to law—this is why the participation of non-lawyers is essential. We must denounce the hegemony and the mystification of the law. Sometimes we have been caught in a response solely and purely legal ... The discussion must go further than the black letter of law, to delve further into the analysis of the social facts.[47]

The experience of the Place des Fêtes law shop also gave rise to tensions. People generally came to it in order to find concrete answers to everyday legal problems (problems of health insurance, lodging, illegal immigrants seeking regularisation, etc). Yet, they were faced with the requirement of participation in a collective debate conducted with broader political goals. The vast majority of those who came to a law shop would have liked to see a regular lawyer. On the contrary, the approach of the organisers of the law shop at Place des Fêtes was to encourage individuals to take charge of their own problem. This approach questioned the delegation of legal problems to the lawyer, which is at the heart of the lawyer–client relationship. It sought to eradicate the professionalisation of the law, by challenging the monopoly of lawyers and calling for limited participation of professionals in law shops. The Bars did not take long to react, sometimes taking disciplinary measures against their members who participated in law shops, such as in

[46] H Leclerc, *Un combat pour la justice, Entretiens avec Marc Heurgon* (Paris, La Découverte, 1994).

[47] C Revon, *Boutiques de Droit* (Paris, Éditions Solin, 1978).

Strasbourg or Chateauroux. The law shop at Place des Fêtes even promoted the theme of self-defence of the accused person in the trial. Indeed, the radical approach to the issue of access to law in the end entailed advising non-lawyers to specialise on legal matters.

The theme of access to law gave rise to the most innovative forms of organisation that were associated with the mobilisation of lawyers in the 1970s. Such forms of organisation were more or less experimental, and sustainable only with the involvement of a sufficient number of activists. Yet, the declining number of activists over time contributed to the demise of their activities. The theme of access to the law also progressively lost its radical overtones when it was institutionalised through the development of State-funded legal aid programmes during the 1970s and the early 1980s. But besides the wide-ranging legal organisations created in the 1970s on a political basis to promote access to law, groups focusing on other issues also emerged in the same period, building on the rising appeal of rights in the French context. In these circumstances, the immigration domain was certainly one of the more fruitful, as is evidenced in the example of the GISTI, which exemplifies how various strands of legal mobilisation came together to acquire an organised form. This is developed in the next section.

III. HELPING IMMIGRANTS WITH LAW: THE CASE OF THE GISTI

The GISTI (Information and Support Group for Immigrant Workers) is the best example of a social movement relying on legal strategies, which emerged in the early 1970s.[48] Recent studies view the GISTI as epitomising the creation of the field of immigration law, in the terrain of the State.[49] Yet, as will be shown, the invention of the GISTI was mainly problem-oriented, linking a political question with legal expertise. The GISTI did not seek to construct an autonomous sub-profession or anything as large as a field, but instead, it remained voluntarily small, and largely based on pro bono advocacy.[50] In order to understand the professionalisation of lawyering in favour of immigrants, it is necessary to take into account the broader context and to analyse how some lawyers and non-lawyers specialised progressively on immigrants' issues for political purpose.[51] The creation of the GISTI is

[48] For a detailed account, see L Israël, 'Faire émerger le droit des étrangers en le contestant, ou l'histoire paradoxale des premières années du GISTI' (2003) 16 *Politix* 115.

[49] L Kawar, 'Legal Mobilization in the Terrain of the State: Creating a Field of Immigrant Rights Lawyering in France and the United States' (2011) 2 *Law and Social Inquiry* 354.

[50] Even if the term *pro bono* is rather anachronistic and not idiomatic in the French context, lawyers involved in the cases brought by the GISTI were almost always volunteer, and sometimes anonymous.

[51] JP Tonneau, 'Pratiquer le droit des étrangers, défendre une cause. Le syndicat des avocats de France initiateur d'un nouveau domaine du droit' (2010) 14 *Savoir/Agir* 29.

significant primarily because it exemplifies a new form of collective action based on law.

From an analytical perspective, important distinctions must be drawn among organisations that are generally depicted through a law and social movements frame. Some, like the GISTI, are built directly on a legal frame that shapes the way in which a social problem is raised and addressed politically. Others, like the allies of the GISTI in various political struggles—unions, associations, NGOs, etc—are focused on a social or political problem (discrimination, social assistance, workers' living conditions) and choose to occasionally use the law—which is not their master frame—as an instrument, often jointly with lawyers. A third kind of organisation is exemplified in the lawyers' and magistrates' unions described earlier: it is built on the basis of the profession of their members. The answer to Michael McCann's question 'How does law matter for social movements?'[52] must then draw some important distinctions. Movements can be distinguished first, on the basis of whether they mainly use legal tools, and secondly, on whether they mainly address the legal profession or act as an advocacy group on behalf of a social cause.

Concerning the GISTI, the legal framing that defined the creation of the organisation was at the heart of its identity and special competence, but at the same time it entailed a problematic relationship with the State. For GISTI, to seek to establish legal control over immigration meant to assume a role in the production of case law and to become a co-producer in the legal process, goals that contradicted the more radical conceptions of social change held by some of its members.

More broadly, the growth of law in the domain of immigration was Janus-faced: on the one hand, it gave opportunities to contest decisions concerning immigrants that would have been totally discretionary without the law. At the same time though, as we will see, the progressive legalisation of immigration also permitted the authorities to restrict drastically the conditions of access to residence or work.

A. Birth of the GISTI

Following the World War II, the new French government created a new higher education institution devoted to the training of the administrative elite, the ENA (National School of Administration). After May 1968, some of its students decided to protest against a law designated as *anti-casseurs* (against rioting demonstrators). When the director asked those students

[52] M McCann, 'How Does Law Matter for Social Movements' in B Garth and A Sarat, *How Does Law Matter?* (Evanston, IL, Northwestern University Press, 1998).

to quit the ENA,[53] they refused. Instead, they created informal groups reflecting on various political or social issues. One of these groups focused on the status of immigrant workers in France, questioning why this issue was handled administratively but was not approached through a legal perspective. The students interested in this did not intend to found a new organisation. They believed it was the duty of unions to take into account the fate of immigrant workers, whose living and working conditions were particularly poor at that time.[54] But the unions, and in particular the CFDT (Confédération Française du Travail), which was the closest to their beliefs, did not respond to their suggestion. Convinced that their legal competence was of value, the young civil servants decided to take action themselves, and began to organise small meetings and hold discussions on the topic. The idea of forming a group was motivated less by their experience in dealing with the problem, and more by a purely intellectual question, typical of a (French?) lawyer: was it acceptable to leave a gap in the juridical net that was supposed to provide protection to the entire world? For them, adopting a law that provided some protection was better than nothing, especially for immigrant workers whose position was extremely precarious.[55]

It is then on the basis of political and social networks that four young civil servants began to gather with various professionals: social workers based in the shanty towns that surrounded Paris, legal professionals who were members of the French Human League and of the newly created Magistrates' Union, and members of non-profit organisations such as the CIMADE.[56] The first formal gathering took place on 18 December 1971.[57] The first stage of the group's creation was not based on collective interest (none of the founders was an immigrant worker), and it was not a response to a particular demand either. The original nucleus of the soon-to-be GISTI then was something like an intellectual vanguard, as Lenin and then Gramsci defined it. It comprised a group of intellectuals, most of them lawyers, who decided to take charge of the problem of immigrant workers as the most marginalised and the least organised group among the working class. This group intended to support a social movement on behalf of immigrant workers, by employing legal strategies. Its approach as such contradicted the logic of collective action as expounded by Mancur Olson: the social and

[53] ENA students are considered as civil servants, and they receive a corresponding salary.

[54] A Sayad, *The Suffering of the Immigrant* (Cambridge, Polity Press, 2004).

[55] Historical data based on archives from organisations, interviews with several founders of the GISTI, and observation of a day-long meeting dedicated to the memory of the association organised by its members (Journée Histoire et Mémoire du GISTI, 8 December 2000). I made a transcript of this day-long meeting that was a major basis for the making of this history. Kawar (n 50) drew from this extensively for her study but failed to cite it among her sources.

[56] Comité Inter-Mouvement Auprés des Évacués, Christian organisation created in the late 1930s to help refugees.

[57] Report of the meeting, GISTI archives.

legislative changes produced by the movement would not directly benefit any of its members in contrast to the assumptions of Olson's utilitarian model.[58]

The choice of the name GISTI in 1972 must be understood in relation to other leftist groups, which combined activism and professional ability, and whose names also began with 'GI'. The most prominent among them was the GIP (Groupe d'Information Prison—Information Group on Prison), which was created in 1972 and led by the philosopher Michel Foucault. Others were the GIS (Groupe d'Information Santé—Information Group on Health) and the GIA (Groupe d'Information Asile—Information Group on Asylum). All of those groups were directly influenced by the Foucauldian criticism of institutions, and largely comprised activists who were themselves professionals. Even though the members of the nascent GISTI chose a name signifying that they were part of a larger movement, unlike other GIs (and especially the GIP led by Foucault), they did not want to be composed of leading personalities and public figures. Indeed, several civil servants involved in the GISTI, including some of its founders, never appeared in public. The alliance between expert training and activism led the GISTI as a cause lawyering organisation to progressively adopt a legal framing to analyse the political problems of immigrants, who epitomised the exploited workers of the leftist rhetoric. It was also a way to convert a professional juridical ability usually associated with conservatism into a liberal political resource.

B. Between Political Radicalism and Legal Technique: the Use of Law

Law has been deployed through various channels by the GISTI: legal services, publication of handbooks, and legal activism. The decision to offer legal services through telephone counselling was taken in April 1972. Underlying this alternative legal work was, again, the will to put into question the traditional lawyer–client relationship, as in the law shops. Legal counselling allowed for the collection of real cases involving immigrants' legal problems. In this way, members of the GISTI were able to link their theoretical reflection to real-life cases that could eventually be mobilised.

The second main activity of the GISTI was to translate into legal terms the political denunciation of immigrant workers' living conditions. Some lawyers had already experimented with this when they defended immigrant homes or shanty-town inhabitants. One of the shanty towns in the city of Nanterre was especially well known: it was near Paris, close to a university

[58] M Olson, *The Logic of Collective Action* (Cambridge, MA, Harvard University Press, 1971).

that had been one of the main centres of the May 1968 events, and in a working-class town administrated by the Communist Party. After 1968, shanty towns and immigrants' homes were especially targeted by leftist social workers as a field of action. Some lawyers, such as Simone Pacot from the Cabinet d'Ornano, began to take into account legal problems: did those who offered very expensive rooms to poor workers contravene the hotel industry legislation? Could houses in shanty towns benefit from the legal protection accorded to private homes? Would it then be possible to define as offences private property intrusions and destruction of houses by the police? While apparently purely technical, these questions were intrinsically provocative: they considered slums, where immigrants lived, as regular lodging, and therefore as subject to legal rules as any other hotel or home. Those questions were discussed in the first publications of the GISTI, in the journal *Actes*.[59]

Legal materials were used both to help citizens to deal with legal issues, and to enable them to deconstruct official discourses. The exegesis of immigrants' legal situation is typically found in those texts, together with references to official documents, such as administrative circulars. These circulars were obtained through the networks of members of the GISTI in the high echelons of public administration, from which its members had initially been recruited. Being able to obtain and to analyse circulars, the GISTI could enter into the inside processes of administration. The links of this leftist organisation with the public administration permitted it to clarify the legal status of immigrant workers. Indeed, the founding members of the GISTI believed, as many socio-legal scholars did, that 'marginalized groups benefit from more formalized processes, where codified procedural rights and substantive standards can be employed'.[60]

The GISTI soon came across and reflected on the contradiction between the case and the cause, well established in the cause lawyering literature. 'Inserting individual cases into collective mobilisation',[61] as it was described in their *Le petit livre juridique des travailleurs immigrés* (The small handbook of immigrant workers) published in April 1974 by Maspero, was typically at the core of attempts to politically mobilise the French legal system, since procedures such as class actions did not exist (and do not exist yet) in French law. In this way, GISTI sought to distinguish itself from other organisations, such as the French Human Rights League, which mainly provided legal assistance by intervening in individual cases.[62] By contrast, the legal

[59] A special issue was edited by the GISTI in 1974 with the title: 'Immigrant Workers: Unequal Rights'.

[60] McCann (n 52) 95.

[61] Introduction to Collectif d'alphabétisation et GISTI, *Le petit livre juridique des travailleurs immigrés* (Paris, Maspero, 1974).

[62] E Agrikoliansky, *La ligue française des droits de l'homme et du citoyen depuis 1945. Sociologie d'un engagement civique* (Paris, L'Harmattan, 2002).

discourse about immigration advanced by the GISTI was a new frame of analysis of the problem. Following David Snow's analysis, framing here can be understood as the cognitive operation that creates shared meanings and motivations among actors.[63] The GISTI provided an opportunity for radical lawyers to develop a subversive use of their abilities that was at the same time critical and powerful. This was manifested mainly in litigation.

C. The Use of Litigation: Between Legal Struggle and Recognition of Legal Competence

Litigation is the domain in which the distinctive features of the GISTI become more apparent. The use of legal competence in the field of political struggle, still controversial in the leftist movements of the 1970s, was necessary to demonstrate the legitimacy of this strategy. Legal problems raised by immigrants' living conditions have been central since the birth of the GISTI. Lawyers and social workers had already engaged in advocacy on behalf of those populations. The GISTI gave an opportunity to private lawyers engaged in the counselling of immigrants to get together and share their experience, that is—in their words—to collectivise the fight. This collective dimension (analysis of new laws, alerting to new procedures, etc) countered the fact that law individualises responsibilities and sentences. By doing so, the GISTI coordinated a collective legal fight among lawyers politically oriented to the radical left. The GISTI solicited lawyers, whom it already knew from dealing with cases, especially through legal counselling. The organisation selected the cases that presented an opportunity to change the case law. It could not support all the legal demands brought to it. At the same time, lawyers took advantage of the knowledge accumulated by the GISTI when they needed it.

One example of mobilisation is the movement called 'immigrants' homes strike' (*grève des foyers*) in the mid-1970s. A lawyer, Christian Bourguet, was called to defend immigrants' home residents.[64] Immigrants' homes owned by the State were associated with bad living conditions, a colonial attitude towards residents, including many racist managers, often former servicemen in Algeria, and coercive rules for inhabitants.[65] According to Bourguet, the first claim was lodged thanks to an incredible opportunity. A magistrate, member of the newly founded SM, met residents of an immigrants' home who protested against excessive rents. Sympathetic to their cause, the magistrate helped them to write a complaint, translating

[63] D Snow and R Benford, 'Ideology, Frame Resonance, and Participant Mobilization' (1988) 1 *International Social Movement Research* 197.

[64] Interview with C Bourguet, 17 January 2002, Paris.

[65] Notably concerning access to their rooms.

a grievance into an appropriate legal claim. He then assigned the hearing of the case to himself, to be sure that it would be accepted. Other claims, lodged notably by Bourguet, soon followed this first successful one.

The movement protesting against high rents charged to immigrants spread among various residences in France, and developed into a general rent strike. By the end of the 1970s, as many as 4,000 residents refused to pay their rent. Some were expelled from their homes, others from the country, and two immigrants' homes were destroyed by the authorities. Yet, the problem was now exposed and the living conditions improved in some ways. A coordination committee enlisted organisations that supported the movement. The GISTI helped it to organise an operational platform among lawyers involved in similar rental disputes in other parts of France, and supported the political negotiation led by immigrants' representatives with public authorities. At the same time, the GISTI refused to be officially present in the negotiations. While it was willing to support the movement, it refused to take action, which it considered that immigrants themselves must assume.[66] When the left came to power in 1981, the rent strike came to an end, even though problems remained outstanding.

GISTI also engaged in litigation before the Conseil d'État (Council of State), the highest administrative court. Petitions before the Conseil d'État require far more specialised and technical legal skills, closer to those of law professor-members of the GISTI than to those of private lawyers. The first action before the Conseil d'État was decided on 13 January 1975, surprisingly in favour of the claims put forth by the GISTI.[67] The decision was based on the abrogation of a *circulaire* and had implications that were not clearly intelligible, especially for non-lawyers. It involved a legal technicality and it was not at all linked to 'legal norms [that] can become important elements in the process of forging a sense of collective aspiration and identity among diversely situated citizens'.[68] This demonstrated that cause lawyering may be 'more effective in attacking the peripheries of power than the core', particularly considering that 'law prefers to articulate procedural rules rather than dictate outcomes'.[69] The GISTI immediately issued a leaflet explaining the consequences of the decision, both in practical and more policy-oriented terms. It condemned the repressive attitude of the State towards immigrants, and considered the court's decision as a victory over the illegality of this public policy. This first success before the Conseil d'Etat revealed an underlying ambiguity: winning a case meant more or less becoming an indirect partner of the State.

[66] *Journée Histoire et Mémoire* (n 55).

[67] CE, 13 January 1975, nos 90193, 90194, 91288, *Lebon* (Dondoux).

[68] McCann (n 52) 83.

[69] R Abel, 'Speaking Law to Power: Occasions for Cause Lawyering' in Sarat and Scheingold (n 7) 103.

These examples show that the victories before the Conseil d'Etat established the legal skills of an association like the GISTI. They did so despite the fact that the latter had a political background apparently incompatible with the stuffy atmosphere of the Council described as a venerable institution, removed from this world.[70] The recognition of the GISTI's legal skills by the most authoritative judicial institution in the administrative domain created an ambiguous situation. The possibility for interference in public policies through juridical decisions, unusual in France where case law is traditionally less important than legislation in the development of the law, apparently had the potential to exert influence, especially in the administrative domain. At the same time though, the shift of the GISTI to legal and juridical strategies, led some of its lawyers, such as Jean-Jacques de Felice,[71] to claim that its members had abandoned their original critical posture.

More broadly, the focus on litigation tended to create a confrontation with the State at the same time that it strengthened the State's control over immigration. By asking for a more explicit and clear delimitation of the State's policy over immigration, the GISTI participated in the definition of this domain of policy action. As any socio-legal scholar would admit though, law is both a constraint and a resource. The founders' objective of transforming immigration into a field in which one could rely on legal rules was undoubtedly attained. At the same time that GISTI accomplished this though, it also participated in strengthening the legal instruments of political control over immigration in France. It also made this deprived population more dependent on the legal tools provided by the GISTI and generally by lawyers.

The GISTI always remained relatively small, comprising around 100 individuals, most of whom worked on a voluntary basis. It never really became a professional association in the sense of '... possessing a purposive organization, whose leaders identify with the preferences of an unmobilized constituency which they attempt to mobilize in direct action in relation to a target of influence in the political system'.[72] Indeed, the goal was not really to mobilise directly: practically the target was professionals interested in immigration questions, lawyers or social workers. The GISTI engaged in action in two directions: it provided technical legal support for professionals, and at the same time legal counselling to social movements.

In the intellectual and political domains, the GISTI provided—and still provides—to social movements the analytical tools to struggle against the legitimacy of the State through its most potent tool—law. The legitimacy it acquired as the State recognised its legal skills helped convince contentious

[70] B Latour, *La fabrique du droit. Une ethnographie du Conseil d'État* (Paris, La Découverte, 2002).

[71] Interview with the author, 14 January 2002, Paris.

[72] McCann (n 52).

actors to use law against the State. The judicial victories, especially before the Conseil d'État, confirmed that 'rights consciousness develops in conjunction with the development and clarity of legally enforceable rights sanctioned by officials'.[73]

Immigration was a sector that the unions had neglected in the 1950s and 1960s, focusing instead on national workers. It became a central piece of the leftist criticism of capitalism in the 1970s, when leftist activists came into conflict with the traditional representatives of the working class. In the following years, the issue of immigration maintained a central place in the political debate. First, the economic crisis in the 1970s and 1980s, and the presence of immigrant workers in a context of rising unemployment, became a source of sharp political controversy and tensions, paving the way for the rise of a far-right party, the National Front. During the same period, numerous legislative reforms, mostly against illegal immigration, highlighted further the significance of the legal competence acquired by the GISTI. For example, legal skills enabled it to stop people from being deported back to their countries, especially when asylum policy became restrictive.

In the context of growing globalisation, the legal struggles related to immigration have extended at the European and international level.[74] In 2003, in the wake of the mobilisation around the camp of Sangatte (north of France), Claire Rodier, a jurist belonging to the GISTI, was one of the founders of Migreurop. Migreurop is 'a network of activists and scholars aimed at spreading knowledge about the generalisation of retention for undocumented foreigners as well as the increasing number of camps, which is at the centre of the EU migration policy'.[75] In this new context, the GISTI is still nowadays a leading actor in the advocacy of immigrants' living conditions.

IV. CONCLUSION

In this chapter I have analysed how social movements learned progressively to use the law and to incorporate it into their strategies in the post-1968 era in France. My main argument is that the mass protests constituted a major political event that transformed the legal consciousness of lawyers in universities, and of those lawyers committed to the defence of students and activists. The backlash of the political right in the early 1970s, as

[73] C Epp quoted in ibid, 84.

[74] V Guiraudon, 'Weak Weapon of the Weak? Mobilizing around Migration at the EU-level' in D Imig and S Tarrow (eds), *Contentious Europeans: Protest and Politics in an Emerging Polity* (Lanham, MD, Rowman and Littlefield, 2001).

[75] Migreurop's website can be accessed at www.migreurop.org/article643.html, last accessed 7 July 2013.

well as ongoing social conflicts and social movement mobilisation in the country, led to new forms of lawyering, and the rise of a new generation of committed lawyers. New alliances were created between jurists and social and political movements, through various channels and in cooperation with legally oriented organisations or with more activist groups that had a broader orientation and approach. The example of the GISTI, as well as the difficulties encountered by the law shop movement, show that the use of law as a political tool was powerful enough to convince a growing number of individuals and organisations to refer to it, and to mobilise it. While this success reinforced the power and legitimacy of lawyers, it overlooked the limits of litigation and legal strategies in bringing about social change. Those French cause lawyers inadvertently helped to create a 'myth of rights' in France, even if their original goal was to criticise the law.

In conclusion, if the analysis developed in this chapter is correct, the rise of legal mobilisation in Europe must be understood and explained primarily in reference to national level developments. It has grown as a result of the new conceptions of law developed by young jurists willing to reconcile their professional aspirations and their political beliefs. Similar trends in several countries (including West Germany—at that time, Italy, the Netherlands and the United Kingdom) are to be analysed as a reflection of the Europeanisation of social and professional conditions—notably what Maria Malatesta describes as 'Professional Europe'[76]—in the wake of a global event such as May 1968 and its aftermath.

The emergence of new legal instruments at the European level, albeit criticised by the same activists in such cases as anti-terrorist laws, was no doubt considered important by social movements—as appears in their publications, notably *Actes* in the French case. In turn, the actual cases with which lawyers and social activists were confronted and the problems that they raised led them to envisage new ways of solving them, politicising law in the process. In doing so, European law could provide opportunities, especially when it was not anticipated by the national authorities. But their utilisation was only possible because of the transformative processes in the understanding and practice of law, which had already been taking place locally in the interstices of social struggles. Accordingly, the bottom-up approach followed in the foregoing analysis is an invitation to reconsider the claim that the 'rights revolution' has been driven by European-level developments. Instead, this chapter argues that if legal instruments can open up new opportunities for action, they must always be understood in reference to their respective social and historical context.

[76] M Malatesta, *Professional Men, Professional Women. The European Professions from the 19th Century until Today* (Thousand Oaks, CA, Sage, 2010).

Part II

European Courts as Arenas for Legal Mobilisation

5

A Tool-box for Legal and Political Mobilisation in European Equality Law[1]

MARK DAWSON, ELISE MUIR AND MONICA CLAES

IN HER ADDRESS at the XXV Congress of the 'Fédération Internationale pour le Droit Européen' (FIDE), the Vice-President of the European Commission Viviane Reding acknowledged the ambivalent role of the EU Charter of Fundamental Rights after the Lisbon Treaty.[2] It has been both a powerful tool to enhance the fundamental rights dimension of EU legislation and a disappointment for citizens whose expectations for greater fundamental rights were not met.[3] There may be several reasons for such disappointment;[4] one of them—which this contribution seeks to address—relates to the complexity of the mechanisms for the enforcement of EU law.

Whereas fundamental rights were almost totally absent from the original text of the EU Treaties, the development of the EU as a human rights actor[5] is accelerating and is likely to enhance public expectations for greater protection. The last decade has seen a proliferation of rights catalogues, legislation and mechanisms for the protection of fundamental rights in the EU legal order. The available *mechanisms* to protect EU fundamental rights are expanding. The Union now carries its own binding Charter of Fundamental Rights, and will—if all goes well—also accede to the European Convention on Human Rights (ECHR). At the same time, the *substantive scope* of the

[1] This contribution is based on an earlier publication by M Dawson, E Muir and M Claes, 'Enforcing the EU's Rights Revolution: The Case of Equality' (2012) 13 *European Human Rights Law Review* 276–91. All websites below have last been accessed 14 December 2012.

[2] V Reding, 'Observations on the EU Charter of Fundamental Rights and the Future of the European Union', XXV Congress of FIDE, Tallinn (30 May 2012), http://europa.eu/rapid/press-release_SPEECH-12-403_en.htm.

[3] Ibid 3.

[4] Such as the restrictions on the substantive scope of EU law, eg, Art 51 of the Charter.

[5] For a sceptical appraisal of the EU's evolution in this direction, see A von Bogdandy, 'The European Union as a Human Rights Organization? Human Rights and the Core of the European Union' (2000) 37 *Common Market Law Review* 1307–38.

fundamental rights enjoyed by individuals in the EU is growing. A human rights policy is developing, led by a Human Rights Commissioner and overseen by a Fundamental Rights Agency. Finally, fundamental rights and the Charter are ever more frequently being invoked before European and national courts.[6]

This stronger fundamental rights mandate of the European Union presents both a challenge and an opportunity. The challenge is that the expansion of EU fundamental rights has the potential to create considerable confusion.[7] Alongside the multiple mechanisms at the EU level mentioned above, one must add into the mix the peculiar 'multi-level' nature of the EU legal order. Raising a successful legal claim may involve navigating an interlocking maze of related, but distinct, legal systems. Hence people risk 'knocking at the wrong door'[8] when they seek to enforce their fundamental rights. An NGO or individual seeking to use EU law to bolster their fight against breaches of fundamental rights faces a potentially bewildering array of mechanisms and rights to choose from, each coming with their own features, strengths and limits.

Instead of being a source of disappointment, however, the very expansion of EU fundamental rights can also create unique opportunities. The very 'multi-level' features of the EU legal order that make legal action complicated, eg the ability of EU law to create direct entitlements for individuals in the national order, are also the features which may enable groups and individuals to use EU law as a new site for legal and political mobilisation. For social actors with the know-how to take advantage of it, the consolidated array of fundamental rights instruments available at the EU level offers a new landscape in which to contest practices of inequality and discrimination across Europe.

Turning the risk of disappointment into a set of opportunities demands a clearer map or toolkit as to how EU fundamental rights claims can be raised and enforced. Building on earlier work,[9] this chapter seeks to provide such a map, exploring the various remedies available under EU law to enforce EU fundamental rights, and analysing their various strengths and weaknesses. It considers remedies for the enforcement of EU fundamental rights not just in individual terms, ie as a means of seeking redress for a concrete legal claim, but in broader political and societal terms, examining how and

[6] Eg, Joined Cases C-92/09 and C-93/09 *Schecke* [2010] ECR I-11063; Case T-85/09 *Kadi II* [2010] ECR II-5177; Case C-61/11 *PPU El Dridi* [2011] ECR I-03015.

[7] Eg, V Pop, 'EU Charter creating "confusion" on human rights', *EU Observer*, 11 November 2011, at http://euobserver.com/institutional/114247.

[8] By analogy, Reding(n 2) 7.

[9] See Dawson, Muir and Claes (n 1). See also M Dawson and E Muir, 'Individual, Institutional and Collective Vigilance in Protecting Fundamental Rights in the EU: Lessons from the Roma' (2011) 48 *Common Market Law Review* 3.

whether enforcement mechanisms for EU fundamental rights can contribute to processes of legal and political reform.

The focus is on a specific domain of EU fundamental rights policy, EU equality law.[10] EU equality law—as an area of European law in which enforcement mechanisms are embedded in both primary[11] and secondary[12] European law—offers a fertile ground to reflect on the mobilisation of EU rights in order to effect political and social change in the European Union.[13] The objective of our contribution is not to provide an exhaustive toolkit of the relevant procedures available to combat inequalities and the use made of them. Such a task, in a European Union with 28 Member States, would be close to impossible. Instead, we will outline the systemic nature of the various avenues for enforcement and outline the challenges as well as opportunities for mobilisation they provide. Parallels with mechanisms for the enforcement of other EU (fundamental) rights will also occasionally be made to illustrate the broad relevance of our approach.

In carrying out this task, this chapter is structured on the basis of two main axes of analysis. First, one can distinguish between three key categories of actors who can bring actions based on EU equality law: (i) private parties, (ii) institutions (either EU or Member State institutions), and (iii) collective actors such as NGOs or trade unions, all of whom have been active in protecting given minority rights. Each of these actors holds a share of the tools for the enforcement of EU equality law; we will thus analyse them in turn. Secondly, for each category of applicants a second variable will be introduced: separate sub-sections will distinguish *against whom* they may bring an action (EU institutions, Member States or private parties).[14]

The chapter argues that EU law has considerably enhanced the possibilities for individuals and groups to challenge breaches of fundamental rights to equality. Our analysis, though, also identifies some important weaknesses in the system of remedies provided by EU law. First, the autonomy provided by EU law for domestic orders to develop their own remedies and

[10] See B de Witte, 'From a "Common Principle of Equality" to EU Equality Law' (2010) 53 *American Behavioral Scientist* 1715–30.

[11] See the development of equality norms both as general principles of EU law and through Art 21 of the Charter; eg, Case C-149/77 *Defrenne* [1978] ECR 1365; Case C-144/04 *Mangold* [2005] ECR I-9981.

[12] See, eg, Directive 2006/54 on the implementation of the principle of equal opportunities and equal treatment of men and women in matters of employment and occupation [2006] OJ L204/23; Directive 2000/43 implementing the principle of equal treatment between persons irrespective of racial or ethnic origin [2000] OJ L180/22; Directive 2000/78 establishing a general framework for equal treatment in employment and occupation [2000] L303/16.

[13] The prohibition of nationality discrimination is left aside for the purpose of this contribution. In the current state of EU law, it is not considered as a fundamental right of the same nature as the right not to be discriminated against on other grounds, eg, sex, race etc.

[14] The institutional enforcement of equality law against individuals has not been included in the analysis owing to the limited capacity of the EU institutions to enforce fundamental rights claims against private parties.

rules of access creates significant discrepancies in enforcing fundamental rights across the Member States. Secondly, while institutional and collective mechanisms for enforcing EU equality law will be explored, its enforcement remains primarily based on individual litigation and complaints. Not only may this leave 'gaps' in protection for vulnerable and under-resourced groups but it may also make it difficult to address 'systemic' problems of discrimination that are irreducible to individual legal claims.

I. ENFORCEMENT OF EU EQUALITY LAW BY PRIVATE PARTIES

One of the key features that makes EU law unique as an international legal system is the ability of individuals to directly invoke provisions of EU law before national courts.[15] These courts are under a duty to set aside conflicting national law. This mechanism is by now taken for granted among EU lawyers. Yet, its radical consequence has been a heightened ability for ordinary citizens to use provisions of EU law (be they Treaty provisions or articles of directives) to challenge both national measures and even the action of private parties.

We will go on to consider how direct effect can be used by individuals both vertically against national law—and hence the Member States—and horizontally in private relations. We must first, however, clarify how EU primary law (such as the equality rights contained both in the Treaty itself and in the EU Charter of Fundamental Rights) can also be invoked by individuals to challenge acts of EU secondary law (eg EU regulations, directives or decisions).

A. Private Parties v EU Institutions

Where a provision of EU secondary law violates EU primary law, the act in question may be challenged before the Court of Justice of the European Union (CJEU).[16] To give an example relevant to equality law, one could bring a challenge—on the basis of Art 157 TFEU on sex discrimination—against EU legislation providing an exception to the general prohibition on sex discrimination. This could be the case where a piece of EU legislation

[15] Note that several researchers have also explored the direct effect of the ECHR in European domestic legal orders. See H Keller and A Stone Sweet, *The Reception of the ECHR in Europe* (Oxford, Oxford University Press, 2008); G Martinico and O Pollicino, *The National Judicial Treatment of the ECHR and EU Law. A Comparative Constitutional Perspective* (Groningen, Europa Law Publishing, 2010).

[16] In this chapter we use the name CJEU to refer to the entire institution, encompassing the Court of Justice, the General Court and the Civil Service Tribunal, as well as to the Court of Justice, without further specification, unless where relevant.

would allow insurance premiums to be set at different rates for men and women.[17] Even explicit opt-outs to equality within secondary EU law remain subject to the equality rules contained in the primary law itself. A direct legal challenge provides an opportunity, which individuals are able to exploit to obtain the annulment of the relevant provision of EU law, as well as of the corresponding provision of national law. This illustrates the significant consequences for EU law and policy—and even for private contracts—that EU equality law can bring.

Challenging acts of the EU institutions can be carried out through two routes. The first possibility is to challenge EU law via a national court. Where the *validity* of an act of EU law is in question, national courts are obliged to make a preliminary reference to the ECJ.[18] The example of the discriminatory exception for insurance premiums above illustrates this route: elimination of the exception to the general principle of equal treatment could be the consequence of a private applicant who challenged a domestic law implementing EU legislation before a national court. The national court, realising that questioning the validity of the national measure also involves questioning the EU measure which authorises it, must then refer the matter to the ECJ. While only the ECJ can rule an act of EU law invalid, the decision to make a reference in the first place remains in the hands of the national court (ie, applicants themselves cannot compel the national court to make a reference).[19] On the basis of national law, national courts determine which individuals or groups can have standing in the initial litigation.[20] An example of a successful challenge of the validity of a EU secondary law provision for breach of a fundamental right via the national route may be found in the *Schecke* case involving the right to data protection.[21]

A second, more direct, route is to challenge acts of EU law which violate equality principles before the European Court itself via an annulment action. This procedure is elaborated in Art 263 TFEU. While this route could seem more promising than the laborious mechanics of the preliminary reference

[17] See, by analogy, Case C-236/09 *Test-Achats* [2011] ECR I-773 (discussed further in section III below).

[18] Art 267 TFEU.

[19] On the first principle, see Case C-314/85 *Fotofrost* [1987] ECR 419. The ECJ has limited the justifications national courts can invoke in refusing to make a reference such as the 'acte clair' doctrine. Controversially, failures by national courts to refer questions where under an obligation to do so, could lead to a claim for damages or an infringement action. See Case C-224/01 *Köbler* [2003] ECR I-239 and Case C-154/08 *Commission v Spain* [2009] ECR I-187.

[20] See section I(B) below. The standing of individual litigants before national courts when invoking EU law obligations has often been rather unclear—the Court has indicated that 'national Courts are required, so far as possible, to interpret and apply national procedural rules ... in a way that enables natural and legal persons to challenge before the Courts the legality of any decision'. Nonetheless, the Court has also made clear that it will not sanction national courts for failing to adapt *locus standi* rules to meet this requirement; see Case C-263/02 P *JégoQuéré* [2004] ECR I-3424 [32].

[21] Joined Cases C-92/09 and C-93/09 *Schecke* [2010] ECR I-11063.

procedure, the practical ability of private parties to challenge EU law in this manner is questionable. As part of the Court's infamous *Plaumann* doctrine, private parties may normally only challenge an act of EU law where it is of 'direct and individual concern' to them.[22] In effect, the consequence of this rule is that private applicants carry standing only where they can distinguish their legal situation from that of *all other applicants*. This may be a particularly high hurdle to meet in equality law, where a discriminatory practice may be felt by a wide group of individuals.[23]

As a consequence, the ability of individuals to directly challenge EU law on equality grounds is heavily circumscribed. To again return to the example of discriminatory exceptions in the case of insurance premiums, it seems highly unlikely that a consumer of insurance premiums could challenge the EU Directive in question directly before the European Court—it was, after all, a legislative measure, while consumers of insurance premiums are one among many actors affected by the exception. The primary option for the consumer instead would be to challenge the national law implementing the Directive before domestic courts (a possibility that will be discussed in section II(B) below). However, examples of successful direct annulment actions against EU instruments may be found in other fields of EU law involving fundamental rights breaches such as the well known *Kadi I* case involving the fundamental rights to property and the right of defence.[24]

B. Private Parties v Member States

As is clear from the previous paragraph, EU primary law can be invoked to question the validity of EU acts in litigation before a domestic court. In a similar fashion, an individual can invoke EU law to challenge the validity of a national law before domestic courts. The ECJ has asserted that, by virtue of the primacy of EU law over national law,[25] any domestic act that runs counter to EU law is inapplicable and must be removed by the relevant national authority or set aside by domestic judges.[26] In the view

[22] See Art 263 TFEU, 5th indent; Case C-25/62 *Plaumann* [1963] ECR 95. For the purpose of this chapter, the specific situation of challenges to regulatory acts that do not entail implementing measures are left aside: see Case T-18/10 *Inuit* [Order of 6 September 2011] (appeal pending in Case C-583/11 P), and Case T-212/10 *Microban* [Order of 25 October 2011].

[23] Privileged applicants, such as the other principal EU institutions and the Member States, enjoy a much better situation—they carry automatic standing. A further category of 'semi-privileged' actors—the European Central Bank, the Committee of the Regions and the Court of Auditors—may act where their institutional prerogatives are affected.

[24] Here the applicant was individually concerned since his name was explicitly mentioned in the annex of the EU instrument challenged. See Cases T-315/01 *Kadi I* [2005] ECR II-3649 and C-402/05 P *Kadi I* [2008] ECR I-6351.

[25] Case C-6/64 *Costa v ENEL* [English special edition] ECR 585.

[26] Case C-106/77 *Simmenthal* [1978] ECR 629.

of the European Court, this rule holds true for any domestic norm that would conflict with any provision of EU law, irrespective of whether it is primary or secondary EU law (ie, the Treaty, the Charter but also EU anti-discrimination legislation).[27]

An individual can thus seek the annulment of a domestic legal instrument on the grounds that it violates EU equality law. One could, for example, seek the annulment of a supplementary retirement pension scheme that would distinguish between registered partners and married couples in a comparable situation for breach of the EU prohibition on discrimination on grounds of sexual orientation.[28] Alternatively, in litigation between two individuals based on domestic law, a party may argue that the domestic rule should be judged inapplicable because it conflicts with EU law. In both cases, a finding of incompatibility of the domestic provision with EU law will lead to it being deprived of its effects.[29]

Individual enforcement of EU law against the state can go beyond the mere questioning of the validity of domestic rules (ie, legal action against the state *qua* public institution). Individuals can also invoke EU law against the Member States *qua* private actors, for example when the state acts as an employer. Such a use of EU law requires either that the EU right is given effect through national law (in which case claims can be based directly on the domestic rule which must be interpreted in the light of EU law[30]) or that the EU provision is itself sufficiently clear, precise and unconditional to allow judges to identify the existence of a specific right. Several provisions of EU equality law clearly fulfil these conditions.[31] In that second scenario, the relevant provision of EU law is capable of having direct effect.[32]

In both settings, individuals willing to invoke their EU rights before a national court will have to comply with the procedural rules applicable in the state at hand. The rules for standing to challenge the validity of acts

[27] Case C-11/70 *Internationale Handelsgesellschaft* [1970] ECR 1125. On the reluctance by domestic constitutional courts to accept this view, see M Claes, *The National Courts' Mandate in the European Constitution* (Oxford, Hart Publishing, 2006).

[28] See, by analogy, Case C-147/08 *Römer* [2011] ECR I-3591.

[29] This is complemented by a subsequent duty for the relevant authority to repeal or amend the provision that is not compatible with EU law. See Case C-197/96 *Commission v France* [1997] ECR I-1489.

[30] This duty of consistent interpretation 'requires the referring court to do whatever lies within its jurisdiction, having regard to the whole body of rules of national law, to ensure that [EU rights are] fully effective'. See Joined Cases C-397/01 and C-403/01 *Pfeiffer* [2004] ECR I-8835 [118].

[31] Eg, Art 157 TFEU, Arts 4, 5 and 14 of Directive 2006/54, and Arts 3(1) and 4 of Directive 2004/113; Case C-152/84 *Marshall* [1986] ECR 723.

[32] Case C-26/62 *Van Gend en Loos* [1963] ECR 1. The ECJ has adopted a broad understanding of the notion of the State in this context (Case C-188/89 *Foster* [1990] ECR I-3343), mitigating some of the difficulties connected with enforcing EU law against private parties (although such difficulties have been considerably reduced after the *Kücükdeveci* case—see section I(C) below).

of Parliament, time limits to bring legal action or sanctions are defined differently in each Member State by virtue of what is commonly referred to as the principle of procedural autonomy. The national procedural rules applicable for the enforcement of EU law should however be equivalent to those applying for the enforcement of domestic law and must ensure the effective protection of the EU right at hand.[33] Procedural rules should thus not make it virtually impossible or more difficult to claim rights conferred by EU law than to claim rights protected under national law.

Despite the requirements for equivalence and effectiveness, the variety of domestic remedies may lead to important discrepancies in the possibility for victims of discrimination in different countries to bring claims.[34] It is in order to address this concern that the EU Equality Directives provide a set of minimum procedural rights.[35] Among the key features of these procedural guarantees: the burden of proof on the claimant ought to be partly shifted;[36] a system of sanctions, which may include compensation to the victim, must be created to ensure that sanctions are effective, proportionate and dissuasive.[37] The Directives also seek to provide protection for individuals against victimisation.[38] Finally, a special body for the promotion of equal treatment must be designated in each Member State to provide independent assistance to victims of discrimination on the grounds of race/ethnic origin and sex.[39] These procedural rules enhance the actual enforcement of EU equality law and make it easier for individuals to initiate litigation.[40] At the same time, important divergences in the possibility for individuals to bring remedies either against the state or against private parties before domestic courts remain as we will discuss below.

C. Private Parties v Private Parties

EU equality law is also a powerful tool to claim equal treatment against private parties. This characteristic of the relevant EU legal framework is

[33] See Case C-45/76 *Comet* [1976] ECR 2043.

[34] Note that a complementary and related mechanism to enhance the effectiveness of EU equality law is the general principle of state liability in damages for breaches of EU law (Joined Cases C-46/93 and 48/93 *Brasserie du Pêcheur* [1996] ECR I-1029). In such circumstances, the burden of proof placed on the applicant is particularly high since he must establish the existence of a sufficiently serious violation of EU law.

[35] See section I(C) below.

[36] Eg, Art 8 of the Race Equality Directive.

[37] Ibid, Art 15.

[38] Ibid, Art 9.

[39] Ibid, Art 13(1).

[40] G de Búrca, 'EU Race Discrimination Law: a Hybrid Model?' in G de Búrca and J Scott (eds), *Law and New Governance in the EU and the US* (Oxford, Hart Publishing, 2006) 100; L Waddington and M Bell, 'More Equal Than Others: Distinguishing European Union Equality Directives' (2001) 38 *CMLR* 3, 608.

particularly important in those Member States where the prohibition of discrimination was not enshrined in domestic legislation or it was not of such a broad scope as it is now as a result of the EU Equality Directives adopted in the past decade.[41] In these countries, where the principle of non-discrimination was enshrined only in constitutional norms, and legislative implementation was lacking, the possibility to rely on the relevant equality rights against a private party was limited and controversial.[42]

The EU Equality Directives address this problem and extend the protection against discrimination to private relationships. They are designed to be transposed into national law and thereby be made applicable in litigation between private parties. Once the implementation period of an anti-discrimination directive has expired, the equality rights that it is intended to protect must be given effect through national law. Regular reports on developing anti-discrimination law in Europe[43] provide a valuable overview of the relevant instruments adopted to give effect to the EU Directives in national legal orders. Any complaints against private parties can then be directly based on the domestic provision giving effect to the EU right, which should ideally ensure the optimal effectiveness of the EU right.

Even if a Member State has failed to adequately give effect to the equal treatment clauses contained in the Directives, the ECJ has asserted that individuals may rely directly on the general principle of non-discrimination as given expression by EU equality legislation against a private party in domestic courts.[44] Ms Kücükdeveci, for example, successfully claimed that her employer could not rely on national law to exclude the early years of her employment contract in the calculation of the notice period for her dismissal. A system disregarding the work period completed before the employee reached the age of 25 was constitutive of age discrimination prohibited by EU law and had to be set aside.[45]

Despite procedural rules to ensure effective enforcement of EU equality rights at the national level, their differences across countries raise fears that the level of protection against discrimination in the EU actually depends

[41] For a schematic overview see Annex IV of Commission Communication 'Certain Community measures to combat discrimination' COM(1999)564, see eur-lex.europa.eu/LexUriServ/LexUriServ.do?uri=COM:1999:0564:FIN:EN:PDF, accessed 8 June 2013.

[42] See M De Mol, 'The Novel Approach of the ECJ Towards the Horizontal Direct Effect of the EU Principle of Non-discrimination: (Unbridled) Expansionism of EU Law?' (2011) 48 *Maastricht Journal of European and Comparative Law* 109. For a comparative overview see A Sajo and R Uitz, *The Constitution in Private Relations: Expanding Constitutionalism* (The Hague, Eleven International Publishing, 2005).

[43] Drafted by the European network of legal experts on the non-discrimination field, see www.non-discrimination.net/publications.

[44] E Muir, 'Of Ages in—and Edges of—EU law' (2011) 48 *CMLR* 1, 39–62.

[45] Case C-555/07 *Kücükdeveci* [2010] ECR I-365. For further discussion on the exact reach of this case, see De Mol (n 42).

on where one lives.[46] A recent comparative study on access to justice in gender equality and anti-discrimination law identifies important differences in the procedural rules applicable to anti-discrimination claims within each Member State. They may, for instance, vary depending on the ground of discrimination alleged.[47] EU legislative intervention could certainly help in addressing at least some of these concerns by harmonising further procedural rights and/or bringing more coherence in the procedural safeguards available for each ground of discrimination. However, the latest attempt at enhancing the effectiveness and scope of the EU prohibition on discrimination has now been stuck in the pipelines of the EU legislative process for a few years.[48]

Besides these procedural challenges, there may also be deeper social and psychological barriers that prevent individuals from actually deciding to bring legal action. This is particularly true for victims of discrimination, who are more likely to be weakened and marginalised than most ordinary claimants. An important recent example of this is the position of vulnerable ethnic minority groups in the EU, such as the Roma minority.[49] In the summer of 2010, the European Commission (using a procedure that will be discussed below) contemplated acting against the French government owing to its decision to seek the deportation of almost 1,000 individuals of Roma descent from France. While the seemingly systemic nature of these deportations led many to question their compatibility with EU law, a surprisingly low number of individuals chose to contest their deportation orders in national courts.[50]

Such vulnerable groups may lack the financial resources, or the necessary knowledge of their legal rights, to make an individual claim in court. These difficulties for victims to actually gain access to justice and obtain redress are a source of concern for the enforcement of other EU fundamental rights. The recent Commission proposal to modernise the EU data protection regime, for example, places great emphasis on '*remedies, liability and sanctions*'

[46] EU efforts to organise cross-border remedies have focused exclusively on civil and commercial litigation: Regulation 44/2001 on jurisdiction and the recognition and enforcement of judgments in civil and commercial matters [2001] OJ L12/1 and Regulation 2201/2003 concerning jurisdiction and the recognition and enforcement of judgments in matrimonial matters and the matters of parental responsibility [2003] OJ L338/1.

[47] Milieu, 'Synthesis report: Comparative study on access to justice in gender equality and anti-discrimination law' (February 2011), section 7.1.

[48] Commission proposal for a Directive on implementing the principle of equal treatment between persons irrespective of religion or belief, disability, age or sexual orientation, COM(2008)426. See also press release of 3053rd Council meeting on Employment, Social Policy, Health and Consumer Affairs, Brussels (6–7 December 2010).

[49] See Dawson and Muir (n 9).

[50] J-P Lhernoud, 'L'éloignement des Roms et la directive 2004/38 relative au droit de séjour des citoyens de l'UE' (November 2010) 11 *Droit Social* 1024; A Math, 'Roms et autres: la protection sociale des ressortissants communautaires' (November 2010) 11 *Droit Social* 1037.

for breaches of the relevant EU rules.[51] This points to the added value of complementary enforcement mechanisms in EU law—mechanisms that are not initiated by individuals but by institutions, either at the national or at the European level.

II. THE ENFORCEMENT OF EU EQUALITY LAW BY INSTITUTIONS

The reason for the justified fame of the *Van Gend en Loos* decision of the ECJ is its radical decision to allow individuals to play a key role in the enforcement of EU law. What is often forgotten in the rush to consider EU law in individual terms, however, are the bodies originally envisaged as its main enforcing actors—the EU institutions. The two sections below consider the possibility of the EU institutions raising actions either against the Member States, or against each other, for infringements of EU equality law.[52]

A. Institutions v EU Institutions

Under the annulment action of Art 263 TFEU, it is possible for the EU institutions to challenge acts of EU law that they consider invalid. While this option is often used by the EU institutions in order to protect their institutional prerogatives (for example, their role in the legislative process) it has also been used where questions of fundamental rights are at stake. To take one example, the European Parliament challenged exceptions to Directive 2003/86 on family reunification, which allowed Member States to require non-EU nationals to be lawfully resident for two years before their family could join them. It did so on the grounds that these exceptions violated the right to family life protected in both the ECHR and the EU Charter of Fundamental Rights.[53]

While the right to initiate such proceedings rests with the EU institutions—not with the individual citizens they represent—exerting political pressure on institutions, or mobilising through political parties and groupings, may be useful. It may prompt political initiatives but also encourage institutions like the European Parliament to take a more pro-active role in enforcing EU

[51] Commission Proposal for a Regulation of the European Parliament and of the Council on the protection of individuals with regard to the processing of personal data and on the free movement of such data, COM(2012)11, chapter 8.

[52] This structure leaves one further possibility out—the institutional enforcement of equality law against individuals. Examples of the EU institutions using procedures such as the Art 258 TFEU procedure for private infringements of EU equality law are, so far, non-existent. However, in other fields, the Court has indicated its willingness to accept the Commission's claim that *the state itself* may be responsible for infringements of EU law committed by private parties (eg, Case C-265/9 *Commission v France (Spanish strawberries)* [1997] ECR I-6959).

[53] Case C-540/03 *Parliament v Council* (family reunification) [2006] ECR I-5796.

equality norms.[54] The mechanisms of EU law in this sense create institutional possibilities to challenge both EU and national law, which, although limited, ought not to be overlooked.

B. Institutions v Member States

Two procedures within EU law—the infringement procedure of Art 258 TFEU and the inter-state infringement procedure of Art 259 TFEU—allow Member States to be brought before the ECJ in order to bring violations of EU law to an end. As has been made clear by the Commission, infringements of the EU Charter of Fundamental Rights could also constitute a basis for infringement proceedings.[55] The power to bring an action remains solely at the discretion of the Commission (or the Member State concerned). The Commission cannot be held liable for a 'failure to act' nor can its reasons for either raising an action or failing to raise one be the subject of judicial proceedings.[56] For social and civil society actors, the ability to petition the Commission to bring such an action therefore represents a limited opportunity.

At the same time, the Commission has taken upon itself a number of procedural obligations in relation to complaints raised by private actors. In response to complaints before the EU Ombudsman, the Commission adopted a Communication (essentially a code of practice) on procedural rights for complainants.[57] While the rights that private complainants hold are limited,[58] it remains true that many infringement actions—including some raising fundamental rights questions—were initially brought to the Commission's attention by ordinary citizens.[59]

By far the least used of the two procedures is the Art 259 TFEU procedure.[60] Copying an approach common to international treaties, it allows Member States to raise actions against each other. This is complemented by a specific procedure for violations of fundamental rights and the other fundamental

[54] See D Acosta, 'The Good, the Bad and the Ugly in EU Migration Law: Is the European Parliament Becoming Bad and Ugly?' (2009) 11 *European Journal of Migration and Law* 1.

[55] See '2010 Report on the Application of the EU Charter of Fundamental Rights' SEC(2011) 396 final, 3. The situation must fall within the scope of EU law.

[56] See Cases C-416/84 *Commission v United Kingdom* [1988] ECR 3217; C-247/87 *Star Fruit* [1989] ECR 291.

[57] Commission Communication 'On Relations with Complainants in respect of Infringements of Community Law', COM(2002)141.

[58] R Rawlings, 'Engaged Elites: Citizen Action and Institutional Attitudes in Commission Enforcement' (2000) 6 *European Law Journal* 4.

[59] For example, a clash between religious rights and values and commercial rights to develop genetically modified food, as in Case C-165/08 *Commission v Poland* [2009] ECR I-6843.

[60] For a recent and rare example, see Case C-364/10 *Hungary v Slovak Republic* [16 October 2012] (not yet reported).

values mentioned in Art 2 TEU and contained in Art 7 TEU, which was introduced via the Treaty of Amsterdam. This procedure allows voting and other rights of a Member State to be suspended where there is a 'clear risk of a serious breach' of the fundamental values listed in Art 2 TEU.

As illustrated by the reluctance of EU institutions to make use of the Article 7 TEU procedure against Hungary and Romania in 2012,[61] the use of both procedures is likely to be exceptionally rare. Fearing the negative impact this could have on bilateral relations, Member States have been far keener to allow the Commission (an autonomous and independent body) to instigate infringement proceedings than to start proceedings themselves. The use of Art 7 TEU has been even rarer; in fact, the procedure has never been successfully invoked.[62] This has less to do with the complete absence of fundamental rights violations in the Member States than with the very high substantive conditions and voting thresholds required to start the procedure. The procedure is not apt to tackle fundamental rights violations that do not qualify as 'serious and persistent breaches'. Furthermore, under the terms of Article 7(2) and (3) TEU, a successful suspension of rights would require both unanimous agreement in the European Council and a qualified majority vote in the Council of Ministers, as well as the approval of the European Parliament, to succeed. Only the most excluded and isolated Member State need ever fear such a procedure.

While this may seem unsatisfactory to the extent that the EU does not seem to dispose of powers to enforce compliance with its basic values, the power and ability of the Commission to enforce EU equality law, as well as EU law more broadly, should not be underestimated.[63] For example, in recent months, the Commission initiated an accelerated infringement procedure against Hungary for the reform of the retirement age of judges leading to the early retirement of 236 judges in a particularly sensitive political context.[64] Hardly more than 10 months after the first official announcement by the Commission, the CJEU found Hungary to be in violation of the EU prohibition on age discrimination.[65] The speed of the procedure as well as

[61] See M Dawson and E Muir, Editorial: 'Enforcing Fundamental Values: EU Law and Governance in Hungary and Romania' (2012) 19 *Maastricht Journal of European and Comparative Law* 469–76.

[62] For an innovative, though not unproblematic proposal to enhance the relevance of Art 2 TEU see A von Bogdandy et al, 'Reverse *Solange*—Protecting the Essence of Fundamental Rights against EU Member States' (2012) 49 *Common Market Law Review* 489, and the Report of the High Level Group on Media Freedom and Pluralism, 'A free and pluralistic media to sustain European democracy' (January 2013).

[63] It should be emphasised that Art 258 TFEU proceedings cannot be used to enforce compliance with the values in Art 2 TEU, for which Art 7 TEU provides a special procedure.

[64] European Commission, 'Statement of the European Commission on the situation in Hungary' Memo/12/9 (11 January 2012), see europa.eu/rapid/pressReleasesAction.do?reference=MEMO/12/9&format=HTML&aged=0&language=EN&guiLanguage=en, accessed 8 June 2013.

[65] Case C-286/12 *Commission v Hungary* [6 November 2012] (not yet reported).

the Commission's clear intent to stress the unacceptable nature of broader threats to the rule of law in Hungary (for example by announcing a bundle of infringement actions and strongly condemning the situation[66]) exemplify how powerful institutional enforcement mechanisms could be if used to tackle fundamental rights violations falling within the scope of EU law.

Apart from individual enforcement and remedies, the CJEU has indicated its willingness to allow infringement actions which target general and persistent infringements of EU law (GAPs).[67] This approach—allowing the Commission to tackle underlying structural problems of non-compliance with EU law—could be a powerful tool in the context of endemic violations of equality law.[68] This could help in addressing situations where 'the remedy ... lies not merely in taking action to resolve a number of individual cases ..., but where this situation of non-compliance can only be redressed by a revision of the general policy and administrative practice of the Member State'.[69] While actions against Member States on the basis of general and persistent breaches of equality law have not yet been brought by the Commission, equality law may be a classical example in which breaches of fundamental rights are rarely confined to individual cases but are instead part of a wider societal practice of discrimination.

The ability of the Commission to bring such cases though, crucially depends on its political will to act. As already indicated, the right of initiative under Art 258 TFEU rests with the Commission alone. On this count, much depends on the dual role which the Commission plays within the EU's institutional system. On the one hand, the Commission is an independent 'prosecutor' of EU law via the infringement procedure. At the same time, it is also a political actor, the body with the sole right to initiate EU legislation in most policy fields. The problem may be the temptation to trade one role for the other. Significant resistance on the part of one or more powerful Member States to particular equality principles could either slow down the Commission's legislative agenda, or damage its political standing. The result may be a reluctance on the part of the Commission to pursue to the fullest extent infringement proceedings based on violations of fundamental rights.

One possible example of this is once again the dispute in the summer of 2010 between France and the Commission over the deportation of almost

[66] European Commission, 'Statement of the European Commission on the situation in Hungary' (n 63).

[67] P Wenneras, 'A New Dawn for Commission Enforcement under Articles 226 and 228 EC. General and Persistent (GAP) Infringements, Lump Sums and Penalty Payments' (2006) 43 *Common Market Law Review* 1.

[68] By analogy, see L Prete and B Smulders, 'The Coming of Age of Infringement Proceedings' (2010) 47 *Common Market Law Review* 23–24.

[69] Opinion of AG Geelhoed (23 September 2004) in Case C-494/01 *Commission v Ireland* [2005] ECR I-3338 [48].

1,000 Bulgarian and Romanian citizens of Roma descent from France.[70] Following the publication in the French media of an administrative act specifically targeting Roma as the object of removal procedures,[71] the Commission threatened France with infringement proceedings in September 2010. One month later, however, after intense resistance from France, as well as concerns from other Member States, the Commission announced that it would not take legal action against France '*for the time being*'.[72] Rather than pursue legal proceedings, the Commission focused on building an extensive package of other measures to better integrate Roma communities, including better targeting of EU funding towards projects benefiting the Roma.[73]

While the Commission's response to the Roma dispute may produce tangible benefits for a vulnerable minority, it illustrates the political dilemmas of relying upon the Art 258 TFEU procedure.[74] While enforcement based on the latter provides a remedy for vulnerable groups unable to prosecute violations of EU fundamental rights on their own, it also leaves the protection of EU equality law in the hands of an uncertain, and potentially political, process.

III. THE ENFORCEMENT OF EU EQUALITY LAW BY 'COLLECTIVE ACTORS'

In recent years, much attention has been devoted to a third set of enforcement mechanisms that fall in between individual and institutional tools. They may be referred to as 'collective' enforcement mechanisms in so far as they rely either on an individual acting on behalf of a group, or associations (eg NGOs) and other special bodies entrusted with this function, who may act to defend collective interests.[75] The debate on collective enforcement of EU law has so far mostly focused on consumer law and competition law,[76] as well as the enforcement of environmental interests.[77] These

[70] See Dawson and Muir (n 9).

[71] Ministère de l'Intérieur, de l'Outre-mer et des Collectivités Territoriales, Circulaire 'Evacuation des campements illicites' (5 August 2010) IOC/K/1017881/J.

[72] European Commission press release on recent developments in France (29 September 2010); statement by V Reding (19 October 2010); Human Rights Watch, 'France: One Year On, New Abuses against Roma' (29 September 2011) and A Rettman, 'EU executive leaves Roma problem to France' (*EU Observer*, 30 September 2011).

[73] Commission Communication, 'The Social and Economic Integration of the Roma in Europe' COM(2010)133 final. See also: Commission Staff Working Document 'Community Instruments and Policies for Roma Inclusion' SEC(2008)2172.

[74] See Dawson and Muir (n 9).

[75] Ibid.

[76] Eg, European Commission, 'Public Consultation: Towards a Coherent Approach to Collective Redress' SEC(2011)173 final.

[77] Eg, Art 9 of the Convention on Access to Information, Public Participation in Decision-making and Access to Justice in Environmental Matters; Proposal for a Directive of the European Parliament and of the Council on access to justice in environmental matters COM(2003)624 pending.

efforts contrast with the lack of initiative by the Commission to strengthen the collective enforcement of EU equality law. This has been a disappointment for many academics and stakeholders in respect of the main Equality Directives adopted to enhance EU equality law in 2002.[78]

Collective enforcement may serve three key purposes. First, it can be used to *support, represent or replace* action by an individual victim who does not have the resources to take action: especially in the case of vulnerable groups there may be a yawning gap between them and the law.[79] In these circumstances collective enforcement assists and empowers individuals to have their rights protected. Secondly, in contrast to enforcement initiated by private individuals, who are already victims, collective enforcement may act as a *preventive* tool. It may be used to discourage future violations of fundamental rights. Finally, collective enforcement can be used *strategically*, as a way to encourage political and societal change by forcing the political institutions to take action, or by drawing the public's attention to violations of EU rights that may be of particular importance to society as a whole. It is then a mechanism for strategic 'public interest' litigation: litigation designed to advance the common good.[80] Although notable progress has been made, such enforcement mechanisms remain to a large extent insufficient.

A. Collective Actors v EU Institutions

As in the case of individuals, two routes are available to collective actors: direct actions before the CJEU and indirect challenges via the national courts. Where the validity of EU law is at stake, national courts must make a reference to the CJEU. With respect to direct actions, associations and special bodies are likely to encounter the same obstacles as individuals challenging acts of the EU institutions. The hurdle of having to prove that the applicant is directly and individually concerned by the EU act being challenged applies to organisations, as well as to individual applicants. In fact, associations and special bodies are by definition unlikely to meet the *individual* concern

[78] On the relevance of collective action mechanisms for claims on equal treatment in employment, see R Mulheron, 'Reform of Collective Redress in England and Wales: A Perspective of Need', Research Paper for submission to the Civil Justice Council of England and Wales (February 2008), chapter 18, at www.judiciary.gov.uk/JCO%2FDocuments%2FCJC%2FPublications%2FOther+papers%2Freform-of-collective-redress.pdf.

[79] This is a key justification in respect of the Commission's proposals for consumer protection and competition law too: European Commission (n 75).

[80] Eg, JA Goldston and M Adjami, 'The Opportunities and Challenges of Using Public Interest Litigation to Secure Access to Justice for Roma in Central and Eastern Europe' in Y Ghai and J Cottrell, *Marginalized Communities and Access to Justice* (London, Routledge, 2010) 205–31.

test.[81] Despite vivid criticisms, the CJEU has so far explicitly declined to relax its standing rules,[82] holding that it is for the Member States to establish a system of legal remedies and procedures ensuring effective judicial protection of EU rights.[83]

The more common route for collective actors to challenge EU acts, as it is for individuals, is therefore the indirect route. Organisations representing collective interests, however, precisely because they have no self-standing (or individual) right, meet additional difficulties. National legal systems have very diverse rules on the standing of organisations depending on the rights at stake.[84]

Yet, owing to certain domestic laws having generous standing rules, EU equality law could be significantly improved. A recent action brought by a Belgian organisation called Test-Achats provides an example of the successful use of indirect challenges to EU acts. This consumers' association and two private applicants challenged a Belgian law implementing EU legislation before the Belgian constitutional court. The national court, aware that questioning the validity of the national measure amounted to questioning the EU Directive[85] on which it was based, referred the matter to the ECJ. This gave the European Court the opportunity to review and declare invalid the provisions of the Directive in breach of the principle of equal treatment between men and women.[86]

This example confirms that collective actors can usefully complement the role of EU institutions in the safeguarding of EU fundamental rights.[87] Here, EU institutions had not exercised their right to bring an annulment action against the provisions of the said Directive directly before the ECJ although they would have had standing.[88] Test-Achats would not have had standing before the ECJ due to the lack of individual concern; yet, the challenge of the Directive was successful through the indirect route (ie through

[81] On the limited standing of associational bodies: Case T-585/93 *Greenpeace* [1995] ECR II-2205. On the pros and cons of heavy restrictions on association standing: C Harlow, 'Public Law and Popular Justice' (2002) 65 *Modern Law Review* 13, 1.

[82] Note however developments following the entry into force of the Lisbon Treaty, which are mentioned above (n 22).

[83] Case C-50/00 P *Unión de Pequeños Agricultores* [2002] ECR I-6677 [44].

[84] M Ilieva, 'Legal standing for civil society legal entities to litigate against discrimination in the member states of the European Union and candidate countries'. Paper presented at the Jean Monnet Conference 'One for all and all for one? The role of collective actors in enforcing European Law', Hertie School of Governance, Berlin, 23 May 2013.

[85] Directive 2004/113 implementing the principle of equal treatment between men and women in the access to and supply of goods and services (2004) OJ L373/37.

[86] The legal problem at hand in this case is elaborated upon in section I above (text accompanying n 16).

[87] See also S Carrera and B Petkova, 'The Role and Potential of Civil Society and Human Rights Organizations Through Third Party interventions before the European Courts: The Case of the EU's Area of Freedom, Security and Justice' in M Dawson, B de Witte and E Muir, *Judicial Activism at the Court of Justice* (Cheltenham, Edward Elgar, 2013).

[88] See section II(A) above.

national courts) thanks to the coexistence of three exceptional procedural circumstances. First, Belgian law allowed standing to Test-Achats as a collective actor. Second, Belgian law, in contrast to most European systems, provides for direct access for private actors before the constitutional court to challenge primary legislation. And third, the Belgian constitutional court is one of the few constitutional courts willing to involve the ECJ through the preliminary reference procedure.

As was observed in relation to actions triggered by individuals against EU acts,[89] whether or not a case brought by an organisation at the domestic level will reach the ECJ depends on many variables. The uncertainty thereby created is often considered as a restriction to access to judicial review and to justice in general. The Compliance Committee of the Aarhus Convention recently came to the conclusion that, in so far as the enforcement of EU environmental law is concerned, the EU does not actually guarantee access to judicial review.[90] The strict standing rules under *Plaumann* (above), combined with the fact that the indirect route via preliminary references from national courts is so uncertain, led the Committee to hold that a new direction of the jurisprudence of the EU Courts should be established in order to ensure compliance with the Aarhus Convention on access to justice for the enforcement of environmental law.

While environmental law is a unique field—one where the beneficiaries of protective measures may be inanimate objects, or future generations unable to directly claim their rights in the present—the same deficiencies in terms of access to justice are of concern when we turn to the question of equality rights. Violations of equality rights may often fall upon vulnerable parties without the means or knowledge to enforce their rights in court. The hurdles for organisations to be granted standing before national courts are thus particularly problematic. Finally, due to variations in national procedural rules, collective actors in some states are able to bring legal claims that in others states are completely prohibited. Similar observations can be made when turning to the next level of enforcement.

B. Collective Actors v Member States or Private Parties

The Equality Directives target both states and private discriminatory practices. They provide for a set of mechanisms designed to trigger and encourage social change in the Member States through the intervention of collective actors. The Directives, for example, require the dissemination of information

[89] See section I(A) above.

[90] Report of the Compliance Committee (14 April 2011). Findings and recommendations with regard to communication ACCC/C/2008/32 (Part I) concerning compliance by the European Union.

on EU anti-discrimination law,[91] and the promotion of social dialogue, while they also encourage the conclusion of collective agreements laying down anti-discrimination rules.[92] In so far as race and sex equality are concerned, they also require the designation of bodies for the promotion of equal treatment, notably with a reporting and information dissemination purpose.[93]

Furthermore, the EU has developed several instruments designed to help eliminate discriminatory practices, which operate as a complement to the mechanisms provided for in the Equality Directives. These initiatives complement what de Búrca has called a hybrid model for the fight against discrimination at the EU level.[94] The model is hybrid because it combines multiple techniques of governance with an aim to achieve a given policy goal. As an example of such EU non-judicial approaches to anti-discrimination, the EU 'Progress' programme provides funding to develop (a) research activities, (b) mutual learning, awareness and dissemination activities and (c) support for main actors such as networks of legal experts.[95] Initiatives concerned with anti-discrimination, diversity and gender equality comprise 35 per cent of this section of the EU budget (an overall budget of 743.25 million euro for seven years (2007–2013)).[96]

Despite these valuable initiatives, when it comes to judicial remedies, EU anti-discrimination law remains primarily centred on individual litigation and requires the victims' active involvement. Since such litigation should take place before domestic courts, the relevant procedural rules are to a large extent decided at the national level. The Directives only request that Member States allow associations, organisations or other legal entities having a legitimate interest as defined by national law to 'engage either on behalf or in support of the complainant, with his or her approval' in judicial or administrative procedures for their enforcement.[97] Also, the equality bodies required by the Race and Sex Equality Directives[98] shall provide independent assistance to actual *victims* when they bring a complaint.[99] Legal remedies are thus seen largely in individual terms; the role of collective actors is mostly concerned with supporting actual victims who thus need to carry the claim or approve of it.

Some Member States, however, have been generous in granting access to courts for collective actors active in the field of anti-discrimination. This is

[91] Eg, Art 10 of the Race Equality Directive.
[92] Ibid, Art 11.
[93] Ibid, Art 13.
[94] De Búrca (n 39) 97.
[95] Decision 1672/2006 establishing a Community Programme for Employment and Social Solidarity—Progress (2006) OJ L315/1, Arts 7, 8 and 9.
[96] Ibid, Art 17.
[97] Eg, Art 7(2) of the Race Equality Directive.
[98] See n 12.
[99] Race Directive (n 12) Art 13(2).

well illustrated by the *Feryn* case in which recruitment practices that were discriminatory on grounds of racial or ethnic origin were brought before Belgian domestic courts by the national equality body and led to a preliminary question to the ECJ *in the absence of* a specific victim supporting the case.[100] Nevertheless, the Member States retain a large degree of discretion to regulate collective actors' access to domestic courts.

Once again, similar issues have in recent years been the subject of much attention in the context of EU environmental law, as a consequence of the EU's accession to the Aarhus Convention. In a recent ruling, the ECJ insisted that, although Article 9(3) of the Convention does not itself grant a right of action to environmental groups, domestic courts should interpret, '*to the fullest extent possible*', the national procedural rules in the light of the objectives of Art 9(3) and the objective of effective judicial protection of the rights conferred by EU law. This shall be done '*in order to enable*' an environmental protection organisation to challenge before a court a decision taken following administrative proceedings liable to be contrary to EU environmental law.[101] In a later case, the ECJ even held that Article 10(a) of Directive 85/337 on the assessment of the effects of certain public and private projects on the environment[102] precludes national law from barring environmental associations from access to courts. It does so on the ground that the relevant rules specifically protect the interests of the general public (and not the interests of individuals). Restricting access to justice to individuals affected by a breach of environmental law would have prevented such groups from having access to the judicial system for the protection of the environment.[103]

These rulings suggest that the ECJ is willing to provide a dynamic interpretation of EU law, setting minimum procedural rights to environmental organisations in order to enhance access to courts. Such developments should be kept in mind when reflecting on the legal framework setting minimum procedural rules for the enforcement of EU equality law.[104] It is worth reflecting on whether EU law should provide for a set of minimum procedural rules applicable to regulate collective action in support or on behalf of the victim. Bell has for example[105] drawn attention to the mechanism for

[100] Case C-54/07 *Centrum voor gelijkheid van kansen en voor racismebestrijding v Firma Feryn NV* [2008] ECR I-5187 [27].

[101] Case C-240/09 *Lesoochranárskezoskupenie* [2011] ECR I-1255, especially [46]–[52].

[102] Directive 85/337 on the assessment of the effects of certain public and private projects on the environment (1985) OJ L175/40 as amended by Directive 2003/35 (2003) OJ L156/17.

[103] Case C-115/09 *Trianel* [2011] ECR I-3673. Note that the case relies heavily on the very specific wording of Art 10(a) of Directive 85/337 as amended; such a provision has no equivalent in EU Equality Law.

[104] It is important to recall that such a legal framework is currently less detailed than the one existing for environmental law. Milieu (n 46).

[105] M Bell, 'Walking in the Same Direction? The Contribution of the European Social Charter and the European Union to Combating Discrimination' in G de Búrca and B de Witte (eds), *Social Rights in Europe* (Oxford, Oxford University Press, 2005) 273.

collective enforcement of the European Social Charter, an instrument of the Council of Europe. This Charter contains extensive anti-discrimination provisions and allows a specific route for collective complaints where national breaches are found. In circumstances where states may have common reasons to ignore or downplay a particular breach of the Charter, the vigilance of interested and representative collective organisations may step in to fill the monitoring gap.[106]

It is doubtful whether the European Commission will intervene in this field in the short term.[107] Its recent efforts on modernising collective enforcement mechanisms, as mentioned before, have focused on consumer and competition law—fields in which the competences of the EU vis-à-vis its Member States are far more established. In the current state of EU law on the matter, it is therefore important to stress the possibility of strategic litigation. Collective entities could be invited to select and support cases in Member States in which procedural rules are more flexible in order to concentrate their efforts on the most promising procedures in terms of actual redress and enhancing societal change. The European Roma Rights Centre—as one pioneering actor in this field—coordinates litigation in a number of Member States of the EU where practices of discrimination have been identified as endemic to several states, looking for the best litigation choices to maximise the societal impact of each procedure.[108]

Through this example, both the benefits and limits of the EU's decision not to harmonise national procedural rules becomes apparent. On the one hand, the ability of NGOs to utilise strategic litigation is uniquely dependent on national legal structures. Those NGOs established in states with restrictive standing rules can do little more than support and provide advice for individual claims. On the other hand, NGOs, and other bodies that have an established *pan-European* presence, can engage in their own variety of 'forum shopping', challenging discriminatory practices in states that are open to collective claims. Where these challenges are then referred to higher courts—for example through the preliminary reference procedure—such cases may establish useful precedents for similarly affected actors in other states. For organisations with the skills and resources to coordinate their legal action transnationally, the diversity of the EU's procedural rules may not be an insurmountable barrier.

[106] See for example, European Committee of Social Rights, Complaint No 63/2010 *Centre on Housing Rights and Evictions (COHRE) v France* [28 June 2011] on evictions of Roma from their dwellings and expulsions from France in the summer of 2010.

[107] Commission proposal for a Directive (n 47).

[108] See European Roma Rights Centre and the Migration Policy Group, 'Strategic litigation of race discrimination in Europe: from principle to practice', available at http://www.migpolgroup.org/public/docs/57.StrategicLitigationofRaceDiscriminationinEurope-fromPrinciplestoPractice_2004.pdf, accessed 16 July 2013, especially 50–51 and 54.

C. Equality Bodies and the Court of Justice of the European Union: the *Belov* Case

A final illustration of the contemporary importance of the 'collective' route for the enforcement of EU equality law comes from the recent *Belov* case. In this case, the Court was asked to rule on the applicability of EU provisions on equal treatment on grounds of racial or ethnic origin in the relationship between an individual and a service provider.[109] The case was referred to it by the Bulgarian Commission for Protection Against Discrimination (the KZD), a body created to promote equal treatment and to defend the rights of victims of discrimination under Directive 2000/43. The KZD had received a complaint from Mr Belov, a Rom living in an area of a Bulgarian city predominately populated by Roma, acting on his own behalf and for the people of Roma ethnic origin living in the relevant districts. Mr Belov's complaint challenged the practice of the local (former state) electricity company in placing electricity meters in his district at a height of 8 metres, rather than in consumers' homes. Ostensibly, this practice was conducted to avoid tampering with the meters, but its effect was to make checking of the meters by consumers on a regular basis impossible.

For the purposes of this chapter, the most interesting issue at stake in the *Belov* case concerned the capacity of the KZD to ask the Court for a preliminary ruling.[110] The KZD is precisely an example of an equality body mandated under the Race Equality Directive mentioned in Section I(B) above. Such bodies were set up with the explicit mission of aiding victims of discrimination and monitoring national compliance with equality principles. Advocate General Kokott argued that the KZD qualifies as a 'court or tribunal' under Art 267 TFEU and can thus make preliminary references to the Court. This line of argument would provide these bodies with a significant new weapon in the armoury against infringements of EU equality norms. Allowing equality bodies to refer possible violations of equality norms to the ECJ would give these bodies significant political and legal leverage to advance EU equality claims at the national level. Strikingly, both the Bulgarian government and the Commission considered the KZD in this case to constitute 'a court or tribunal' for the purposes of Art 267 TFEU.

It is not unusual for national bodies, entrusted with different categories of functions, to be regarded as a court or tribunal within the meaning of Art 267 TFEU when performing judicial functions, but not when exercising functions of an administrative nature.[111] In *Belov*, the CJEU disagreed with the Bulgarian Commission for Protection Against Discrimination and the Advocate General. It held that the decision that this equality body was to

[109] Case C-394/11 *Belov* [Opinion of 20 September 2012] (not yet reported).
[110] See Case C-394/11 *Belov* [31 January 2013] (not yet reported) [23]–[53].
[111] Case C-192/98 *ANAS* [1999] ECR I-8583.

give at the end of the proceedings was essentially an administrative decision, thus disqualifying it as a 'court or tribunal' in the sense of Art 267 TFEU.

Had the Court taken the direction indicated by Kokott, this would have represented a significant advance for the 'collective' enforcement of EU equality law via the equality bodies. Nevertheless, it is worth concluding with some minor reservations.[112] One of the dangers of such an approach could be that it would have the potential to alter their very nature. In order to qualify as a court or tribunal for the purposes of Art 267 TFEU, such equality bodies must have a very specific set of features.[113] Settled case law requires such a referring body to be established by law, to be permanent, to follow *inter partes* procedures, to apply rules of law under a compulsory jurisdiction and to be independent.[114] The question is whether it is desirable for equality bodies to be organised in such a way. One of the distinctive features of many equality bodies, for example, is their distinct presence as a body designed to represent and forward the claims of victims of discrimination.[115] This requirement sits uneasily with the need, implicit in the Art 267 TFEU requirements, to act as an impartial and adversarial body—a body concerned with 'adjudicating' claims rather than advancing a particular equality agenda. In this sense, the Court in the *Belov* case may have been wary of allowing references from equality bodies since it would give them a position not obviously suited to some of their foundational objectives.[116]

IV. CONCLUSION

For individuals who face discrimination, the very complexity of the EU law machinery presents both a challenge and an opportunity. The opportunity comes from the ability of affected individuals and groups to rely on EU rights against the state. This may be particularly important in circumstances where the State machinery—including national courts—has failed to provide an adequate level of protection. An example would be the use of the infringement procedure to bring an end to widespread discriminatory practices at the national level.

The level of sophistication of the machinery, however, comes with *complexity*, which may threaten the efficient enforcement of the rights it seeks to protect. EU fundamental rights are transposed domestically but they interrelate with national rights in so far as they are dependent upon national procedural rules. They also coexist with and are influenced by

[112] See also Dawson and Muir (n 60).

[113] See *Belov* [26].

[114] See Case C-61/65 *Vaassen Goebbels* [1966] ECR 261.

[115] See B de Witte, 'National Equality Institutions and the Domestication of EU Non-discrimination Law' (2011) 18 *Maastricht Journal of European and Comparative Law* 1–2.

[116] See Dawson and Muir (n 60).

the rights and principles deriving from the ECHR and other international treaties, each of which comes with its own mechanisms and logic. The incorporation of EU equality law in 28 national systems leads to substantial diversity in the available mechanisms for protection and opportunities for enforcement between the Member States. While this diversity is inherent in the EU method, it may seem disturbing in a field like equality, especially where parties seek to enforce equality rights against the EU itself.

At the same time, diversity between legal systems may also offer opportunities. It allows for learning and emulation, as well as benchmarking and competition between legal systems. This may be little comfort for private applicants, but it should motivate interest groups and collective actors to network and cooperate transnationally. In this way, each opportunity presents its own dangers and limitations. The ability of individuals to access the full gamut of individual rights remains dependant on the very national systems that may fail to adequately protect important equality rights. These individuals may also be placed in situations that make it difficult for deeper social reasons to even seek access to courts. Collective actors could play a role in compensating for the weakness of individual enforcement, yet this too depends on the openness of national legal orders towards a collective role in enforcing equality rights. Furthermore, as the *Belov* case illustrates, enhancing the role of collective actors as a tool for greater enforcement of EU rights may require a careful analysis of their exact role either as a support for victims of breaches of EU law or as independent problem-solving authorities.

EU equality law is a special case in so far as it provides for a set of minimum procedural rights regarding access to justice in addition to the substantive rights it grants. These procedural rights are not equally applicable to other fundamental rights. However, the same strengths and weaknesses may be. To take the example of data protection, EU efforts in this area have a significant impact on the right to privacy and freedom of expression.[117] They could also form the basis of actions by individuals, by institutions via the Commission's enforcement powers, or for example through collective actions by consumer organisations such as Test-Achats. This merits further academic attention if the EU's nascent 'rights revolution'[118] is to extend across the full range of EU fundamental rights.

[117] See, eg, European Commission, Proposal for a Regulation on the protection of individuals with regard to the processing of personal data and on the free movement of such data (General Data Protection Regulation) COM(2012)11 final.

[118] The idea of a rights revolution, used regularly in US and Canadian literature, refers to the gradual extension of fundamental rights to virtually all human interactions, combined with new patterns of mobilisation, engaging the courts ultimately in policy choices: CR Sunstein, *After the Rights Revolution: Reconceiving the Regulatory State* (Cambridge, MA, Harvard University Press, 1990); M Ignatieff, *The Rights Revolution*, 2nd edn (Toronto, House of Anansi Ltd, 2007).

6

European Courts and the Rights of Migrants and Asylum Seekers in Greece

EVANGELIA PSYCHOGIOPOULOU

THE POWER OF courts to steer policy making and influence how governments abide by fundamental rights guarantees has become the subject of lively scholarly debates in recent years. Key areas of inquiry have been the mobilisation of law through litigation by both individuals and groups in order to seek redress for the curtailment of their rights, and the use of judicial means to pursue policy reform and trigger social change in support of fundamental rights protection.[1] Research on legal mobilisation and the ability of courts to influence public policy has long been focused on the United States. During the past 15 years or so though, a flourishing body of literature on European integration has studied legal mobilisation and the use of judicial tactics to diffuse human rights norms into public policies in Europe.[2] In this context, the European Court of Human Rights (ECtHR)

[1] See in particular M McCann, *Rights at Work. Pay Equity Reform and the Politics of Legal Mobilization* (Chicago, University of Chicago Press, 1994); M McCann, 'Law and Political Struggles for Social Change: Puzzles, Paradoxes and Promises in Future Research' in DA Schultz (ed), *Leveraging the Law. Using the Courts to Achieve Social Change* (New York, Peter Lang, 1998) 319; GN Rosenberg, *The Hollow Hope: Can Courts Bring About Social Change?* 2nd edn (Chicago, University of Chicago Press, 2008).

[2] See mainly K Alter and J Vargas, 'Explaining Variation in the Use of European Litigation Strategies' (2000) 33(4) *Comparative Political Studies* 452; D Anagnostou, 'Does European Human Rights Law Matter? Implementation and Domestic Impact of Strasbourg Court Judgments on Minority-Related Policies' (2010) 14 *The International Journal of Human Rights* 721; D Chalmers, 'The Positioning of EU Judicial Politics within the United Kingdom' (2000) 23 *West European Politics* 169; R Cichowski, *The European Court and Civil Society: Litigation, Mobilization and Governance* (Cambridge, Cambridge University Press, 2007); L Conant, *Justice Contained: Law and Politics in the European Union* (Ithaca, Cornell University Press, 2002); RD Kelemen, 'Suing for Europe: Adversarial Legalism and European Governance' (2006) 39 *Comparative Political Studies* 101; A Sweet, *Governing with Judges. Constitutional Politics in Europe* (Oxford, Oxford University Press, 2000); L Vanhala, 'Anti-discrimination Policy Actors and their Use of Litigation Strategies: The Influence of Identity Politics' (2009) 16 *Journal of European Public Policy* 738.

and the Court of Justice of the European Union (CJEU, former European Court of Justice) have received significant attention. Both courts have increasingly served as platforms of support for organised interests and individuals who seek to affect government policies by asserting their rights.

Over time, the two European courts have developed a substantial body of case law related to fundamental rights. This is hardly surprising for the ECtHR. On the basis of the European Convention on Human Rights (ECHR), the ECtHR has sought to consolidate the rule of law in Europe, specifically from a fundamental rights perspective. The CJEU, for its part, has enriched its jurisprudence with a fundamental rights component from an early stage, despite the fact that the founding Treaties of the European Communities in the 1950s did not contain a commitment to human rights protection. Seeking to respond to national allegations that constitutionally safeguarded human rights should act as a limitation on the powers of the European Communities, the CJEU employed a fundamental rights discourse in its early case law.[3] This became both a cause and catalyst for changes brought to primary European Union (EU) law for the protection of fundamental rights. In the 1990s, fundamental rights, as guaranteed by the ECHR, and resulting from the constitutional traditions common to the EU Member States, were recognised as general principles of EU law, binding not only the European institutions but also national authorities when these act within the scope of EU law. More recently, in 2009, the Charter of Fundamental Rights of the European Union (CFR) was given binding legal status by the Treaty of Lisbon and the EU was required to accede to the ECHR.

The attractiveness of the two European courts for the exposure of the hurdles that third country migrants (ie nationals of non-EU countries) and asylum seekers encounter in Europe has expanded throughout the years. Resort to the ECtHR has revealed a number of deficiencies in the protection of migrants' rights across a number of countries party to the Council of Europe.[4] The CJEU has also been confronted with cases that raise serious concerns about the level of protection afforded to the rights of third country nationals and asylum seekers in the EU Member States.[5] Some of the most important cases brought before the two courts concern the Greek state, which during the past few decades has faced a vast immigration influx.

[3] See in particular CJEU, Case 29/69 *Stauder v City of Ulm* [1969] ECR 419; Case 11/70 *Internationale Handelsgesellschaft v Einfuhr und Vorratsstelle für Getreide und Futtermittel* [1970] ECR 1125; and Case 4/73 *Nold v Commission* [1974] ECR 491.

[4] See indicatively N Mole and C Meredith, *Asylum and the European Convention on Human Rights*, Human Rights Files, no 9 (Strasbourg, Council of Europe Publishing, 2010); H Lambert, 'The European Convention on Human Rights and the Protection of Refugees: Limits and Opportunities' (2005) 24 *Refugee Survey Quarterly* 39.

[5] See indicatively E Guild and P Minderhoud (eds), *The First Decade of EU Migration and Asylum Law* (Leiden, Brill, 2012).

Since Greece accepted the individual right to petition the ECtHR in the mid-1980s, a growing number of cases brought against Greece have originated in applications by non-Greek nationals.[6] Of 62 judgments, delivered before 1 January 2013 and declaring a violation of the ECHR on the basis of applications filed by foreigners (either alone or together with Greek citizens),[7] 51 have stemmed from claims raised by third country nationals.

[6] See N Sitaropoulos, 'Η προστασία από την Ελλάδα θεμελιωδών δικαιωμάτων των αλλοδαπών μέσα από το πρίσμα της νομολογίας του Ευρωπαϊκού Δικαστηρίου Δικαιωμάτων του Ανθρώπου. Σχετικά ζητήματα ουσίας και εφαρμογής της ΕΣΔΑ στην Ελλάδα [The Greek State's Protection of Migrants' Fundamental Rights under the Jurisprudence of the European Court of Human Rights. Substantive Issues and the Application of the ECHR in Greece] (2003) 29 *To Syntagma* 233.

[7] *Hornsby v Greece* App no 18357/91 (ECtHR, 19 March 1997); *Twalib v Greece* App no 24294/94 (ECtHR, 9 June 1998); *Portington v Greece* App no 28523/95 (ECtHR, 23 September 1998); *Biba v Greece* App no 33170/96 (ECtHR, 26 September 2000); *Dougoz v Greece* App no 40907/98 (ECtHR, 6 March 2001); *Peers v Greece* App no 28524/95 (ECtHR, 19 April 2001); *Yagtzilar and Others v Greece* App no 41727/98 (ECtHR, 6 December 2001); *Sajtos v Greece* App no 53478/99 (ECtHR, 21 March 2002); *Alija v Greece* App no 73717/01 (ECtHR, 7 April 2005); *Jarnevic Profit v Greece* App no 28338/02 (ECtHR, 7 April 2005); *Kurti v Greece* App no 2507/02 (ECtHR, 29 September 2005); *Mohd v Greece* App no 11919/03 (ECtHR, 27 April 2006); *Papa v Greece* App no 21091/04 (ECtHR, 6 July 2006); *Allushi v Greece* App no 3525/04 (ECtHR, 13 July 2006); *Kaja v Greece* App no 32927/03 (ECtHR, 27 July 2006); *Alsayed Allaham v Greece* App no 25771/03 (ECtHR, 18 January 2007); *Vasilev v Greece* App no 2736/05 (ECtHR, 18 January 2007); *Perlala v Greece* App no 17721/04 (ECtHR, 22 February 2007); *John v Greece* App no 199/05 (ECtHR, 10 May 2007); *Noel Baker v Greece* App no 32155/04 (ECtHR, 21 June 2007); *Peca v Greece* App no 14846/05 (ECtHR, 21 June 2007); *Celniku v Greece* App no 21449/04 (ECtHR, 5 July 2007); *Gjashta v Greece* App no 4983/04 (ECtHR, 18 October 2007); *Behar Metushi v Greece* App no 34148/05 (ECtHR, 25 October 2007); *Luan Metushi v Greece* App no 34643/05 (ECtHR, 25 October 2007); *Sekseni v Greece* App no 41515/05 (ECtHR, 6 March 2008); *Kabili v Greece* App no 28606/05 (ECtHR, 31 July 2008); *Sossoadouno v Greece* App no 29845/06 (ECtHR, 31 July 2008); *Angelov v Greece* App no 22035/05 (ECtHR, 6 November 2008); *Nerattini v Greece* App no 43529/07 (ECtHR, 18 December 2008); *Kola v Greece* App no 1483/07 (ECtHR, 2 April 2009); *Bigaeva v Greece* App no 26713/05 (ECtHR, 28 May 2009); *Elyasin v Greece* App no 46929/06 (ECtHR, 28 May 2009); *SD v Greece* App no 53541/07 (ECtHR, 11 June 2009); *Chuwunonso v Greece* App no 43407/06 (ECtHR, 2 July 2009); *Ekonomi v Greece* App no 39870/06 (ECtHR, 2 July 2009); *Elezi and Others v Greece* App no 33863/07 (ECtHR, 9 July 2009); *Shuvaev v Greece* App no 8249/07 (ECtHR, 29 October 2009); *Tabesh v Greece* App no 8256/07 (ECtHR, 26 November 2009); *Peca v Greece (No 2)* App no 33067/08 (ECtHR, 10 January 2010); *Popovitsi v Greece* App no 53451/07 (ECtHR, 14 January 2010); *Bala v Greece* App no 40876/07 (ECtHR, 1 July 2010); *AA v Greece* App no 12186/08 (ECtHR, 22 July 2010); *Bubullima v Greece* App no 41533/08 (ECtHR, 28 October 2010); *Fawsie v Greece* App no 40080/07 (ECtHR, 28 October 2010); *Saidoun v Greece* App no 40083/07 (ECtHR, 28 October 2010); *MSS v Belgium and Greece* App no 30696/09 (ECtHR, 21 January 2011); *Rahimi v Greece* App no 8687/08 (ECtHR, 5 April 2011); *RU v Greece* App no 2237/08 (ECtHR, 7 June 2011); *Efraimidi v Greece* App no 33225/08 (ECtHR, 21 June 2011); *Taggatidis and Others v Greece* App no 2889/09 (ECtHR, 11 October 2011); *Takush v Greece* App no 2853/09 (ECtHR, 17 January 2012); *Zontul v Greece* App no 12294/07 (ECtHR, 17 January 2012); *Mathloom v Greece* App no 48883/07 (ECtHR, 24 April 2012); *Buyan and Others v Greece* App no 28644/08 (ECtHR, 3 July 2012); *Lica v Greece* App no 74279/10 (ECtHR, 17 July 2012); *Mahmundi and Others v Greece* App no 14902/10 (ECtHR, 31 July 2012); *Ahmade v Greece* App no 50520/09 (ECtHR, 25 September 2012); *Bygylashvili v Greece* App no 58164/10 (ECtHR, 25 September 2012); *Lin v Greece* App no 58158/10 (ECtHR, 6 November 2012); *Nieciecki v Greece* App no 11677/11 (ECtHR, 4 December 2012); *Tzamalis and Others v Greece* App no 15894/09 (ECtHR, 4 December 2012).

Forty-one of these rulings were issued in the period 2007–2012, pronouncing breaches of various ECHR provisions: Article 2 (right to life), Article 3 (prohibition of torture), Article 5 (right to liberty and security), Article 6 (right to a fair trial), Article 8 (right to respect for private and family life), Article 13 (right to an effective remedy), Article 14 (prohibition of discrimination); Article 1 of Protocol 1 to the ECHR (protection of property) and Article 1 of Protocol 7 to the ECHR (procedural safeguards relating to expulsion of aliens). Although some of these judgments addressed general deficiencies of the Greek legal and judicial order affecting nationals and non-nationals alike, others brought to the surface highly sensitive matters concerning the regulation of migrants' and asylum seekers' entry and stay in Greece.

Although Greece lacks a tradition of *public interest litigation*,[8] there have been instances of *strategic* use of the ECHR regime with a clear focus on law and policy reform.[9] In these instances, recourse to the ECtHR principally took place with a view to challenging restrictive existing laws and administrative or judicial practices, besides seeking redress for the violations suffered by the applicants. A series of religious freedom cases, for instance, were filed by petitioners belonging to non-Orthodox religious groups, and others were brought to the ECtHR by individuals from the Turkish Muslim community living in Greece.[10] Those cases were carefully selected and their submission to the ECtHR was prepared or supported by human rights organisations and other civil society or political associations.[11]

Litigation in the ECtHR in relation to migrants' and asylum seekers' rights on the other hand, has for the most part lacked such a strategic dimension. Yet, during the past few years, increased reliance has been placed on the ECHR and its judicial arm as a means to document injustices and advocate changes in the formation of policies affecting migrants' rights. Interestingly, recourse to the ECtHR has gained weight not only as a means to exert pressure for altering national laws and practices but also as a means to stress the importance of developing policies at the EU level that promote the protection of migrants' rights. The jurisprudence of the

[8] Public interest litigation generally refers to litigation that is not focused on vindicating private interests but on raising, through legal action, matters of general public interest in the pursuit of systemic policy change and broad political/social reform.

[9] See E Psychogiopoulou, 'The European Court of Human Rights in Greece: Litigation, Rights Protection and Vulnerable Groups' in D Anagnostou and E Psychogiopoulou (eds), *The European Court of Human Rights and the Rights of Marginalised Individuals and Minorities in National Context* (Leiden, Martinus Nijhoff Publishers, 2010) 115, 126–28.

[10] See D Anagnostou and E Psychogiopoulou, 'Under What Conditions Do National Authorities Implement the European Court of Human Rights' Rulings? Religious and Ethnic Minorities in Greece' in D Anagnostou (ed), *The European Court of Human Rights: Implementing Strasbourg's Judgments on Domestic Policy* (Edinburgh, Edinburgh University Press, 2013) 143.

[11] Ibid.

CJEU concerning the rights of third country nationals and asylum seekers in Greece has been less voluminous and varied in terms of subject matter. It has, nevertheless, been of unprecedented significance as it has served to exemplify the importance that the CJEU ascribes to the application of EU law in a manner that is congruent with fundamental rights, while complementing in varying ways the jurisprudence of the ECtHR.

This chapter examines litigation strategies that originate from Greece before the two European courts. The following sections investigate the migrant-related litigation patterns before the ECtHR and the CJEU, identifying the type of claims brought before the two judiciaries, and the nature and degree of support that litigants received. In doing so, the analysis pinpoints and examines those cases that could be considered as instances of strategic litigation in the pursuit of legal and social change. It also explores whether the ECHR and EU fundamental rights have provided litigants with a critical resource enabling the contestation of particular policies and practices. Some concluding remarks follow on the ability of the two European courts to impact on policy making and promote policy change that boosts fundamental rights protection.

I. EVOLVING PATTERNS OF LITIGATION IN THE ECTHR

A number of cases brought to the ECtHR against Greece by migrants have dealt with the excessive length of domestic proceedings, the lack of an effective remedy in this respect, and impairments to the right to a fair trial or the right of access to court. Many cases further concerned acts of police brutality, excessive use of force by the police and procedural shortcomings in the investigation of the incidents under dispute. Applicants have also criticised State authorities for unlawful and lengthy detention, for debasing detention conditions in police stations and in holding facilities for migrants and prisons, for interference with the right to one's correspondence while kept in detention and for the failure to have the lawfulness of detention pending expulsion reviewed by a national court. Complaints about asylum seekers' degrading living conditions and deficiencies in the Greek asylum procedure were also made. Additionally, claims criticising impediments to the protection of property and breach of the right to respect for one's private and family life were put forward.

In the kinds of claims advanced by migrants against the Greek state, litigation in the late 1990s and the early 2000s was hardly characterised by strategic motivation aimed at policy change. Although many local migrants' associations and human rights organisations advocated increased protection of the rights of migrants and asylum seekers, litigation in the ECtHR was the result of the sole determination of the victims to seek redress. Accordingly, the applicants did not receive support in a concerted, systematic or coordinated manner.[12] Most of the lawyers selected to represent the litigants in the ECtHR were individually chosen on the basis of their qualifications or they had been appointed by the court in the context of domestic proceedings, following the applicants' difficulties to afford legal costs. A partial exemption in this regard was the Greek Helsinki Monitor (GHM), a local non-governmental organisation that monitors human rights in Greece. The GHM engaged in litigation involving migrants' rights, mostly concerning Albanians,[13] drawing on the experience it had obtained by successfully litigating cases in the ECtHR in relation to the rights of Roma.[14]

Although these first instances of litigation in the ECtHR lacked strategic impetus, they proved highly influential in terms of legal mobilisation, increasing incentives to litigate in Strasbourg. By finding Greece in breach of its human rights obligations, the case law of the ECtHR profoundly influenced perceptions about legal tactics and the use of the ECHR normative system to push for changes in the domestic authorities' treatment of migrants. Early cases finding breach of Article 6 ECHR, for instance due to lengthy proceedings, unfair trial or impairments to the right of access to court,[15] paved the way for a new set of applications from the mid-2000s onwards, which led to a number of findings of a violation of the ECHR.[16]

The ECtHR rulings emanating from applications filed in the late 1990s and the early 2000s concerning breach of Articles 3 and 5 ECHR similarly triggered a wave of new applications. With respect to Article 3 ECHR, in particular, following the judgments in *Dougoz* and *Kaja*, which concerned migrants' degrading detention conditions in prisons and police facilities,[17] the number of applications made to the ECtHR on similar grounds grew rapidly in number. Thus, in the period 2007–12, the ECtHR delivered numerous judgments declaring breach of Article 3 ECHR on account of degrading detention conditions in prisons, police stations and other holding facilities

12 Although some local organisations offered legal services, these concerned for the most part domestic issues and procedures (for example, explaining the Greek legal framework, assisting in the preparation of legal documents, including asylum requests, and representing migrants before Greek administrative and judicial authorities).

13 The GHM represented the applicants in *Celniku v Greece* and *Gjashta v Greece* (n 7). The former concerned an Albanian national fatally wounded at the age of 20 during an attempted police arrest. The latter dealt with an Albanian national who complained about the length of criminal proceedings against him.

14 See in particular, *Bekos and Koutropoulos v Greece* App no 15250/02 (ECtHR, 13 December 2005); *Zelilof v Greece* App no 17060/03 (ECtHR, 24 May 2007); *Karagiannopoulos v Greece* App no 27850/03 (ECtHR, 21 June 2007).

15 See *Twalib v Greece*; *Biba v Greece*; *Yagtzilar and Others v Greece*; *Alija v Greece*; *Kurti v Greece*; *Papa v Greece*; *Allushi v Greece* (n 7).

16 See *Perlala v Greece*; *Peca v Greece*; *Behar Metushi v Greece*; *Luan Metushi v Greece*; *Gjashta v Greece*; *Sekseni v Greece*; *Sossoadouno v Greece*; *Kabili v Greece*, *Kola v Greece*; *Elyasin v Greece*, *Chuwunonso v Greece*; *Ekonomi v Greece*; *Elezi v Greece*, *Peca v Greece (No 2)*, *Buyan v Greece* (n 7).

17 See *Dougoz v Greece*; *Kaja v Greece* (n 7).

for migrants.[18] In several of these (eg *Rahimi*, *RU*, *Lica* and *Mahmundi and Others*[19]), besides breach of Article 3 ECHR, the ECtHR also found a violation of Article 13 ECHR due to the absence of an effective remedy enabling the applicants to complain about their detention conditions.

In the same vein, in the wake of *Dougoz*, *Mohd* and *John*,[20] which led to the finding of a violation of Article 5 ECHR in view of the applicants' unlawful detention, the ECtHR's case law on Article 5 ECHR developed dramatically. In doing so, it revealed a number of improper state practices. In *Dougoz*, for example, the ECtHR declared breach of Article 5 ECHR because the applicant's detention pending expulsion lacked a proper legal basis. In *SD*, *AA*, *RU*, *Efraimidi* and *Ahmade*,[21] the ECtHR also found a violation of Article 5 ECHR. It did so because although domestic legislation precluded the deportation of individuals who had applied for asylum status until their asylum application had been examined, the applicants—all asylum seekers—had been detained with a view to expulsion. In *John*, the ECtHR held a violation of Article 5 ECHR on account of the illegal extension of the applicant's detention pending expulsion, in breach of the time limit prescribed by national legislation. *Tabesh* concerned an irregular migrant who was detained for the maximum period allowed by domestic legislation in order to be expelled but was not deported given the national authorities' failure to make proper arrangements for his repatriation.[22] In *Rahimi*, in turn, the Greek authorities' failure to give consideration to the best interests of the applicant as an unaccompanied minor (by exploring, for instance, the possibility of replacing detention with a less burdensome measure) led the ECtHR to affirm a violation of Article 5 ECHR.[23]

Along the same lines, in the aftermath of *Dougoz*, which led to the finding of a violation of Article 5(4) ECHR for lack of judicial review of the lawfulness of the applicant's detention, several petitions to the ECtHR alleged similar breaches, leading to an array of condemning judgments in the period 2010–12.[24] Some of these dealt with the absence of domestic legislation conferring on courts the power to examine the lawfulness of migrants' detention pending expulsion. Others concerned impediments

[18] See *SD v Greece*; *Shuvaev v Greece*; *Tabesh v Greece*; *AA v Greece*; *MSS v Greece*; *Rahimi v Greece*; *RU v Greece*; *Efraimidi v Greece*; *Taggatidis and Others v Greece*; *Ahmade v Greece*; *Bygylashvili v Greece*; *Lica v Greece*; *Lin v Greece*; *Mahmundi and Others v Greece*; *Mathloom v Greece*; *Nieciecki v Greece*; *Tzamalis and Others v Greece*; *Zontul v Greece* (n 7).

[19] See *Rahimi v Greece*; *RU v Greece*; *Lica v Greece*; *Mahmundi and Others v Greece* (n 7).

[20] See *Dougoz v Greece*; *Mohd v Greece*; *John v Greece* (n 7).

[21] See *SD v Greece*; *AA v Greece*; *RU v Greece*; *Efraimidi v Greece*; *Ahmade v Greece* (n 7).

[22] See *Tabesh v Greece* (n 7).

[23] See *Rahimi v Greece* (n 7).

[24] See *Bala v Greece*; *AA v Greece*; *Bubullima v Greece*; *Rahimi v Greece*; *RU v Greece*; *Efraimidi v Greece*; *Ahmade v Greece*; *Mathloom v Greece*; *Mahmumdi and Others v Greece*; *Lica v Greece*; *Lin v Greece* (n 7).

undermining the applicants' ability to defend themselves against detention or the failure of domestic authorities to decide in a speedy manner on the applicants' request to be released.[25]

Interestingly, many of the lawyers and legal practitioners who prepared the applications filed with the ECtHR from the mid-2000s onwards were among those who had successfully litigated some of the early cases brought to the ECtHR. Encouraged by the legal victories obtained until then, and driven by professional ambition and personal commitment to migrants' rights, this group of lawyers progressively provided systematic support to petitioners wishing to bring their cases in the ECtHR. This enabled a new set of issues to be placed under the ECtHR's supervision. Alongside the stream of cases focusing on irregular migrants' and asylum seekers' rights, litigation gradually expanded to cases concerning migrants who are legally resident in Greece, regarding, for instance, their access to employment[26] or public assistance funds.[27] Concurrently, the attention that the successful cases received by the legal profession led a new generation of Greek lawyers to develop an interest in, and engage with, European human rights law, which has diversified legal support structures for litigation in the ECtHR.

Legal support has also been increasingly provided from abroad. Cases that led to important ECtHR judgments sometimes derived from the active engagement of lawyers and associations established in other countries. A clear example in this respect is *Zontul*,[28] a case concerning an illegal migrant who was sexually abused after being intercepted by Greek coastguards. REDRESS, a human rights organisation established in the UK and dedicated to helping torture survivors obtain justice and reparation, represented the applicant before the ECtHR, which found breach of Article 3 ECHR. In addition to holding that the treatment to which the applicant had been subjected amounted to an act of torture, the ECtHR condemned the Greek state for the ineffectiveness of the investigation carried out into the incident. It also deplored the inability of the Greek criminal justice system to provide adequate redress to the applicant, and the failure of domestic authorities to keep the applicant informed of the progress of proceedings to the extent that he had been unable to exercise his rights as a civil party and claim damages.

Notably, several international, European and national bodies and non-governmental organisations also supported migrants' litigation in the ECtHR. They did so in an indirect manner, through documentation, which informed and corroborated the Court's judgments. For example, in appraising the facts of *SD* concerning the deportation of an individual whose asylum application

[25] See *Bala v Greece*; *Bubullima v Greece*; *Mathloom v Greece* (n 7).
[26] See *Bigaeva v Greece* (n 7).
[27] See *Fawsie v Greece*; *Saidoun v Greece* (n 7).
[28] See *Zontul v Greece* (n 7).

was still pending, the ECtHR took note of a variety of reports published by the Hellenic Office of the UN High Commissioner for Refugees (UNHCR), the European Committee for the Prevention of Torture and Inhuman Treatment or Punishment (CPT), the Council of Europe Commissionaire for Human Rights, Human Rights Watch, the Greek Ombudsman and the Greek section of Amnesty International.[29] All of these had expressed concern about irregular migrants' detention conditions due to overcrowding and the absence of basic welfare and hygiene standards. Similarly, in *AA v Greece*, the ECtHR drew attention to several documents disclosing humiliating detention conditions, produced by the European Parliament's Committee on Civil Liberties, Justice and Home Affairs, the Hellenic Office of the UNHCR, the CPT, the Parliamentary Assembly of the Council of Europe, Pro Asyl and the Athens Group of Lawyers for the Rights of Migrants and Refugees.[30]

Although the preceding analysis shows that legal support structures spread and multiplied, most of the cases brought to the ECtHR were not the result of a deliberate strategy devised to advocate changes in domestic policies and state practices to the benefit of migrants' rights and freedoms. The vulnerability of migrants and asylum seekers hampered collective mobilisation aimed at policy reform, including through legal means. However, there are some instances of litigation in the ECtHR that clearly had a strategic component, with goals that went far beyond individual remedy and redress. The case of *MSS v Belgium and Greece* is an exemplary instance of strategic litigation, which principally took place with a view to exercising political pressure for changes in the European system of asylum management and in the rights of asylum seekers.[31]

II. THE *MSS* CASE AND THE CHALLENGE TO THE DUBLIN REGULATION

The *MSS* case was filed with the ECtHR in June 2009 against both Belgium and Greece. It concerned an irregular migrant of Afghan nationality who had entered the EU through Greece and had subsequently filed an asylum application in Belgium. The EU Dublin Regulation establishes a set of criteria for the determination of the EU Member State responsible for examining an asylum application made in one of the Member States.[32] On the basis of this regulation, the Belgian authorities had requested the Greek state to take charge of the applicant's request and had transferred him to Greece. Upon

[29] See *SD v Greece* (n 7) [33]–[40].
[30] See *AA v Greece* (n 7) [34]–[38].
[31] See *MSS v Belgium and Greece* (n 7).
[32] Council Regulation No 343/2003 of 18 February 2003 establishing the criteria and mechanisms for determining the Member State responsible for examining an asylum application lodged in one of the Member States by a third-country national [2003] OJ L50/1.

his arrival, the applicant had been placed in detention and after his release, had lived in the street with no means of subsistence.

To reach a better understanding of the strategic motivation that characterised litigation in the *MSS* case, due consideration must be given to the principal features of the EU common asylum system,[33] particularly as regards the allocation of responsibility between the EU Member States for deciding asylum claims. According to the legal framework introduced by the Dublin Regulation, responsibility for examining an asylum application rests with the Member State where a family member of the applicant is already legally present, the state that has provided the applicant with a valid residence or visa document, or the state where the third country national first entered the EU illegally.[34] Where no state can be designated on the basis of these criteria, responsibility is assigned to the first Member State where an asylum application is lodged.[35] The aim is to avoid multiple applications and to guarantee that each asylum seeker's case is dealt with by a single Member State. By way of derogation, Article 3(2) of the regulation, the so-called 'sovereignty clause', allows a Member State to take charge of an asylum application even though another Member State is responsible for it in accordance with the criteria of the regulation.

Although the Dublin Regulation is based on the premise that all EU Member States treat asylum seekers in a fair, efficient and fundamental rights-compliant manner, its implementation in Greece—a main country of entry in the EU for a considerable number of migrants—has been controversial. Following the enactment of the regulation in February 2003, concerns that asylum seekers returned to Greece might be subject to immediate pre-removal detention and deportation, without benefiting from a substantive examination of their asylum claim, were increasingly voiced. Such grievances, alongside complaints for other deficiencies of the country's asylum system, were expressed by international and European organisations and bodies such as the UNHCR,[36] the Council of Europe Commissioner for

[33] Besides Council Regulation No 343/2003, the EU common asylum system comprises Council Directive 2001/55/EC of 20 July 2001 on minimum standards for giving temporary protection in the event of a mass influx of displaced persons and on measures promoting a balance of efforts between Member States in receiving such persons and bearing the consequences thereof [2001] OJ L212/12; Council Directive 2003/9/EC of 27 January 2003 laying down minimum standards for the reception of asylum seekers [2003] OJ L31/18; Council Directive 2004/83/EC of 29 April 2004 on minimum standards for the qualification and status of third country nationals or stateless persons as refugees or as persons who otherwise need international protection and the content of the protection granted [2004] OJ L304/12; and Council Directive 2005/85/EC of 1 December 2005 on minimum standards on procedures in Member States for granting and withdrawing refugee status [2005] OJ L326/13.

[34] See Arts 6–12 of Council Regulation No 343/2003 (n 32).

[35] Ibid, Art 13.

[36] See for instance UN High Commissioner for Refugees, 'Note on Access to the Asylum Procedure of Asylum-Seekers Returned to Greece, Inter Alia, Under Arrangements to Transfer Responsibility With Respect to Determining an Asylum Claim or Pursuant to Application of the Safe

Human Rights[37] and the CPT,[38] human rights advocates such as Human Rights Watch and Amnesty International,[39] and domestic bodies such as the Greek Ombudsman.[40]

Shortcomings became more widely documented and eventually, in 2008, led the UNHCR to recommend that EU Member States refrain from returning asylum seekers to Greece and take responsibility for their asylum applications in line with Article 3(2) of the regulation.[41] It should thus come as no surprise that in some EU Member States (eg Germany, Denmark and Luxembourg) domestic authorities issued instructions prohibiting transfers to Greece. In others (eg Austria, France, Hungary, Italy and Romania), national courts suspended 'Dublin transfers' in individual cases.[42] The issue also reached the ECtHR, which from 2008 onwards, in the light of the UNHCR recommendations, received an increasing number of requests for the adoption of provisional measures suspending transfers to Greece, on the basis of Rule 39 of the Court Rules concerning interim measures. For instance, between 14 May and 16 September 2008, Rule 39 was applied in a total of 80 cases brought to the ECtHR by applicants in the United Kingdom (UK) who were to be removed to Greece.[43]

Third Country Concept', November 2004, www.unhcr.org/refworld/docid/46d52b3d2.html, accessed 5 January 2013.

[37] See T Hammarberg, Council of Europe Commissioner for Human Rights, Report following his visit to Greece, 8–10 December 2008, Issue Reviewed: Human Rights of Asylum Seekers, CommDH(2009)6, 4 February 2009 wcd.coe.int/ViewDoc.jsp?id=1401927&Site=CommDH&BackColorInternet=FEC65B&BackColorIntranet=FEC65B&BackColorLogged=FFC679, accessed 5 January 2013.

[38] See European Committee for the Prevention of Torture and Inhuman or Degrading Treatment or Punishment, Report to the Government of Greece on the visit to Greece from 27 August to 9 September 2005, CPT/Inf(2006)41, www.cpt.coe.int/documents/grc/2006-41-inf-eng.pdf, accessed 5 January 2013.

[39] See Human Rights Watch, 'Stuck in a Revolving Door. Iraqis and Other Asylum Seekers and Migrants at the Greece/Turkey Entrance to the European Union', November 2008, www.hrw.org/sites/default/files/reports/greeceturkey1108web_0.pdf, accessed 5 January 2013; Amnesty International, Amnesty International Report 2009, http://report2009.amnesty.org/sites/report2009.amnesty.org/files/documents/air09-en.pdf, accessed 5 January 2013, 156.

[40] Greek Ombudsman, 'Έκθεση αυτοψίας στους χώρους κράτησης παρανόμως εισερχομένων αλλοδαπών και αιτούντων άσυλο στην περιοχή του Ν. Έβρου και Ροδόπης' [Report concerning the detention premises of irregular migrants and asylum seekers in the prefectures of Evros and Rodopi], 29 October 2007, http://www.synigoros.gr/resources/_autopsia_thraki_29_01.pdf, accessed 5 January 2013.

[41] UN High Commissioner for Refugees, 'UNHCR Position on the Return of Asylum-Seekers to Greece under the "Dublin Regulation"', 15 April 2008, www.unhcr.org/refworld/docid/4805bde42.html, accessed 5 January 2013.

[42] UN High Commissioner for Refugees, 'UNHCR Information Note on National Practice in the Application of Article 3(2) of the Dublin II Regulation in particular in the context of intended transfers to Greece', 16 June 2010, www.refworld.org/cgi-bin/texis/vtx/rwmain?docid=4c18e6f92, accessed 5 January 2013.

[43] See *KRS v United Kingdom* App no 32733/08 (ECtHR, 2 December 2008).

The first substantiated ECtHR decision came in December 2008 in *KRS v UK*.[44] The *KRS* case concerned an Iranian national who had sought asylum in the UK after travelling through Greece. The applicant had challenged his removal to Greece under the Dublin Regulation as contrary to Article 3 ECHR. The complaint asserted, among other things, that the UNHCR had found a number of structural deficiencies in the Greek asylum procedures, and had recommended a halt of asylum seekers' transfers. However, the ECtHR declared the application inadmissible, taking the view that the UNHCR concerns, when translated into ECHR terms, could not be relied upon to preclude the UK from transferring the applicant to Greece. First, concerning the applicant's argument that removal to Greece entailed a risk of immediate expulsion to his country of origin, the ECtHR noted that on the basis of the information before it, there was no evidence to ascertain that Greece actually deported people to Iran.[45] As to whether removal to Greece entailed a real risk of ill-treatment, the presumption should be upheld that Greece would abide by its obligations under the EU common asylum system, adhering to minimum standards in asylum and reception procedures. At any rate, should the Greek state fail in its obligations, returnees would be in a position to appeal to the domestic courts and if necessary, apply to the ECtHR for interim measures and/or redress. The ECtHR's stance in *KRS* was essentially the following: on the one hand, reception conditions were a matter for the receiving state and did not engage the responsibility under the ECHR of the sending state; on the other hand, in the absence of proof to the contrary, it should be assumed that the receiving state complied with the obligations imposed by EU law, and that it would conform to Article 3 ECHR.

The *MSS* case was filed six months later and was directed *both* against Greece as the receiving state and Belgium as the transferring state. In reviewing this case, the ECtHR significantly departed from *KRS*. Concerning Greece, in particular, besides finding that the conditions of the applicant's detention amounted to ill-treatment, the ECtHR ruled that the applicant's living conditions after his release also violated Article 3 ECHR. The applicant had spent months living in the street in extreme poverty and had received no assistance despite the obligations incumbent on the Greek authorities by virtue of EU law,[46] especially as regards the provision of accommodation and decent material conditions. Domestic authorities were also held accountable for breach of Article 13 ECHR, read together with Article 3 ECHR, due to the deficiencies in the examination of the applicant's asylum request

[44] Ibid.

[45] Should Greece commence removals to Iran, the Dublin Regulation, the ECtHR stressed, allowed the UK authorities, if they considered it appropriate, to exercise their right to examine asylum applications under Article 3(2) of the regulation.

[46] See Council Directive 2003/9/EC above (n 33).

and the risk he faced of being removed to his country of origin without an examination of his application on the merits and without having access to an effective remedy.

The Greek asylum procedure was marked by such structural shortcomings, the ECtHR noted, that asylum seekers had generally very little chance of having their applications seriously assessed. Major hindrances included the provision of insufficient information about the procedures to follow; impediments concerning access to the asylum system in general; the absence of a reliable system of communication with the applicants and the lack of legal aid; the shortage of interpreters; the lack of training of the responsible staff; excessively lengthy delays in reaching a decision; and the fact that almost all first-instance asylum decisions were negative while being drafted in a stereotyped manner without any justification. Also, concerning the possibilities available for a judicial review of a potential rejection decision, the authorities' failure to ensure communication with the applicants, the ineffective legal aid system in place and the excessive duration of appeal proceedings, all entailed the absence of an effective remedy, and the lack of substantive guarantees that asylum applications would be examined on their merits.

The *MSS* case, as prepared and filed with the ECtHR, reflected the full gamut of problems and constraints facing asylum seekers in Greece. Quite importantly, these were substantiated by numerous reports and materials made available to the ECtHR. In its judgment, the ECtHR referred to no less than 23 documents from international and regional organisations, as well as international and local non-governmental organisations, including the UNHCR, the CPT, the Council of Europe Commissioner for Human Rights, Amnesty International, Human Rights Watch, Pro Asyl, the European Council on Refugees and Exiles, the Greek Council for Refugees, the Greek National Commission for Human Rights and the GHM.[47] Published at regular intervals since 2006 and with greater frequency in the period 2008–09, these reports, based on field surveys, had fiercely criticised the detention and reception conditions of asylum seekers in Greece. They also revealed the deficiencies of the asylum system in general and the practice of direct or indirect *refoulement* on an individual or a collective basis. Proof of the failure of the Greek state to respect the requirements of the ECHR had thus become widely available since the *KRS* case, and this played a crucial role for the adjudication of the *MSS* case.

Given its importance for the protection of asylum seekers' rights, the *MSS* case mobilised a wider set of actors and institutions that were convinced that the impugned practices should be corrected. The Council of Europe Commissioner for Human Rights and the UNHCR requested leave to intervene in the ECtHR's oral procedure and also submitted written

[47] See *MSS v Belgium and Greece* (n 7) [159]–[160].

observations. Written observations were further received by the Centre for Advice on Individual Rights in Europe (the AIRE Centre), Amnesty International and the GHM, which supported the applicant's arguments.

The mobilisation of these actors and institutions, and the reports and materials made available to the ECtHR, assumed significance also in the context of the ECtHR's evaluation as to whether Belgium had similarly breached the ECHR. The Belgian government argued that they had sought sufficient assurances from the Greek authorities that the applicant faced no risk of treatment contrary to the ECHR in Greece. Nevertheless, the ECtHR considered that the systemic deficiencies of the Greek asylum procedure and the degrading detention and living conditions of asylum seekers in the country had been known and documented in a reliable manner. They were therefore known or ought to have been known by the Belgian authorities. By transferring the applicant to Greece and by exposing him to the detention and reception conditions prevailing there, the Belgian authorities had thus breached Article 3 ECHR.[48]

The filing of the *MSS* case in the ECtHR shortly after the *KRS* inadmissibility decision and the attention it triggered from the broader legal and human rights advocacy community show that the case was far from being solely concerned with the applicant's redress, important as this may be. Litigation in the ECtHR purposefully sought to bring to the surface the hurdles asylum seekers are confronted with in Greece. But beyond this, it also marked a harsh critique of the EU Dublin system, particularly as regards the mechanism of attribution of responsibility between the EU Member States for asylum requests and the ensuing uneven distribution of asylum seekers between the Member States at the external borders of the EU and the rest. In doing so, it underscored the point that those EU Member States, relieved for the most part from responsibility for examining asylum claims, should not be absolved from their fundamental rights' responsibilities as well. Indeed, and though not framed as such, the underlying problem in the *MSS* case was not just the poor level of protection afforded to asylum seekers in Greece, but also the arrangements made at the EU level for the screening of asylum applications more broadly.

Pursuant to Article 46(1) ECHR, states party to the ECHR must abide by the ECtHR final judgments in which they are parties. Although the ECtHR may occasionally provide directions on the domestic measures required, especially in cases reflecting structural shortcomings, national authorities enjoy a wide margin of appreciation in relation to the means through which they may discharge their obligations under Article 46 ECHR. These

[48] The ECtHR also found that in the absence of domestic provisions allowing for a close, rigorous and substantive scrutiny of the applicant's complaint that expulsion to Greece would expose him to treatment prohibited by Article 3 ECHR, Belgium had also breached Article 13 ECHR in conjunction with Article 3 ECHR.

include individual measures adopted to remedy the effects of infringement, and general measures aimed at averting similar human rights violations. Supervision is exercised, in accordance with Article 46(2) ECHR, by the Committee of Ministers (CoM).

In the wake of the *MSS* judgment, Belgium granted the litigant refugee status and also stopped transferring asylum seekers to Greece, assuming responsibility for their asylum requests on the basis of the sovereignty clause of the Dublin Regulation.[49] As to Greece, the changes brought to national legislation and domestic asylum procedures did not eradicate deficiencies. Although Law 3907/2011 introduced a new legal framework on asylum,[50] making arrangements for the establishment of a new Asylum Service for the processing of asylum applications, the Greek state still lacks a functioning asylum system, as stressed by the CoM.[51] In addition, despite the launch of projects, aimed at improving detention conditions and asylum seekers' reception standards and procedures, reforms have proved insufficient. This explains why the CoM has requested the Greek state to intensify its implementation efforts and provide additional information on a number of issues. These include the operation of first reception centres, measures taken to address prolonged and systematic detention of irregular migrants (including unaccompanied minors), domestic remedies allowing for detention conditions to be challenged before domestic courts, and measures taken (or envisaged) to improve the living conditions of asylum seekers.[52]

More broadly, with limited exceptions, most of the detected ECHR violations against Greece in the fields of asylum and immigration remain under the purview of the CoM because the Greek state has not been able to persuade the CoM of the effectiveness of the implementation steps taken. Although a number of administrative and legislative measures have been adopted, these have fallen short of the CoM's implementation standards and therefore monitoring is ongoing.

[49] Ministers' Deputies Information Documents, 'M.S.S. against Belgium and Greece, Assessment of the General Measures presented in the Action Plans of Belgium and Greece, Memorandum prepared by the Department for the Execution of Judgments of the European Court of Human Rights', CM/Inf/DH(2012)19, 29 May 2012. Belgium also started making use of the sovereignty clause in relation to Dublin transfers to countries other than Greece. It does so when asylum seekers claim that the general situation in the responsible, according to the Dublin Regulation, state infringes Article 3 ECHR and this has been proven by the information compiled by international organisations. The Committee of Ministers currently examines the general measures taken by Belgium in response to the finding of a violation of Article 13 ECHR. See Ministers' Deputies Information documents, 'M.S.S. against Belgium and Greece, Assessment of the General Measures taken by Belgium in Response to the Finding of a Violation of Article 13, Memorandum prepared by the Department for the Execution of Judgments of the European Court of Human Rights', CM/Inf/DH(2012)26rev, 24 September 2012.

[50] Law 3907/2011 on the establishment of an Asylum Service and a Service of first reception, FEK A' 7/2011.

[51] Ministers' Deputies Information Documents (n 49).

[52] Ibid.

III. THE MOBILISATION OF EU FUNDAMENTAL RIGHTS

Despite finding both Belgium and Greece in breach of the ECHR, the *MSS* judgment did not go to the heart of the problem. This concerns the uneven allocation of responsibility among the EU Member States for the examination of asylum applications, effected by the EU Dublin Regulation. The Dublin Regulation has been severely criticised for overloading the asylum system of some Member States, while accentuating fundamental rights failings therein. The ECtHR though did not delve into the fundamental rights implications of the regulation. In fact, a ECtHR ruling dealing directly with the regulation and its compliance with fundamental rights would have interfered with the autonomy of EU law,[53] given that the EU has not yet acceded to the ECHR. By way of filling this gap, litigation at the national level, and in the UK in particular, has contested asylum seekers' transfer to Greece pursuant to the Dublin Regulation. In addition, it paved the way for the CJEU to rule on the importance of applying EU asylum law in compliance with fundamental rights. On 21 December 2011, a year after the *MSS* ruling, the CJEU issued the landmark judgment of *NS and ME and Others*.[54] The case stemmed from two disputes, referred for a preliminary ruling, between asylum seekers who were to be returned to Greece, and the UK and Irish authorities, respectively.

The *NS* case concerned an Afghan national who having illegally entered Greece, was arrested and expelled to Turkey. Having escaped detention, he travelled to the UK where he lodged an asylum application. The Secretary of State for the Home Department requested Greece to take charge of the applicant's application. Following the failure of the Greek authorities to respond within the time limit set by the Dublin Regulation, the Greek state was deemed to have accepted responsibility. The applicant requested the Secretary of State to assume responsibility for his asylum claim under the sovereignty clause of the regulation, with the argument that his fundamental rights under EU law, the ECHR and the 1951 Geneva Convention relating to the Status of Refugees would be violated, if he were returned to Greece. However, the Secretary of State upheld the decision for his transfer. The applicant contested this before domestic courts. In appeal proceedings challenging the dismissal of his arguments by the High Court of Justice

[53] CJEU, Opinion 1/91, *Draft agreement between the Community, on the one hand, and the countries of the European Free Trade Association, on the other, relating to the creation of the European Economic Area* [1991] ECR I-6079. On this see also P Gragl, 'The Shortcomings of Dublin II: Strasbourg's M.S.S. Judgment and its Implications for the European Union's Legal Order' in W Benedek, F Benoît-Rohmer, W Karl and M Nowak (eds), *European Yearbook on Human Rights* (Mortsel, Intersentia, 2012) 123–40.

[54] CJEU, Joined Cases C-411 & 493/10 *NS v Secretary of State for the Home Department and ME and Others v Refugee Applications Commissioner, Minister for Justice, Equality and Law Reform*, 21 December 2011, nyr.

(England and Wales), the Court of Appeal of England and Wales identified a number of important questions. In particular, in the light of the Member States' duty to observe fundamental rights, could it be presumed that the responsible state under the Dublin Regulation, to which an asylum seeker is transferred, would observe the asylum seeker's rights under EU law and the minimum standards imposed by EU asylum legislation? Moreover, was a Member State obliged by EU law to make use of the sovereignty clause of the Dublin Regulation and take responsibility for an asylum claim, and if yes, under what circumstances? In need of clarifications, the domestic court stayed proceedings and made a reference to the CJEU for a preliminary ruling.

Litigation in the *NS* case at the national level was meticulously prepared by two charitable organisations providing legal advice and representation on asylum matters in the UK: Refugee and Migrant Justice and the Immigration Advisory Service. When both ceased providing free legal advice and representation services, blaming government changes to the domestic system of legal aid,[55] the case was handed over to the Migrants' Law Project at Islington Law Centre, which represented the litigant before the CJEU.

Before domestic courts, the *NS* case was purposely litigated on the basis of EU fundamental rights. What explains such a strategic choice is the fact that the *MSS* judgment of the ECtHR had not yet been issued when *NS* was subjected to judicial review in the UK. In the aftermath of the *KRS* inadmissibility decision issued by the Strasbourg Court, the legal question of whether the CFR could provide wider protection to asylum seekers, when compared with the ECHR, gained particular significance. Before the Court of Appeal of England and Wales, the appellant indeed contended that the protection conferred by the CFR went beyond that guaranteed by Article 3 ECHR,[56] which could lead to a different judicial outcome than *KRS*. His application for a reference for a preliminary ruling made to the CJEU found support with a number of parties which intervened in domestic proceedings: the UK Equality and Human Rights Commission (EHRC), Amnesty International, the AIRE Centre and the UNHCR. Most of these bodies and organisations claimed before the Court of Appeal that the protection of fundamental rights resulting from the CFR was broader than that provided by the ECHR. Therefore, by taking the CFR into account, transfers of asylum seekers to Greece should be stopped. On this basis, the referring court included among the questions referred to the CJEU a

[55] See J Doward, 'Funding Crisis over Legal Aid Threatens UK Asylum Chaos, Ministers are Warned', *The Guardian*, at www.guardian.co.uk/uk/2010/may/30/asylum-refugee-migrant-justice, accessed 25 March 2013; J Robins, 'Legal Aid Cuts to Immigration Could Mean "Injustice, Hardship and even Loss of Life"', *The Guardian*, www.guardian.co.uk/law/2011/jul/15/immigration-advisory-service-legal-aid-cuts, accessed 25 March 2013.

[56] Joined Cases C-411 & 493/10 (n 54) [48].

question on whether the relevant scope of the protection offered by the general principles of EU law and the CFR was wider than the protection granted by Article 3 ECHR.

NS was conjoined with *ME and Others*, a case concerning five applicants from Afghanistan, Algeria and Iran, who had been arrested in Greece for illegal entry. They had then travelled to Ireland, had claimed asylum, and had requested the Irish authorities to exercise their powers under Article 3(2) of the Dublin Regulation by taking responsibility for the examination of their asylum applications. In related proceedings, the Irish High Court asked the CJEU to clarify two key issues: was a transferring state, within the meaning of the Dublin Regulation, obliged to assess the compliance of the receiving state with fundamental rights and EU asylum law? If yes, what were the consequences, should the receiving state be found to be failing in its obligations? Amnesty International, the AIRE Centre and the UNHCR intervened before the CJEU in relation to *ME and Others* and, together with the EHRC, similarly supported CJEU litigation for *NS*.

Both cases attracted much interest among the Member States. In addition to Ireland, the UK and Greece, Austria, Belgium, the Czech Republic, Finland, France, Germany, Italy, the Netherlands, Poland, Slovenia and Switzerland intervened in the CJEU proceedings. Some of these countries claimed that only in specific cases, and under extraordinary circumstances, should the presumption that the Member State responsible for examining an asylum application will act in accordance with EU and international law be rebutted. Others though argued that they lacked the instruments necessary to assess compliance with fundamental rights by the responsible Member State.

The questions of the referring courts were reframed by the CJEU, which essentially ruled on the interrelationship between fundamental rights and the Dublin transfer mechanism.[57] The CJEU explained that the common asylum system could provide for a clear, rational, swift and legally secure mechanism for the examination of asylum claims in the EU, only if grounded on the presumption that the treatment of asylum seekers in all EU Member States complied with fundamental rights. Solely on the basis of such a presumption could the effective application of the system and thus the effective application of EU law be guaranteed. As a result, the 'slightest' infringement of EU asylum law was not sufficient to prevent the transfer of an asylum seeker to the Member State primarily responsible.[58] At issue, as underlined by the CJEU, was the very 'raison d'être of the European Union and the creation of an area of freedom, security and justice … based

[57] In its judgment, the CJEU also examined whether EU law applied to the decision of a Member State to make use of Article 3(2) of the Dublin Regulation or not.
[58] See Joined Cases C-411 & 493/10 (n 54) [84].

on mutual confidence and a presumption of compliance, by other Member States, with European Union law and, in particular, fundamental rights'.[59]

At the same time, however, it was not 'inconceivable that [the asylum] system may, in practice, experience major operational problems in a given Member State', entailing 'a substantial risk that asylum seekers may, when transferred to that Member State, be treated in a manner incompatible with their fundamental rights'.[60] The presumption that all Member States observed fundamental rights should not therefore be deemed conclusive but rebuttable. Article 4 CFR, in particular, on the prohibition of torture and inhuman or degrading treatment, should be interpreted as precluding the transfer of asylum seekers to the Member State responsible under the Dublin Regulation where there were substantial grounds for believing that there existed systemic flaws in the asylum procedure and reception conditions, resulting in inhuman or degrading treatment. The CJEU observed that information such as that cited by the ECtHR in the *MSS* judgment from non-governmental organisations and international and European institutions enabled national authorities to evaluate the functioning of the asylum system in the responsible Member State and to assess possible risks. Bearing in mind that the ECtHR had found in the *MSS* judgment that a number of structural deficiencies actually existed in Greece, the CJEU concluded that the transfer of asylum seekers there should be deemed incompatible with Article 4 CFR.[61]

As to whether the Member State prohibiting the transfer of an asylum seeker should itself assume responsibility for the processing of the asylum request, the CJEU offered two alternatives. In addition to examining the application itself, in accordance with Article 3(2) of the Dublin Regulation, the Member State concerned could also verify whether a third Member State could be identified as the responsible state on the basis of the criteria of the regulation. The latter solution, however, should ensure that the asylum seeker's situation would not be worsened through use of an unreasonably lengthy designation procedure. If necessary, use of Article 3(2) of the regulation should therefore be made.

The *NS and ME and Others* ruling is important because it shows that systemic deficiencies in the protection of fundamental rights in the EU Member States may override the principle of mutual trust. The transfer of asylum seekers to those Member States that do not systematically abide by their fundamental rights obligations can thus be opposed. But besides this, the ruling is significant because it demonstrates that litigation strategies in

[59] Ibid, [83].

[60] Ibid, [81].

[61] This was so also in the case of the UK because Protocol no 30 on the application of the Charter of Fundamental Rights of the European Union to Poland and to the United Kingdom did not exempt the UK from the obligation to comply with the CFR.

support of asylum seekers' rights have multiplied. They presently draw both on the ECHR and EU fundamental rights and involve both the ECtHR and the CJEU.

One reason for the expansion of litigation strategies stems from the genuine diversification of the fundamental rights sources of EU law, which now benefit from a legally binding CFR, addressed to the institutions and bodies of the EU and the Member States when these act within the scope of EU law.[62] Also, institutional reforms which have extended the scope of the EU preliminary reference mechanism, expanding access to the CJEU, have a crucial role to play. Under former Article 68(1) of the Treaty on the establishment of the European Community, domestic courts against whose decisions a judicial remedy existed under national law could not request the CJEU to give a preliminary ruling on the interpretation of Title IV of the EC Treaty on 'visas, asylum, immigration and other policies related to free movement of persons', and on the validity and interpretation of the EU acts adopted on the basis of the title's provisions. The Treaty of Lisbon has provided the CJEU with general jurisdiction to give preliminary rulings in the area of freedom, security and justice.[63] This in turn has enabled lower courts to seek guidance from the CJEU on asylum matters. Lawyers and legal practitioners defending asylum seekers in court may thus invoke the CFR and build their arguments in ways that favour the referral of questions to the CJEU.

A strong argument explaining resort to the CJEU may also be inferred from the fact that concerns for the level of protection afforded to asylum seekers did not only spring from their inadequate treatment in Greece,[64] but also from the failings of the EU Dublin regime as such. Evidently, the Dublin Regulation cannot guarantee, in its present form, a fair distribution of asylum seekers among the EU Member States. This is a problem that directly emanates from the EU mechanism of attribution of responsibility for the examination of asylum requests. Notably, it exacerbates the human rights failures of those countries, which on account of their geographical

[62] See Art 51 CFR and CJEU, Case C-617/10 *Åkerberg Fransson*, judgment of 26 February 2013, nyr.

[63] See Art 267 of the Treaty on the Functioning of the European Union.

[64] Note for instance that in February 2006, the European Commission took legal proceedings against Greece for failure to transpose the EU Reception Directive (CJEU, Case C-72/06 *Commission v Greece* [2007] ECR I-57). In March 2008 it also started infringement proceedings for failure of the Greek authorities to ensure the examination of the applications of returned asylum seekers, in line with Art 3(1) of the Dublin Regulation (see Action brought on 31 March 2008, Case C-130/08 *Commission v Greece* [2008] OJ C128/25), but these were discontinued on account of the changes brought to the Greek legal framework. In November 2009 and June 2010 letters of formal notice were again sent by the European Commission to the Greek state, alleging infringement of various provisions of the EU common asylum system (see Opinion of Advocate General Trstenjak delivered on 22 September 2011, Case C-411/10 *NS v Secretary of State for the Home Department* [104]).

location, are faced with a volume of requests that far exceeds the capacities of their asylum system.

Although a genuine EU problem, the European institutions proved unable to agree on the modification of the system. Discussions in the Council did not bring changes that could ensure a fairer way of sharing the burden of refugee protection in the EU.[65] Also, they did not advance the harmonisation of rules and procedures, which might have rendered less significant the determination of the EU Member State responsible for the processing of asylum requests, particularly in terms of standards of treatment.[66] Unsurprisingly, the Council's stalled negotiations went hand in hand with a dramatic increase in petitions at the national level for asylum seekers' transfers to be halted. In domestic proceedings concerning the *NS* case, in particular, it was stated that 1,000 'Dublin' cases implicating Greece were in the pipeline across Europe and that 300 or so cases had been stayed in the UK, awaiting the decision of the Court of Appeal.[67]

It becomes evident then that the *NS* case was not merely concerned with individual justice; it primarily sought to bring before the CJEU an issue that Member States had been unable or unwilling to solve in the Council. Importantly, and moving a step further than the *MSS* judgment, yet without compromising the EU asylum system, the CJEU clarified what the practical consequences are when systemic deficiencies are detected in the asylum procedure and the reception conditions in the receiving state. The CJEU explained that the transferring state must refrain from removing the asylum seeker. It must either assume responsibility for the examination of the asylum application made or verify, by means of an efficient and speedy procedure, whether a third Member State may be designated as responsible in accordance with the Dublin Regulation. This suggests that litigation of asylum cases on the basis of EU law and fundamental rights may present advantages when compared to litigation on the basis of the ECHR.

The judgments of the ECtHR are for the most part declaratory, pronouncing breach of the ECHR, which then needs to be rectified via the adoption

[65] In 2008 the European Commission suggested the establishment of a mechanism of temporary suspension of Dublin transfers in cases of particular pressure on certain Member States with limited reception and absorption capacities. This mechanism should also be applied in the case of countries where the level of protection for asylum seekers was not in conformity with EU law, particularly in terms of reception conditions and access to the asylum procedure. The proposal did not find support in the Council. See European Commission, COM(2008) 820, 3 December 2008; Council doc 17223/10, 30 November 2010; Council doc 15055/11, 5 October 2011.

[66] On this see also M den Heijer, 'Joined Cases C-411 & 493/10, N.S. v. Secretary of State for the Home Department and M.E. and Others v. Refugee Applications Commissioner, Minister for Justice, Equality and Law Reform, Judgment of the Court (Grand Chamber) of 21 December 2011, nyr' (2012) 49 *Common Market Law Review* 1735.

[67] Doughty Street Chambers, 'Government Concedes in the Court of Appeal that UK has No Opt-out from the EU Charter of Fundamental Rights', 13 July 2010, www.doughtystreet.co.uk/news/news_detail.cfm?iNewsID=405, accessed 5 January 2013.

of individual and general measures, as mentioned above. Conversely, although the CJEU cannot itself adjudicate on complaints by individuals that their rights under EU law have been infringed, the EU legal system benefits from a range of procedures aimed at ensuring the effective enforcement of EU law, including fundamental rights. Whereas, for instance, the ECtHR can adjudicate a human rights dispute only when all domestic remedies have been exhausted,[68] the mechanism of preliminary references enables the CJEU to intervene at an earlier stage, providing guidance to domestic courts on how to prevent or redress violations.[69] Such earlier intervention, coupled with the primacy of EU law over conflicting national measures and the fact that the CJEU preliminary rulings bind not only the referring court but all national courts in the EU Member States, indicates that fundamental rights under EU law might be more effectively enforced. This, of course, does not mean that the CJEU's rulings automatically entail legal and policy change. The CJEU's case law may serve to resolve uncertainties but its effective implementation requires domestic courts' compliance with the CJEU's pronouncements. Support by a broader range of actors, including domestic governments and legislatures, is also required for legal norms and policy frames to substantively change.[70]

Besides the fact that the CJEU's jurisprudence is not *self-implementing* at the national level, it also betrays an anxiety to openly compare the CFR with the ECHR as regards the breadth of the protection afforded to fundamental rights. In *NS and ME and Others*, the CJEU was expressly requested to pronounce on whether the scope of the protection conferred upon an asylum seeker by the general principles of EU law and Articles 1, 18 and 47 CFR concerning human dignity, the right to asylum and the right to an effective remedy and to a fair trial was wider than the protection offered by Article 3 ECHR. In examining this question, the CJEU made explicit mention of the *MSS* judgment, which had been issued in the meantime. In doing so, it interpreted Article 4 CFR, which replicates verbatim Article 3 ECHR, in accordance with the ECtHR's interpretation of the same Convention provision in the *MSS* ruling. This was to be expected, taking into account that Article 52(3) CFR stipulates that the CFR rights that correspond to the rights guaranteed by the ECHR shall be given the same meaning and scope. However, the CJEU refrained from engaging in a detailed analysis of the protection offered by Articles 1, 18 and 47 CFR, which do not have an exact equivalent in the ECHR. With respect to these rights, the CJEU merely affirmed that they did not lead to a different answer to the questions concerning the interrelationship between the Dublin regime and fundamental rights.

[68] See Art 35 ECHR.

[69] Note that the mechanism of preliminary rulings also affords the CJEU the opportunity of averting or remedying violations before these reach the ECtHR.

[70] Conant (n 2).

IV. CONCLUSION

Litigation in the ECtHR has played an indispensable role in exposing the principal human rights violations committed against migrants and asylum seekers in Greece. The success of early litigation in the ECtHR at least in part accounts for this. It reinforced faith in the Strasbourg Court, steering a number of applications alleging breach of the ECHR on various grounds. Also, support structures providing assistance to the applicants progressively strengthened and multiplied, which facilitated resort to the ECtHR. During the past few years, cases that were driven by strategic intent rather than being simply concerned with individual redress have increasingly been filed with the ECtHR. The malfunctioning of the asylum system and the degrading detention and reception conditions to which asylum seekers are subjected in Greece have been the main issues pursued through strategic litigation in the ECtHR. Reliance on the ECHR and its judicial mechanism in these instances has not only sought to elucidate the need for changes in the asylum system and the treatment of asylum seekers in Greece. It has also sought to contest the uneven distribution of asylum applications in the EU Member States and the cumbersome effect this produces on the EU border Member States.

The mobilisation of the ECHR for the vindication of asylum seekers' rights has been complemented by litigation that drew on EU fundamental rights, particularly the CFR, reaching the CJEU through the preliminary ruling mechanism. The use of the CFR and the involvement of the CJEU in cases similar to those lodged with the ECtHR derived from genuine strategic motivation. What was at stake here was not only an individual remedy but resilience to dispute and bring before the CJEU issues of asylum and migration policy that the EU Member States had been reticent or disinclined to resolve themselves. Additionally, litigation on the basis of EU fundamental rights sought to test the potential offered by the CFR as compared to the ECHR. The CJEU was invited to assess which of these two legal regimes offers wider protection, interpreting the two instruments in convergence with each other.

Although strategic litigation on the basis of the ECHR and the CFR demonstrates that both the Strasbourg and the Luxembourg courts are considered to be influential actors, their power to dictate the direction in which legal reform and public policies should develop has important limits, as the case of Greece discloses. Caught between upholding human rights on the one hand, and coping with excessive migration and refugee flows on the other, Greece has faced serious difficulties in fully aligning its laws, policies and practices with the ECHR standards. Such difficulties are ongoing despite a number of ECtHR judgments finding a violation of the Convention, including the seminal *MSS* ruling. Overall, the strategy of the Greek state concerning migration management and the improvement of asylum mechanisms has been undermined by the absence of concrete steps taken to formulate a comprehensive immigration and border control policy with clear objectives and aims as regards the increase of irregular migrants and asylum seekers in the country.[71] The Greek state has, in fact, openly admitted that it cannot deal with the situation alone and has requested EU assistance, including through a revision of the Dublin Regulation.[72] In a joint communiqué of 19 April 2011, signed together with Cyprus, Italy, Malta and Spain, the Greek government called in particular on the EU Member States to consider adopting 'a mechanism to suspend the transfers to Member States facing particular pressure on their national asylum systems'.[73]

An EU problem par excellence, the mechanism of identifying the Member State responsible for the examination of asylum requests has, however, remained unchanged. Despite the fact that following the *NS and ME and Others* ruling of the CJEU, increased application of the sovereignty clause of the Dublin Regulation has mitigated the adverse effects of the system of allocating responsibility among the Member States, the political will to change the partitioning of asylum applications between the Member States is missing. Discussions in the Council and, following the entry into force of the Treaty of Lisbon,[74] the European Parliament did not result in a radical reform.[75] The European Parliament has convinced the Council to adopt provisions that reflect the *NS and ME and Others* ruling as regards the obligations of the sending state in the case of systemic flaws in the asylum procedure and reception conditions of the receiving state.[76] Yet, a fundamental overhaul of the way in which responsibility for asylum requests is distributed among the Member States did not take place. Only an early warning system has been introduced, which should allow for the early identification of particular pressure on a Member State's asylum system and of problems in its functioning.[77] As to the suspension of transfers as such, in the aftermath of

[71] The parties that submitted observations to the CJEU in the *NS and ME and Others* case are in agreement that Greece was, in 2010, the point of entry in the EU of almost 90 per cent of illegal immigrants. See CJEU, *NS and ME and Others* (n 54) [87].

[72] See Greek Ministry of Citizen Protection, 'Greece sends its National Action Plan for Migration Management to the European Commission', 25 August 2010, www.ydt.gr/index.php?option=ozo_content&perform=view&id=3246&Itemid=443&lang=EN, accessed on 5 January 2013.

[73] Migrants at Sea, 'Cyprus, Greece, Italy, Malta, & Spain Issue Joint Communiqué Regarding Response to North African Migration', migrantsatsea.wordpress.com/2011/04/21/cyprus-greece-italy-malta-spain-issue-joint-communique-regarding-response-to-north-african-migration, accessed 5 January 2013.

[74] The Treaty of Lisbon extended the legislative co-decision procedure, renamed ordinary legislative procedure, to the adoption of measures for a common European asylum system. See Art 78(2) of the Treaty on the Functioning of the European Union.

[75] European Commission, 'A Common European Asylum System', MEMO/13/532, 12 June 2013, europa.eu/rapid/press-release_MEMO-13-532_en.htm, accessed 13 June 2013.

[76] Council doc 11467/12, 20 June 2012. See also Council doc 15605/12, 14 December 2012.

[77] Council doc 15605/12.

MSS and *NS and ME and Others*, the transfers of asylum seekers to Greece might have stopped but no formal EU mechanism was adopted in this regard. This is so despite the fact that following Greece, other countries now appear to come into focus such as Italy, Malta and Hungary.[78]

On the basis of the above, one may conclude that the judgments of the ECtHR and the CJEU do not in themselves prompt legal and policy change. Rather, they may serve as a catalyst for reform. Their ability to do so though is strongly conditioned by a number of factors, including the level of support their rulings enjoy among political elites and the breadth and complexity of the reforms required. At the same time, the authoritativeness and resonance of the judgments of the two European courts provide increased legitimacy to advocates of substantive reform. This renders the justification of failing policies by those that claim or purport to abide by the rule of law extremely difficult and could make a difference.

[78] K Clarke and N Denti, 'The Nascent Impact of the "Greek Transfer" Cases', www.legalaidboard.ie/lab/publishing.nsf/content/The_Researcher_April_2012_Article_6, accessed 5 January 2013. See also *ECHR interim measure suspending the expulsion of the applicant to Hungary* App no 2283/12 (ECtHR, 11 January 2012).

Part III

The Role of NGOs and Transnational Human Rights Networks

7

From Belfast to Diyarbakir and Grozny via Strasbourg: Transnational Legal Mobilisation Against State Violations in Contexts of Armed Conflict

DIA ANAGNOSTOU

THE EMERGENCE OF the European Convention of Human Rights (ECHR or Convention) and the evolution of its judicial arm, the European Court of Human Rights (ECtHR or the Court), has been one of the most remarkable and momentous developments of post- World War II European history. Studies from law, politics and international relations have investigated the historical origins of the Convention as a bulwark against fascism and communism, its shifting significance in the Cold War climate, as well as its entanglement with the processes and politics of decolonisation in the 1950s and 1960s.[1] In the 1970s and 1980s the Convention and the Court underwent a profound transformation away from the 'legal diplomacy' of the early phases and towards a legalised regime, increasingly attuned to delivering justice to individuals whose human rights are violated by states.[2] Since the 1990s, the acceptance of the individual petition mechanism by old contracting states, such as Turkey, and mainly the accession

[1] MR Madsen, 'From Cold War Instrument to Supreme European Court: The ECtHR at the Crossroads of International and National Politics' (2007) 32 *Law and Social Inquiry* 137; E Bates, *The Evolution of the European Convention on Human Rights: From its Inception to the Creation of a Permanent Court of Human Rights* (Oxford, Oxford University Press, 2010), especially chapter 1; S Greer, *The ECHR—Achievements, Problems and Prospects* (Cambridge, Cambridge University Press, 2006); A Moravscik, 'The Origins of Human Rights Regimes: Democratic Delegation in Postwar Europe' (2000) 54 *International Organization* 217, 225.

[2] MR Madsen, 'The Protracted Institutionalization of the Strasbourg Court: From Legal Diplomacy to Integrationist Jurisprudence' in J Christoffersen and MR Madsen (eds), *The European Court of Human Rights between Law and Politics* (Oxford, Oxford University Press, 2011).

of the new states from East and South-East Europe and the former Soviet Union, where rule of law is not firmly consolidated, have marked a new phase in the Court's evolution.

In this latest period, one of the most important challenges the ECtHR has been faced with concerns gross and systemic violations of human rights, a task thoroughly unfamiliar to it in its earlier role as an arbiter of 'good faith' limits of state power.[3] Over the past 15 years, the Court has been inundated with hundreds of complaints from individuals who are victims of state abuses in areas that are sites of political violence and armed conflict. In dealing with systemic infringements and gross violations, the Court has been impelled to shift attention to structural defects, as well as to ingrained practices of abuse and immunity within the new contracting states. By doing so, it has arguably furthered its role as a (quasi)constitutional tribunal[4] and formed the background for debates reconsidering the original architecture and overriding objectives of the Convention.[5] Starting from a broader interest in the institutional evolution of the ECtHR as such, the present study explores its approach and responses in reviewing claims alleging gross violations committed under a state of emergency and in areas witnessing armed conflict.

State governments may declare a state of emergency when they are confronted with minority actions, which they perceive as threatening to national security and public order. Exceptional powers are transferred to the executive, which in normal times would belong to the judiciary or the legislature.[6] A state of emergency though is supposed to be only a temporary departure from normal conditions characterised by enduring democratic controls. The UK was the first European country to declare a state of emergency in the 1960s and 1970s in the context of the inter-community conflict between Catholics and Protestants in Northern Ireland and the political violence that erupted. In the second half of the 1980s, Turkey also declared a state of emergency in the south-eastern part of the country where the army sought to suppress the militant movement of Kurdish separatism. Scores of cases linked to rights violations claimed by individuals from Northern Ireland and from Kurds have been filed with and reviewed by the ECtHR. More recently, while not formally pronouncing a state of emergency, Russia has taken military actions against the separatist movement in

[3] R Harmsen, 'The Reform of the Convention System: Institutional Restructuring and the (Geo-) Politics of Human Rights' in Christoffersen and Madsen (eds) (n 2).

[4] W Sadurski, 'Partnering with Strasbourg: Constitutionalisation of the ECHR, the Accession of Central and East European States to the Council of Europe, and the Idea of Pilot Judgments' (2009) 9 *Human Rights Law Review* 397.

[5] S Greer, 'What's Wrong with the European Convention on Human Rights?' (2008) 30 *Human Rights Quarterly* 680.

[6] S Marks, 'Civil Liberties at the Margin: the UK Derogation and the ECtHR' (1995) 15 *Oxford Journal of Legal Studies* 69, 85.

Chechnya that have given rise to scores of applications in the Strasbourg Court alleging violations such as torture and disappearances.

A review of the relevant case law and how it has evolved over time shows that the judicial attentiveness of the ECtHR to alleged violations in a state of emergency and armed conflict has notably increased. 'Judicial attentiveness' here is understood in the way conceptualised by Charles Epp, to refer to the Court's increased willingness to review such cases, as well as to the varying degree of judicial support to the rights claims that they raise.[7] In the 1970s and for the most part during the 1980s the Court remained largely unconvinced by applicants who were claiming that their rights had been curtailed under the state of emergency that had been declared in Northern Ireland at the time. With the exception of an inter-state complaint submitted by Ireland against the United Kingdom, the ECtHR remained unconvinced by applicants, and upheld the claims put forward by the British authorities.[8]

Over time though, the ECtHR case law concerning abuses under a state of emergency has progressively moved away from its approach of the 1970s and 1980s,[9] which was timid and deferential to national governments. Since the 1990s, the Court has increasingly reviewed complaints linked to a state of emergency on the merits. In over a hundred cases, it has found states such as the UK, Turkey and Russia to be in violation of the Convention, despite maintaining its high standards of proof. In this period, the rapidly rising number of petitions linked to contexts of armed conflict saw an impressive rate of admissibility by the Convention bodies (the Commission and the Court), in comparison to the average rate of admissibility of individual applications overall.[10] In response, the approach of the Commission (now defunct), and the Court since the 1990s, has displayed a gradual, even if not always consistent, tendency to scrutinise deeper state actions and to attach greater weight to the claims of individuals.

[7] C Epp, *The Rights Revolution* (Chicago, University of Chicago Press, 1988) 7.

[8] The inter-state case was *Ireland v UK* App no 5310/71 (ECtHR, 18 January 1978). Other cases considered by the Court were: *Donnelly and others v UK* App nos 5577/72, 5583/72 (Commission decision, 5 April 1973); *McFeely v UK* App no 8317/78 (Commission decision, 15 May 1980); *Farrell v UK* App no 9013/80 (Commission decision, 11 December 1982); *Stewart v UK* App no 10044/82 (Commission decision, 10 July 1984); *Brannigan and McBride v UK* App nos 14553/89 and 14554/89 (ECtHR Plenary, 25 May 1993).

[9] FN Aolain, 'The European Convention on Human Rights and Its Prohibition on Torture' in S Levision (ed), *Torture: A Collection* (Oxford, Oxford University Press, 2004) 213–28.

[10] Out of the 87 applications pertaining to the state of emergency in south-east Turkey in which the Kurdish Human Rights Project (KHRP) was involved, 68 were declared admissible, that is, 80%. This is an impressive admissibility rate in comparison to the various estimates that show a 5–17% admissibility rate of petitions to the ECtHR in general. See C Buckley, *Turkey and the ECHR—A Report on the Litigation Programme of the Kurdish Human Rights Project* (London, KHRP, 2000) 82. It is estimated that just over 2% of applications lodged with the Registry annually are ruled admissible and are actually reviewed by the ECtHR on their merits. See Greer (n 1) 39.

The Court's judgments have increasingly emphasised the rights of victims, while simultaneously reducing the states' margin of appreciation. For example, in dozens of cases concerning the situation in south-east Turkey, the ECtHR has shifted the burden of proof from the individual to the state, requiring state authorities to provide a plausible explanation of the individual's fate in cases in which s/he disappeared while in custody.[11] While originally the Convention's right to life (Article 2) focused on whether the use of force by state agents under particular circumstances was proportionate,[12] it now imposes a duty on the state to investigate alleged abuses occurring with the use of force.[13] In a detailed and balanced analysis, Chevalier-Watts concludes that the ECtHR's approach in alleged killings by state agents has on the whole rigorously applied the requirements of the duty of the state to investigate.[14] To be sure, the approach of the Court and the European Commission of Human Rights (ECommHR) in the 1990s was seen as less than effective and far from proactive in dealing with gross and large-scale violations.[15] Nonetheless, the relevant jurisprudence has moved significantly in the direction of examining the local and national context related to remedies, as well as of placing greater responsibility on the state in investigating alleged abuses.[16]

European human rights review of state actions under a state of emergency and armed conflict is an area in which the expansion of transnational legal authority should have been least expected and it is therefore most intriguing. This is not only because the Convention itself explicitly allows contracting states to derogate from most of their obligations when faced with an emergency or a conflict that is seen to threaten the existence of the nation (Article 15 ECHR). A more lenient and cursory rather than scrutinising kind of European judicial intervention would generally be expected in issues and areas of action that pertain to the most undisputed prerogative of a sovereign state: namely, its ability to quell actions that threaten its public order and territorial integrity. In such areas, a larger rather than smaller margin of appreciation customarily applies. Why then has the ECtHR been increasingly willing to review and vindicate individuals claiming that their rights under the Convention were violated by domestic laws and actions of

[11] Buckely (n 10) 162.

[12] *Stewart v UK* App no 10044/82 (ECommHR, 10 July 1984).

[13] *McCann and Others v the United Kingdom* App no 18984/91 (ECtHR, 5 September 1995); *Kaya v Turkey* App no 22729/93 (ECtHR, 19 February 1998).

[14] J Chevalier-Watts, 'Effective Investigations under Article 2 of the ECHR: Securing the Right to Life or an Onerous Burden on a State?' (2010) 21 *European Journal of International Law* 701.

[15] A Reidy, F Hampson and K Boyle, 'Gross Violations of Human Rights: Invoking the European Convention on Human Rights in the Case of Turkey' (1997) 15 *Netherlands Quarterly of Human Rights* 161.

[16] J Chevalier-Watts, 'The Phenomena of Enforced Disappearances in Turkey and Chechnya: Strasbourg's Noble Cause?' (2010) 11 *Human Rights Review* 469.

authorities under a state of emergency? What factors have influenced the ECommHR and the ECtHR to pay increasing attention to such claims and scrutinise state actions?

The increasing attentiveness of the Strasbourg Court to alleged abuses under a state of emergency and armed conflict may be seen as a direct consequence of European supervision exercised in contracting states where democracy and rule of law are not fully consolidated. It may be that in the face of egregious and mass violations, the ECtHR has been inclined to exercise greater judicial activism and scrutiny vis-à-vis states whose democratic credentials are doubted or suspect (ie Turkey or Russia).[17] It must be noted though that more so than in other areas of law and action, large numbers of petitions must be brought to the attention of the Court in order to enable it to detect and scrutinise gross violations in contexts of armed conflict. Yet, legal scholars and experienced practitioners in this field have pointed to the pervasive limits and weaknesses of the individual complaints mechanism in such contexts; factors such as fear and intimidation, among others, prevent victims from bringing abuses to the attention of the Strasbourg Court.[18] Therefore, the question why the Strasbourg Court has over time displayed increasing judicial attentiveness to related alleged violations cannot merely be attributed to the fact that it now exercises human rights review in unconsolidated democracies lacking well entrenched rule of law. It must also look carefully at the processes and forms of legal and political action that bring such abuses to the attention of the Court.

In this direction, this chapter explores the evolution of the ECtHR case law concerning gross violations in a state of emergency and armed conflict by focusing on the processes of litigation and legal mobilisation in the ECtHR. It argues that expanding processes of legal mobilisation, originating in particular national contexts and spreading transnationally, in tandem with human rights activism, have prompted the Court to become more attentive to and investigative of alleged abuses and gross violations in a state of emergency. Over time, systematic, repeat and often strategically targeted legal action paved the way for the Court to extend its jurisdiction and authority from Belfast to the Kurdish centre of Diyarbakir in south-east Turkey and to the Chechen capital of Grozny. The first part of the chapter reviews insights from a socio-legal perspective for understanding the institutional and jurisprudential evolution of the ECtHR as part of the broader European institutional architecture. The second and third parts of the chapter examine the petitions claiming violations under a state of emergency, the

[17] FN Aolain, 'Transitional Emergency Jurisprudence: Derogation and Transition' in A Buyse and M Hamilton (eds), *Transitional Jurisprudence and the ECHR* (Cambridge, Cambridge University Press, 2011) 39.

[18] Reidy, Hampson and Boyle (n 15).

shifting forms of legal action in tandem with human rights activism, and the evolving approach of the Strasbourg Court.

I. A SOCIO-LEGAL PERSPECTIVE ON THE CONSTRUCTION OF EUROPEAN HUMAN RIGHTS LAW

Historical and international relations accounts on the origins and subsequent construction of a European legal system and its growing authority, including in the human rights field, have centred on the will of governments and states.[19] Legal scholars, on the other hand, have dwelled upon judicial creativity and activism in order to explain how and why the ECtHR has relied on, but also moved beyond, precedent to expand its interpretations.[20] Its judicial activism has primarily been manifested in areas of rights, in which an overall social consensus among the signatory states was deemed to exist.[21] By contrast, judges are expected to be least assertive when respondent states are confronted with large-scale political or separatist violence. More recently, a group of scholars has compellingly shifted attention to the social-legal processes that underpin the evolution and expansion of the ECtHR. In particular, they emphasise the role and professional interests of lawyers and jurists in the expansion of European law and transnational justice more broadly,[22] as well as of activists in the human rights field.[23] These socio-legal analyses have shed new light in understanding the evolution of EU and ECHR law. They reveal the importance of social agency and legal actors in the creation and functioning of a transnational legal and political order, which had been obscured in state-centred and judge-centred approaches.

The above-mentioned socio-legal approaches, however, primarily focus on professional elites and the interests vested in the construction and development of EU and human rights law. Therefore, they do not bring to light the local, national and transnational synergies that are often forged between lawyers, civil society and human rights actors. More importantly,

[19] Moravscik (n 1).

[20] A Mowbray, 'The Creativity of the European Court of Human Rights' (2005) 5 *Human Rights Law Review* 57; P Mahoney, 'Judicial Activism and Judicial Self-Restraint in the European Court of Human Rights: Two Sides of the Same Coin' (1990) 11 *Human Rights Law Journal* 57.

[21] For example, in *Tyrer v UK* App no 5856/72 (ECtHR, 25 April 1978), the UK was found to have violated Article 3 ECHR in maintaining judicial corporal punishment in the Isle of Man. The different standards taking hold in most other countries was explicitly noted by the Court as a reason for finding an infringement.

[22] A Cohen and A Vauchez, 'Introduction: Law, Lawyers, and Transnational Politics in the Production of Europe' (2007) 32 *Law and Social Inquiry* 75; Y Dezalay and BG Garth, 'Introduction—Constructing Transnational Justice' in Y Dezalay and BG Garth (eds), *Lawyers and the Construction of Transnational Justice* (London, Routledge, 2011) 3–13.

[23] Madsen (n 2).

existing studies do not trace whether and how lawyers' actions and social-legal processes are able to extend their reach and influence over the Court's human rights review and the justice that it delivers; and how the Court, in turn, sends back signals to social and legal actors, prompting or foreclosing further legal action. In sum, the interactions and causal connections between social action on the one hand, and legal-judicial institutions and norms on the other, have not been sufficiently explored. An exception here is Cichowski's study that explores how, in response to litigation and social action, the European Court of Justice (ECJ) incrementally developed a set of rights related to gender equality and environmental protection, which were not explicitly enshrined in the Treaties. In this process, judicial decisions created new opportunities for litigation but also for other forms of political and social action, in so far as they established new rules and expanded the scope of rights.[24]

Judges are more likely to be attentive to a set of claims when they are confronted with a large number of petitions raising specific rights claims. In so far as they are receptive, even to some degree, to complaints and vindicate individuals, court rulings act as an incentive for further legal challenges. This study traces the dynamic interaction between growing litigation and legal mobilisation on the one hand, and greater judicial attention and receptivity displayed by the ECtHR on the other, over time, in order to understand and explain the evolution of the Court's relevant case law. Do litigation processes influence the Strasbourg Court's case law related to abuses under a state of emergency and armed conflict? If so, in what ways do they do so, and who are the actors who are involved in legal mobilisation in this area?

Recourse to the ECtHR in regard to petitions related to a state of emergency has involved mobilisation by a variety of actors such as NGOs, cause lawyers and human rights activists. They have often mobilised and collaborated across different states to resist and condemn gross state violations. In exploring patterns of legal mobilisation in the ECtHR, this chapter draws on the concept of transnational advocacy networks, expounded in the influential analysis of Keck and Sikkink. Such networks are organised across state borders in order to bypass national governments condoning or tolerating human rights violations, and to bring international pressure to bear upon them. They operate through open relations among committed and knowledgeable actors working in specialised areas, such as human rights.[25] Abuses involving bodily harm to vulnerable individuals is an issue area around which transnational advocacy networks have organised most frequently around the world.[26] The

[24] R Cichowski, *The European Court and Civil Society: Litigation, Mobilization and Governance* (Cambridge, Cambridge University Press, 2007).

[25] ME Keck and K Sikkink, *Activists Beyond Borders* (Ithaca, Cornell University Press, 1998) 7.

[26] Ibid, 19.

analysis of Keck and Sikkink does not explicitly consider international legal structures among the institutional frames within which they see transnational networks emerge and grow. More recent studies though show that networks of legal and social actors form and actively mobilise in international adjudicatory mechanisms such as those set up to review labour disputes in the North American Free Trade Association (NAFTA) for example, with important consequences for social movement building.[27]

II. ALLEGED VIOLATIONS UNDER A STATE OF EMERGENCY IN NORTHERN IRELAND, 1970S–1980S

Alleged violations under a state of emergency in the ECtHR initially originated from the UK. Britain's acceptance of the ECHR individual petition mechanism in 1966 was anticipated to be inconsequential in the light of its robust civil rights tradition under common law, but this soon turned out not to be the case. Already in 1957, the British government had informed the Council of Europe about a derogation of its commitments within the meaning of Article 15 of the Convention.[28] A national emergency in Northern Ireland was declared in connection with the conflict between the Protestant unionists and the Catholic nationalists (minority), and the activities of the Irish Republican Army (IRA). The state of emergency continued throughout the 1970s along with the imposition of direct rule from London in an attempt to deal with the inter-community violence that had erupted. After 1975, security policy in Northern Ireland abandoned internment without trial and shifted towards a criminal prosecution policy. The latter was aimed at obtaining confessions and convictions, correspondingly downgrading the role of the military and reinforcing that of the police force.[29] A major issue in this new phase was the adequacy and effectiveness of internal police investigations into allegations of abuse.

Emergency measures bolstered executive powers and curtailed the rights of individuals accused or suspected of involvement in terrorist activities, most of whom were Catholics. Many of them sought justice through the legal processes. Yet, while the 1960s civil rights campaign in Northern Ireland inspired a struggle for rights and equality, along the lines of its counterpart in the US,[30] it did not so much impart 'a belief in seeking to pursue change

[27] T Kay, 'Legal Transnationalism: The Relationship between Transnational Social Movement Building and International Law' (2011) 36 *Law and Social Inquiry* 419.

[28] LJ Macfarlane, *Human Rights: Realities and Possibilities* (London, Macmillan, 1990) 33–34.

[29] K Boyle, 'Human Rights and Political Resolution in Northern Ireland' (1982–83) 9 *Yale Journal of World and Public Order* 156, 163–64.

[30] K Boyle, T Hadden and P Hillyard, *Law and State—The Case of Northern Ireland* (London, Martin Robertson and Co, 1975) 11.

through the courts'.[31] The intensification of violence did not help either. Organisations like the Northern Ireland Civil Rights Association largely disintegrated in the wake of the events of Bloody Sunday, which reinforced polarisation and undermined any cross-community alliance around civil rights.[32] Abuses in the application of the security measures fuelled further the psychology of those nationalists committed to achieving their political objectives through violence and reinforced their appeal.[33]

The pursuit of justice through domestic courts proved to be disappointing. Under the state of emergency, domestic judiciaries were significantly constrained in providing effective protection to individuals from abuses in a country that lacked a written bill of rights.[34] Many practices adopted by the police and the army during that period were unlawful, yet hardly any prosecutions were initiated, even if compensation was paid to a number of those affected.[35] British judges acquitted security forces accused of killing at a rate of over 80 per cent, discouraging the bringing of prosecutions.[36] Furthermore, a number of important decisions, in which national courts criticised the actions of security forces, were subsequently reversed legislatively in Parliament. In the context of this analysis there is insufficient space to unravel the complexities defining the role and attitudes of British judges. Most accounts point to an overall disinclination of British judges to scrutinise thoroughly the acts of the executive, the police and the security forces under the state of emergency. In a balanced appraisal, Livingstone attributes this to the complex tensions that national judges were faced with, trying 'to reconcile ideas of judicial independence with fidelity to traditional British constitutional notions of the sovereignty of Parliament'.[37]

In the 1970s and into the 1980s, many individuals whose rights were adversely affected by anti-terrorist legislation in Northern Ireland turned to Strasbourg, in light of the difficulty of finding redress in the domestic judicial system. However, they had little success in convincing the Strasbourg Court and the ECommHR to admit and examine their cases on the merits, not least due to the fact that the claims raised were not formulated and

[31] S Livingstone, 'And Justice for All? The Judiciary and the Legal Profession in Transition' in C Harvey (ed), *Human Rights Equality and Democratic Renewal in Northern Ireland* (Oxford, Hart Publishing, 2001) 131–62, at 141.

[32] M Beirne and A Hegarty, 'A View From the Coal Face: Northern Ireland, Human Rights Activism, and the War on Terror' in J Morison, K McEvoy and G Anthony (eds), *Judges, Transition, and Human Rights* (Oxford, Oxford University Press, 2007) 377–400, at 395–96.

[33] T Hadden, K Boyle and C Campbell, 'Emergency Law in Northern Ireland: The Context' in A Jennings (ed), *Justice Under Fire—The Abuse of Civil Liberties in Northern Ireland* (London, Pluto Press, 1988) 1–26, at 12.

[34] Boyle (n 29) 160–62.

[35] Hadden, Boyle and Campbell (n 33) 6.

[36] Livingstone (n 31) 150–51.

[37] Ibid, 152–53.

managed carefully so as to conform to Convention rules.[38] It was only in an inter-state case brought by the Irish government against the UK in the 1970s, that the ECtHR found British actions in Northern Ireland to be in violation of the Convention.[39] The decision of the ECommHR and the judgment of the ECtHR acknowledged that on the face of it internment without trial breached freedom of liberty (Article 5 ECHR) and the right to a fair trial (Article 6 ECHR). Yet, they proceeded to find no violation on the grounds that the UK had legitimately derogated from its obligations under the Convention in 1957 in the face of inter-community violence and terrorism. The Court declined to examine whether in fact there was an emergency threatening the life of the nation in Northern Ireland.[40] Yet, it found violations of Article 3 ECHR (prohibition of torture and inhuman treatment), expressing particular concern about the failure to carry out internal police investigations and to prosecute those found guilty.

Ill-treatment of detainees by the police was also the charge laid in *Donnelly and Others v UK*,[41] in which human rights lawyers Kevin Boyle and Hurst Hannum were legal representatives. It was a test case that tried to show the existence of a systematic administrative pattern of brutality against individuals detained for suspected involvement in terrorist activities in Northern Ireland. After an initially encouraging admissibility decision, the ECommHR went on to decide that there was no violation on the grounds that the allegations had all been investigated reasonably promptly and effectively at the domestic level. The fact that official investigations were conducted was for the Commission proof that ill-treatment was not condoned or authorised, despite the criticisms levied and despite the fact that few prosecutions or disciplinary actions resulted from such investigations. The lesson taken by lawyers and applicants from this case was that 'proving that a State is systematically failing to comply with its Convention obligations is extremely difficult'.[42]

In general, in the bulk of complaints in the 1970s, the 1980s and until the early 1990s, the adjudicatory organs in Strasbourg did not find a substantive violation for ill-treatment and torture (Article 3) or a violation of the right to life (Article 2). They also held firm to the rule that domestic remedies had

[38] B Dickson, *The European Convention on Human Rights and the Conflict in Northern Ireland* (Oxford, Oxford University Press, 2010) 51.

[39] *Ireland v UK* App no 5310/71 (ECtHR, 18 January 1978). The proceedings in this case concern the scope and the operation in practice of the 'state of emergency' measures declared by the UK and the alleged ill-treatment of persons deprived of their liberty in Northern Ireland. Extra-judicial measures of arrest, detention and internment had been imposed from August 1971 until December 1975 by authorities in response to widespread violence and civil disorder that had erupted in the region. A package of reinforced powers of arrest and interrogation was enacted with the Northern Ireland (Emergency Provisions) Act in 1973. See Hadden, Boyle and Campbell (n 33) 6.

[40] Dickson (n 38) 64–65.

[41] *Donnelly and Others v UK* App no 5577/72 (Commission decision, 15 December 1975).

[42] Dickson (n 38) 146.

to be exhausted for a complaint to be admissible,[43] they were unwilling to challenge findings of fact made by a domestic court, and they deferred to the government's claims that killings and practices to extract confessions were justified in the fight against terrorist violence in Northern Ireland.[44]

Apart from the non-derogable right to life and the prohibition of inhuman treatment though, by the 1980s, the Strasbourg judgments showed signs of internal division. In its judgment in *Brogan and Others v the UK* in 1988, based on a case brought by the Northern Ireland Council for Civil Liberties (NCCL), the ECtHR found that detention periods ranging from four to seven days on suspicion of involvement in terrorist activities contravened Article 5 ECHR.[45] *Brogan* appeared to be a promising shift from the approach of the Strasbourg Court hitherto. However, the UK government refused to abide by the *Brogan* judgment and responded to it by declaring a new derogation from the ECHR in order to evade compliance with it.

Subsequently, *Brannigan and McBride* was lodged with the support of a number of NGOs to challenge the validity of this new derogation and the kind of 'semi-permanent' state of emergency that had seemed to persist since the early 1970s.[46] The Court's judgment in 1993 was a major disappointment and came under fire from human rights critics. It upheld the UK derogation amidst dissent from a small number of its judges (four versus 22), conceding that formal habeas corpus safeguards were sufficient to protect detainees from abuses.[47] The Court seemed to accept the emergency situation as semi-permanent, in essence condoning a process of 'normalisation' of UK anti-terrorist legislation that was 'infecting' ordinary criminal law.[48]

It may be argued that it would be premature to expect the Court and the Commission to be receptive to alleged violations under the state of emergency in Northern Ireland in the 1970s. At least in the early part of that decade, those bodies were still shaped by the political and intergovernmental dynamics that had been in play since their creation in the 1950s. Yet, the legal challenges discussed above, as well as the actors involved in them, did little to challenge the predominantly deferential approach of the Commission and the Court towards the government. In the first place, the attitude of the legal profession in Northern Ireland was characterised by a culture of 'quietism'. While in part attributed to the traditional conservatism of the bar, more importantly, the reluctance of lawyers to denounce

[43] This is the reason that the complaints relating to 22 deaths in the *Ireland v UK* application were declared inadmissible.

[44] *Stewart v UK* App no 10044/84 (ECtHR, 10 July 1984); *Farrell v UK* App no 9013/80 (Commission decision, 11 December 1982); *Kelly v UK* App no 17579/90 (ECommHR decision, 13 January 1993). For a thorough review, see Dickson (n 38), especially chapters 7 and 9.

[45] *Brogan and Others v UK* App no 11209/84 (ECtHR, 29 November 1988).

[46] *Brannigan and McBride v UK* App nos 14553/89 and 14554/89 (ECtHR, 25 May 1993).

[47] Marks (n 6) 80–81.

[48] Ibid, 86.

violations, to mobilise and bring claims in the ECtHR was linked to the hostile climate characteristic of situations of armed conflict, in which engaged lawyers were faced with death threats and intimidation.[49] Lawyers who did engage in litigation in cases linked to the conflict in Northern Ireland were keen to distance themselves from activism and human rights NGOs: 'they were generally content to operate the law as given rather than see it as part of their calling to alter'.[50] As late as 1990, while the Northern Ireland Bar Association condemned the murder of solicitor Pat Finucane by loyalist paramilitaries in 1989, it was far from vocal about it.[51]

Lawyers and public law organisations, which were repeat players like the NCCL/Liberty, insisted on distancing themselves from the political context of the Northern Ireland conflict. Instead of pursuing proactive strategic litigation targeting specific points of human rights law, they litigated in a reactive and haphazard manner, choosing cases that were not always appropriate.[52] The *Stewart* judgment, for instance, which was fought by the NCCL, and which was a major drawback for the rights cause in regard to the state of emergency in Northern Ireland, was arguably a result of misguided legal counsel and action.[53] Jennings sees it as unfortunate that 'the only case in which an inquest had found that a plastic bullet victim was a "rioter" was selected as the test case'.[54] The unreceptive and occasionally only lukewarm, responses of the Court and the Commission undermined a belief that the chances for justice were better in Strasbourg than in domestic courts. After 1990, however, as we shall see in the next section, litigation strategies became increasingly more purposeful and sophisticated, with careful selection of test cases that sought to balance the goal of legal advances with the objective to raise public awareness and support.[55]

III. TRANSNATIONALISING THE STRUGGLE: HUMAN RIGHTS LAW JOINS FORCES WITH ACTIVISM

A few developments in the second half of the 1980s and the early 1990s led some leading human rights lawyers to renew their legal challenges against

[49] K McEvoy and R Rebouche, 'Mobilizing the Professions: Lawyers, Politics, and the Collective Legal Conscience' in J Morison, K McEvoy and G Anthony (eds), *Judges, Transition and Human Rights* (Oxford, Oxford University Press, 2007) 284–85.

[50] Livingstone (n 31) 133.

[51] Ibid, 137; McEvoy and Rebouche (n 49) 284–85.

[52] C Harlow and R Rawlings, *Pressure Through Law* (London, Routledge, 1992) 258; RJ Maiman, '"We've Had to Raise our Game": Liberty's Litigation Strategy under the Human Rights Act 1998' in S Halliday and P Schmidt (eds), *Human Rights Brought Home: Socio-Legal Perspectives on Human Rights in National Context* (Oxford, Hart Publishing, 2004) 94–95.

[53] *Stewart v UK* App no 10044/84 (ECtHR, 10 July 1984).

[54] A Jennings, 'Bullets Above the Law' in A Jennings (ed), *Justice Under Fire—The Abuse of Civil Liberties in Northern Ireland* (London, Pluto Press, 1988) 140.

[55] Maiman (n 52) 98–100.

alleged violations committed in contexts of armed struggle in the UK and beyond. In the first place, the peace process for Northern Ireland that began in the 1990s possibly eased out tensions somewhat and encouraged lawyers to take more cases in the ECtHR. Secondly, in a strategic move expected to enhance the country's prospects for EU membership, for which an application had been lodged in 1987, Turkey accepted the right of individuals to petition the Strasbourg Court. In the same year, though, the Turkish government also declared a state of emergency in the eastern and south-eastern parts of the country, the site of an armed conflict with the Kurdish population. The state of emergency, which was officially abolished only in 2002, set the context for a series of human rights violations committed by security forces against civilians. An equally important development was that in the second half of the 1980s and the early 1990s, many who disagreed with the armed struggle sought to internationalise the Kurdish issue. Perhaps they were also inspired and encouraged to do so by the flourishing standard-setting activities on the European and international plane, for example in the Organization for Security and Co-operation in Europe (OSCE), concerning the protection of minorities through the frame of human rights.

The origins of Kurdish litigation in Strasbourg were critically linked to the pioneer experience that had been gained in the Northern Irish context. Advice from UK lawyers who had been involved in human rights litigation was instrumental in motivating Kurdish lawyers and leaders to consider it as a viable strategy. A meeting held in Diyarbakir in 1992 between lawyers from the Human Rights Centre at Essex University, local Kurdish lawyers and the newly established, London-based Kurdish Human Rights Project (KHRP), proved to be a turning point.[56] The idea of pursuing a legal strategy on behalf of Turkey's Kurds was put down by Fevzi Veznerndaroglu from the Diyarbakir Human Rights Association together with Kevin Boyle from Essex University, who was the legal representative in a number of the earlier Northern Irish petitions in Strasbourg.[57] It was also embraced by the KHRP, which adopted a large litigation programme as the centrepiece of its international strategy and its activities out of London. The transnational connections that were forged enabled Turkish lawyers to launch the first applications in Strasbourg with the assistance of British lawyers like Boyle and Françoise Hampson, who transferred their skills, knowledge and experience with European human rights litigation.

[56] D Kurban, O Erözden and H Gülalp, 'Supranational Rights Litigation, Implementation and the Domestic Impact of Strasbourg Court Jurisprudence: A Case Study of Turkey', report prepared for the JURISTRAS Project funded by the European Commission under the 6th Framework Programme, 2008, 4, available at www.juristras.eliamep.gr/wp-content/uploads/2008/10/casestudyreportturkeyfinal.pdf, accessed 17 July 2013.

[57] MD Goldhaber, *A People's History of the European Court of Human Rights* (New Brunswick, Rutgers University Press, 2007) 123.

Over the years, the KHRP litigation programme significantly expanded the circle of lawyers from the UK and Turkey who got engaged in it.[58] It benefited from the transnational connections established between the KHRP, the Diyarbakir branch of the Human Rights Association of Turkey (DHRA) and the international community. The KHRP defined Convention law and litigation as the primary instrument for awareness raising, advocacy and human rights activism. While it did not itself qualify as a petitioner under the ECHR, the centre was involved in the presentation of a large number of cases in the ECtHR concerning extra-judicial killings, destruction of property, disappearances, ill-treatment and freedom of expression and association. It also provided critical analyses of the government's position and documentary evidence, such as statements from applicants and witnesses, autopsy reports, NGOs' reports, statistical information, etc, as indispensable material to support human rights litigation.[59]

The new wave of legal challenges against violations under a state of emergency in Strasbourg in the 1990s had at least two important advantages related to the socio-legal context of struggle. In the first place, the UK lawyers that spearheaded and were involved in litigation in the first few important cases reviewed by the ECtHR capitalised upon the mistakes and first-hand experience that had been gained in the 1970s and 1980s in the context of Northern Ireland. In particular, it was clear from the start that it would be difficult to persuade the Court and the Commission to condemn state abuses through individual petitions unless the inadequacy of domestic remedies and the systematic nature of violations were compellingly brought out and specifically targeted in the legal argumentation. A further issue, in which the potential for jurisprudential advances was identified, concerned the positive obligations that states had in protecting the right to life and in prohibiting ill-treatment, for example by conducting effective internal investigations into alleged abuses. These points were the lessons that Kevin Boyle had apparently already drawn years earlier as counsel in and commentator on Northern Irish cases, which the ECtHR and the Commission had reviewed.[60]

Therefore, it is not surprising that the first few cases that were taken in Strasbourg in the first half of the 1990s by the KHRP with legal representation by Turkish lawyers and British lawyers from the University of Essex, precisely raised the above points. They led to landmark judgments and set the tone and frame for subsequent litigation. *Aksoy* was the first ECtHR

[58] The KHRP has worked with a large number of lawyers apart from Kevin Boyle and Françoise Hampson, who include Ashling Reidy, Bill Bowring, Tony Fisher, Philip Kirkpatrick, Mark Muller, Nicholas Steward QC, Andrew Collender QC, among others. In Turkey, the KHRP worked together with advocates Osman Baydemir, Kenan Sidar, Mahmut Sakar, Metin Kilavuz and Sinan Tanrikulu, among others. See Buckley (n 10) 2.

[59] See Buckley (n 10) 75.

[60] Boyle (n 29), 166–67.

judgment to confirm an incident of torture anywhere in Europe (violation of Art 3 ECHR), and the first one to put the burden of proof on the state.[61] Significantly, it was also the first case in which the Court considered local courts unreliable for fact finding and sent its own delegates to hold evidentiary hearings in Diyarbakir.[62] In departing from its earlier jurisprudence (see *Brannigan and McBride v the UK*[63]), the Court affirmed in *Aksoy v Turkey* that it is up to it to rule whether state actions under a state of emergency have gone beyond the 'extent strictly required by the exigencies of the crisis'.[64] In *Akdıvar and Others,* which concerned destruction of property during security operations, the Court found Turkey to be in violation of property rights (Article 1, Protocol 1 ECHR). It also recognised here the inadequacy of domestic remedies by pointing out that despite the gravity of village destructions and the multitude of accusations against security forces, no legal remedy was provided and the perpetrators were not held accountable. It therefore exempted applicants from the admissibility criterion of exhausting domestic remedies.[65]

The second advantage that the Kurdish petitions in Strasbourg had in the 1990s was the transnational character of the legal representation, advocacy and activism that defined and supported them, which had not existed—certainly not in the same degree—in Northern Ireland in the 1970s and the 1980s. A well-developed network of human rights organisations in Turkey and abroad ensured a high inflow of complaints, which experienced lawyers and activists were able to frame into well-documented and legally compelling rights claims.[66] Similarly to the Northern Ireland context, bar associations in south-east Turkey for the most part kept their distance and did not provide much support to potential litigants.[67] At the same time, the network of lawyers and activists who supported litigation from abroad helped to somewhat overcome the fear and intimidation with which lawyers and activists in south-east Turkey were confronted. In all these ways, the transnational structures of legal and organisational support enabled scores of petitions to be lodged in Strasbourg in the years following the *Aksoy* and *Akdivar and Others* judgments. The initial successes with these landmark judgments in the mid-1990s prompted lawyers, NGOs and individuals to take more cases to Strasbourg.

[61] See *Aksoy v Turkey* App no 21987/93 (ECtHR, 18 December 1996).
[62] Goldhaber (n 57) 127.
[63] *Brannigan and McBride v UK* (n 46).
[64] See Buckley (n 10) 134–35.
[65] *Akdıvar and Others v Turkey* App no 99/1995/605/693 (ECtHR, 30 August 1996).
[66] K Yildiz and C Brigham, *Human Rights Defenders in Turkey* (London, KHRP and Bar Human Rights Committee of England and Wales, 2006).
[67] Kurban, Erözden and Gülalp (n 56) 9–10.

The vast majority of judgments issued by the ECtHR found Turkey to have violated Articles 2, 3, 5, 6 and 8 of the ECHR and Article 1 of Protocol 1.[68] The violations committed by security officers in the 'fight against terrorism' concerned killings by security forces;[69] ill-treatment,[70] inhuman and degrading punishment[71] or torture;[72] and unlawful detention,[73] among others. Regardless of whether an individual's death occurred during security operations or by an unidentified perpetrator, the Court established that the State has positive obligations under Article 2 to protect life. In particular, it identified a stronger obligation that state authorities had to properly plan State action to protect civilian lives, as well as to conduct an effective criminal investigation where death occurred in suspicious circumstances or where there was a formal complaint about it. In its judgments, the Court concluded that terrorism does not justify holding individuals in incommunicado detention for up to 30 days without access to a judge, lawyer, relative or doctor.[74] It held that the failure to provide detainees the right to bring habeas corpus claims to challenge the legality of their detention violates Article 5(4).[75] It also found the unacknowledged detention of an individual to be a violation of Articles 3 and 5.[76]

Human rights litigation in Strasbourg was part and parcel of the internationalisation and Europeanisation of the Kurdish political strategy that developed at the antipode of the militant struggle. Its resonance grew at a time when the deployment of armed struggle as a means to independent statehood was being discredited and condemned.[77] Instead, this strategy advocated the pursuit of rights of Kurds through democratic reforms and rule of law within the territory of the Turkish state.

[68] For an overview of the ECtHR case law concerning Kurds and other minorities in Turkey, see D Kurban, 'Protecting Marginalised Individuals and Minorities in ECtHR: Litigation and Jurisprudence in Turkey' in D Anagnostou and E Psychogiopoulou (eds), *The European Court of Human Rights and the Rights of Marginalised Individuals and Minorities in National Context* (Leiden, Martinus Nijhoff Publishers, 2010) 159–82.

[69] *Ergi v Turkey* App no 23818/94 (ECtHR, 28 July 1998).

[70] See *Mehmet Emin Yüksel v Turkey* App no 40154/98 (ECtHR, 20 October 2004); *Çelik and İmret v Turkey* App no 44093/98 (ECtHR, 26 October 2004).

[71] *Timurtaş v Turkey* App no 23531/94 (ECtHR, 13 June 2000); *Taş v Turkey* App no 24396/94 (ECtHR, 14 November 2000).

[72] *Salman v Turkey* App no 21986/93 (ECtHR, 27 June 2000); *İlhan v Turkey* App no 22277/93 (ECtHR, 27 June 2000); *Akkoç v Turkey* App nos 22947/93 and 22948/93 (ECtHR, 10 October 2000).

[73] *Kurt v Turkey* App no 15/1997/799/1002 (ECtHR, 25 May 1998); *Çakıcı v Turkey* App no 23657/94 (ECtHR, 8 July 1999); *Taş v Turkey* App no 24396/94 (ECtHR, 14 November 2000); *Çiçek v Turkey* App no 25704/94 (ECtHR, 27 February 2001).

[74] *Aksoy v Turkey* App no 21987/93 (ECtHR, 18 December 1996).

[75] The ECtHR reiterated this principle in subsequent cases which raised similar issues. See ECtHR, *Demir and Others v Turkey* App nos 71/1997/855/1062–1064 (ECtHR, 23 September 1998).

[76] *Kurt v Turkey* App no 15/1997/799/1002 (ECtHR, 25 May 1998).

[77] On the advent and demise of the PKK, see SE Cornell, 'The Kurdish Question in Turkish Politics' (2001) 45 *Orbis* 31.

The systematic litigation programme combined with active campaigning and human rights advocacy targeted European institutions and used the leverage provided by the EU accession process and the pressures it introduced for democratic reforms. In the European Council meeting in Copenhagen in 2002, the KHRP sent a briefing paper on the situation in Turkey to the Danish EU presidency, to the Permanent Representatives of all Member States, and to the European Commission. It contained a detailed evaluation of the situation of Kurds in Turkey and of Turkey's failure to implement the constitutional reform packages.[78] The Commission's progress reports on Turkey's democratisation raised several critical points pertaining to the rights of Kurds and the situation in south-east Turkey, while the European Parliament took strong positions on behalf of the rights of Kurds.[79] Active advocacy and campaigning to spread knowledge and awareness about the situation of Kurds and the conditions in south-east Turkey across European institutions rendered the legal claims raised in Strasbourg even more compelling.

At the same time, a new wave of petitions linked to the actions of the security forces and the police in Northern Ireland reached the ECtHR in the 1990s and early 2000s. In a series of new judgments, the ECtHR found the UK to have violated Article 2 ECHR on grounds that UK authorities had failed to engage in effective and/or timely investigation into the causes of controversial deaths connected with the Northern Irish conflict.[80] Litigation in those cases emerged from a significantly transformed socio-legal context in the UK and dwelled upon the advances made in the landmark judgments that in the meantime had come out in regard to the Kurds. The onset of the peace process helped to ease tensions. The 1998 Good Friday Agreement and the relative decline in inter-community violence prompted more lawyers to get involved and further elevated human rights as a means of seeking redress and facilitating transitional justice in Northern Ireland. In the meantime, a dynamic human rights movement formed to support the domestic incorporation of the ECHR. The passage of the Human Rights Act (HRA) in 1998 reinforced legal mobilisation and rendered human rights litigation a high-in-demand and extremely competitive field of law and social action.[81]

[78] A Blätte, 'The Kurdish Movement. Ethnic Mobilization and Europeanization' in H Kleinschmidt (ed), *Migration, Regional Integration and Human Security* (Aldershot, Ashgate, 2006) 181–202, at 191.

[79] Ibid 192–94.

[80] *McKerr and Others v UK* App no 28883/94 (ECtHR, 4 April 2000); *Shanaghan and Kelly v UK* App nos 37715/97 and 30054/96 (ECtHR, 4 August 2001); *Magee v UK* App no 28135/95 (ECtHR, 6 September 2000); *McShane v UK* App no 43290/98 (ECtHR, 28 May 2002); *Finucane v UK* App no 29178/95 (ECtHR, 1 July 2003); *Jordan v UK* App no 24746/95 (ECtHR, 4 May 2001). For a critical discussion of the UK investigative and prosecutorial processes, see G Anthony and P Mageean, 'Habits of Mind and "Truth Telling": Article 2 ECHR in Post-Conflict Northern Ireland' in J Morison et al (eds), *Judges, Transition, and Human Rights* (Oxford, Oxford University Press, 2007) 185–86.

[81] Maiman (n 52) 100–08.

The new Northern Irish cases in the 1990s, unlike the earlier ones in the preceding decades, were taken in Strasbourg amidst dense and widespread internationalisation activities. These aimed at raising awareness about the fear and intimidation faced by committed human rights lawyers in Northern Ireland but also at criticising the disengagement of bar associations and their timidity to condemn it. They rallied the support of international organisations like Amnesty International, the International Federation of Human Rights, and the International Commission of Jurists, among others, to call for a public inquiry into the investigation into the death of lawyer Pat Finucane, a high-profile case also decided by the Strasbourg Court.[82] In sum, this latest wave of petitions in Strasbourg drew leverage from the rising volume of condemnations issued by the Court in the 1990s concerning abuses by security forces in south-east Turkey, a vibrant local and national human rights context in the UK, as well as from the internationalisation of the conflict in Northern Ireland.

Advancing selected legal claims before Strasbourg by dwelling on points of judicial receptivity or ambivalence displayed in the earlier case law proved an effective strategy. It pushed the Court and the Commission to extend protection of rights, such as the right to life and the prohibition against torture, by broadening state obligations in instances of death in which state agents are allegedly or actually implicated. While the Court's interpretation had originally focused on whether the use of State force under particular circumstances was proportionate (as in *Stewart v UK*), Article 2 was now seen to impose additional obligations on the State. In the seminal case of *McCann and Others v UK*, the ECtHR for the first time set out a requirement for an effective State investigation into deaths,[83] and in subsequent cases further elaborated on what an 'effective' investigation required.[84] Besides conducting a full, effective and timely investigation into the circumstances surrounding the use of force and the resulting loss of life, and prosecuting those State actors found responsible,[85] they further extended to requirements for proper control and organisation of operations resulting in death, in accordance with specific standards.[86]

The very large number of complaints from south-east Turkey and Northern Ireland that reached Strasbourg in the 1990s and into the 2000s critically influenced the expansive interpretations of the ECtHR: they allowed the

[82] McEvoy and Rebouche (n 49) 284–91.

[83] Chevalier-Watts (n 14) 705.

[84] *McKerr and Others v UK* App no 28883/94 (ECtHR, 4 April 2000); *Shanaghan and Kelly v UK* App nos 37715/97 and 30054/96 (ECtHR, 4 August 2001), among others.

[85] Anthony and Mageean (n 80) 184.

[86] This issue was the basis for the finding of Article 2 ECHR violation by the UK in the landmark case of *McCann and Others v UK* App no 18984/91 (ECtHR, 27 September 1995) in which the ECtHR was sharply divided. For a discussion of the judgment and its importance, see Dickson (n 38) 255–58.

Court to acquire thorough knowledge of the local situation and therefore to recognise the systemic nature of abuses and to identify systematic practices, thereby moving beyond the fact-specific and strictly individualised approach to cases. In the second half of the 1990s and early 2000s, the ECtHR's case law related to a state of emergency rapidly evolved, especially around the right to life (Article 2 ECHR) and the prohibition of torture and inhuman treatment (Article 3).[87] It extended their application to cases of forced disappearances and unacknowledged detention. In overcoming the difficulties arising in supplying proof for death when no body is discovered, it shifted the burden of proof to the state when sufficient circumstantial evidence exists.[88] More centrally than ever before, the ECtHR placed great emphasis on the general context of the conflict in south-east Turkey.

In a couple of years, the jurisprudential advances of the Strasbourg Court in regard to rights abuses under the state of emergency in Northern Ireland and Turkey formed key precedents and presented opportunities that inspired and paved the way for another wave of applications, this time from Chechnya. The first few petitions were lodged in the early 2000s, following Russia's accession to the Convention in 1998. They were prepared and submitted to the ECtHR initially on the initiative of the Russian NGO 'Memorial', which filed the first application in 2000 after having conducted thorough research of the case law related to Northern Ireland and south-east Turkey. Together with the support of the Moscow branch of Human Rights Watch (HRW), they also submitted compelling evidence about the degree of immunity enjoyed by Russian servicemen convicted of crimes against the Chechen civilian population.[89] Apart from seeking redress for individual victims, these petitions and the many more that followed had a strategic objective: this was to expose and raise awareness at the European and international level about the gross violations committed by the Russian forces in Chechnya.

Human Rights Watch brought victims from Chechnya into contact with European lawyers who lodged the first few cases. Those initial cases that were litigated formed the nucleus of a separate organisation that was established in 2001, the Stichting Russian Justice Initiative (SRJI) with funding from the Dutch government. The SRJI had a transnational structure with offices in Moscow, Nazran (Chechnya) and Utrecht in the Netherlands. Only two years later, in 2003, a few London-based lawyers, who had been involved in the Kurdish litigation in the ECtHR with the KHRP, set up the

[87] Chevalier-Watts (n 16) 473–76.

[88] *Timurtas v Turkey* App no 23531/94 (ECtHR, 13 June 2000); *Orhan v Turkey* App no 25656/94 (ECtHR, 18 June 2002); *Ipek v Turkey* App no 25760/94 (ECtHR, 14 May 2002).

[89] E Gilligan, *Terror in Chechnya: Russia and the Tragedy of Civilians in War* (Princeton, Princeton University Press, 2009) 186. By 2002, the ECtHR had ruled on 366 cases from Turkey, 44 of which were from Kurds.

Human Rights Advocacy Centre (EHRAC) with EU funding. EHRAC has cooperated with local lawyers and assisted many civilian victims to take cases to the ECtHR.[90] Generally, the vast majority of the Chechen applications are brought by organisations or lawyers (at the local or national level) who have connections with human rights organisations and experts abroad; the bulk of them are lodged by the SRJI and EHRAC in cooperation with Memorial.[91]

Judgments related to Chechnya pertain to torture, bombings, destruction of property, and above all to disappearances.[92] They comprise a significant portion of judgments against Russia, from where the majority of pending applications before the ECtHR come (29 per cent in 2010). The above organisations working on the bulk of the Chechen litigation in Strasbourg have provided legal aid, knowledge and expertise, and generally a structure of support to victims for carrying out the proceedings. It is clear that in the absence of these organisations, which have a transnational structure and connections, applications to the ECtHR by independent lawyers from Chechnya would be few due to limited finances, widespread intimidation and fear.[93] The identification of key points and precedents by human rights organisations and lawyers, on which to press their legal argumentation in Strasbourg, the strategic selection of cases, as well as the sheer number of applications that were lodged, all contributed to important advances in the resulting case law with regard to the rights of victims vis-à-vis state agents in contexts of armed conflict. These merit a thorough and extensive analysis, however, space limitations do not permit more than an indicative and thus cursory review here in relation to disappearances and positive obligations of states.

Disappearances of individuals after being taken to custody were a widespread occurrence in Chechnya and presented a particularly thorny problem for proving a human rights violation due to the lack of evidence, as well as the absence of a body attesting to a killing. As in south-east Turkey before, the large number of applications enabled the Court to acquire a thorough understanding of, and to recognise the specific context of, violence and impunity in Chechnya—this was crucial for deciding cases on incomplete evidence, which characterises most disappearances cases.[94] Building on earlier precedents related to the right to life and the prohibition

[90] Ibid, 187.

[91] F van der Vet, 'Seeking Life, Finding Justice: Russian NGO litigation and Chechen Disappearances before the ECtHR' (2012) 13 *Human Rights Review* 303–25, at 308.

[92] In 2010, SRJI and EHRAC work had resulted in 156 judgments against Russia related to Chechnya, that is, 14% of the total of 1,106 against Russia. Ibid, 309.

[93] O Solvang, 'Chechnya and the ECtHR: The Merits of Strategic Litigation' (2008) 3 *Security and Human Rights* 208–19, at 211.

[94] See *Bazorkina v Russia* App no 69481/01 (ECtHR, 27 July 2006); *Bitiyeva and X v Russia* App nos 57953/00 and 37392/03 (ECtHR, 21 June 2007); *Medov v Russia* App no 1573/02 (ECtHR, 8 November 2007), among many others.

of torture laid in the cases from south-east Turkey and Northern Ireland, the ECtHR has placed even further reliance on inferences drawn and the presumption of fact made in the Chechen cases. In doing so, it loosened the high evidentiary standards that it had maintained in the earlier Kurdish cases, which required the applicants to prove beyond reasonable doubt that the disappeared was dead, as well as government complicity in the killing.[95] The Court also emphasised much more the failure of the Russian government to disclose information and to rebut the applicants' claims, and to provide alternative explanations.[96] The ECtHR has also extended the concept of the victim to relatives of the disappeared, who may be victims of inhuman treatment (Article 3 ECHR) due to the ongoing uncertainty and anxiety that they suffer.[97]

Last but not least, the ECtHR has further extended the positive obligations of the state in the frame of conducting an effective investigation. Apart from the actual or accused perpetrators of the killing, it has also attributed responsibility to those involved in planning an operation (ie whether they ensured a safe exit for civilians).[98] As Chevalier-Watts concludes, the obligation to carry out an effective investigation emphasises the rights of the victim more explicitly in the judgments coming out of Chechnya than previously.[99] The depth of scrutiny and state reprimand from the Court in the Chechen cases has been greater in comparison to the Kurdish and Northern Irish cases, and it may partly be attributed to the fact that existing standards in Russia fell well below the minimum, unlike in the UK.[100]

IV. CONCLUSION

Legal mobilisation claiming violation of Convention rights in a state of emergency and armed conflict emerged from national contexts where domestic channels of judicial redress and government pressure were blocked or ineffective. It did not occur overnight but was rather the progressive culmination of a process that began in the 1970s in the UK, when a small number of lawyers challenged in the Strasbourg Court the actions of security forces in Northern Ireland with limited success. While the expansion of legal aid in the 1970s and 1980s in the UK did not benefit those accused of terrorist

95 I Taqi, 'Adjudicating Disappearance Cases in Turkey: An Argument for Adopting the Inter-American Court of Human Rights' Approach' (2000) 24 *Fordham International Law Journal* 940, at 982.

96 P Leach, 'The Chechen Conflict: Analysing the Oversight of the ECtHR' (2008) 6 *European Human Rights Law Review* 732, 748.

97 Ibid, 760.

98 *Isayeva v Russia* App no 57950/00 (ECtHR, 24 February 2005); *Isayeva, Yusupova and Bazayeva v Russia* App nos 57947/00, 57948 and 57949/00 (ECtHR, 24 February 2005).

99 Chevalier-Watts (n 14) 715.

100 Ibid, 717.

offences, it nonetheless helped public law firms and human rights organisations to engage more in strategic and social cause litigation, and to augment both their expertise and professional commitment in this area. The resulting transformation of the civil rights and human rights field in the UK paved the way for more focused and effective legal tactics before the ECtHR later on. After 1990, legal tactics also spread beyond the UK to Turkey where large-scale strategic use of litigation before the ECtHR was incorporated as the centrepiece of an alternative Kurdish strategy that distanced itself from armed struggle, as well as in another human rights strategy aimed at bringing to light the plight of civilians caught in armed conflict in Chechnya.

Legal mobilisation in regard to gross violations in state of emergency and armed struggle is dominated by transnational networks comprising legal actors, NGOs, activists and academics, similar to those described by Keck and Sikkink. They combine legal expertise, knowledge of, and ties with, an area of conflict, along with principled commitment to, and advocacy in, human rights, in a kind of legal activism that extends across state borders, and which has been instrumental in the Court's institutional and jurisprudential transformation since the 1990s. Lawyers saw the opportunity in points of judicial receptivity or division surfacing in Commission decisions and Court rulings to press with legal and conceptual arguments towards advancing the scope of rights protection. Human rights and civil society activists, on the other hand, were motivated by the need to bypass the state and search for international allies to bring pressure to bear from the outside in redressing gross violations. While such legal activism originated from particular national, legal and social contexts, it subsequently spread in other countries.

Transnational collaborations have enabled a large number of petitions to be brought in Strasbourg by providing external support to counter the risks of human rights litigation in contexts of armed struggle, where applicants and lawyers are confronted with intimidation and threats. Repeat and strategic litigation that targeted points of judicial receptivity or intra-court division displayed in earlier case law pushed the Court to substantially shift its interpretations in a direction of greater scrutiny for state actions and abuses, while paying more attention to the rights of individual victims. It inundated the ECtHR with a constant and growing supply of petitions that raised novel issues of jurisprudence but also social justice. In a number of countries, especially in East Europe and the ex-Soviet Union, such legal mobilisation developed upon, and drew from, a substratum of human rights activism, which had flourished since the 1970s and into the 1980s, largely as a result of the Helsinki process and the movement that it set in train.[101] It also drew from the advent and growth of a new kind of human rights lawyering

[101] For a historical account of the human rights movement that grew with the onset of the Helsinki Process, see S B Snyder, *Human Rights Activism and the End of the Cold War* (Cambridge, Cambridge University Press, 2011).

(or cause lawyering) in the UK and in other countries of Europe characterised by '... a more open acceptance that the intersection between law and politics is a reality in these areas of practice'.[102]

This analysis does not claim that legal mobilisation and activism were the sole or even the main influence on how the Court (re)interpreted the rights in question. Instead, it argues that (a) committed human rights lawyers (or cause lawyers) attended to intra-Court divisions and creatively exploited early advances in the Court's jurisprudence in order to press further claims originating in other national and local contexts; (b) together with human rights organisations at the local-national level and abroad, those lawyers forged transnational networks that engaged both in litigation in the ECtHR and in international advocacy and condemnation of gross violations; and (c) they pursued repeat, proactive and systematic litigation that would not have been possible (or at least would have been very difficult) without the presence and sustained initiative of transnational networks of lawyers and organisations who cooperated with local NGOs, lawyers and bar associations to bring these cases to justice. The large number of cases that they brought to the attention of the Commission and the ECtHR was indispensable in influencing it to adopt a more context-attentive approach, and to elaborate on and extend the obligations and responsibilities of the state in gross violations such as property destructions, torture and inhuman treatment, killings and disappearances.

Increased judicial attentiveness to rights claims linked with gross violations alongside a more thorough scrutiny of state actions, have silently and implicitly moved the Court closer to its constitutionalisation. They have enabled the ECtHR to gradually augment its authority as a court delivering transnational justice par excellence, furthering its own transformation in a constitutional direction. This has brought anew to the fore longstanding concerns about the role of judicial review in relation to the democratic processes, which are particularly apposite with regard to a European court.

Apart from the causes of the Court's jurisprudential and institutional evolution, the question still remains as to what difference its judgments make for state policies and the rights of citizens in the contracting states. State compliance with relevant Court judgments is a complex and multifaceted issue that is beyond the scope of this analysis.[103] Regarding the ECtHR judgments under focus, Turkey, for instance, has undertaken important legislative reforms in response to Article 3 judgments. At the same time, the 2006 amendments to anti-terror law are characterised as regressive.[104] In its correspondence with

[102] McEvoy and Rebouche (n 49) 311.

[103] On this issue, see D Anagnostou (ed), *The ECtHR—Implementing Strasbourg's Judgments on Domestic Policy* (Edinburgh, Edinburgh University Press, 2013).

[104] Ibid. See especially chapter by D Kurban and H Gülalp, 'A Complicated Affair: Turkey's Kurds and the ECtHR', 166–87.

the Committee of Ministers (the body supervising implementation of ECtHR judgments), the KHRP described in detail important gaps in Turkish implementation of reforms to reduce the practice of torture, to enhance procedural safeguards in police custody, and to promote professional training of security forces, among other things.[105] Implementation of the latest wave of Northern Irish judgments in the UK was also hampered by the refusal of British authorities to hold Article 2-compliant public investigations into the deaths of individuals that occurred during the 1980s. Proceedings in domestic courts that appeal to the corresponding provisions in the HRA have not helped break the stalemate as it has been held that the HRA cannot be applied retrospectively (that is, in relation to deaths that occurred before its passage), even in cases that concern the fundamental right to life.[106]

Despite the evasive or resisting responses of national governments, there is no doubt that the ECtHR judgments that vindicate individuals claiming violations by security forces provide considerable leverage to those fighting to end them. They enable human rights defenders and minority activists to draw legitimacy, to expose and to counter state abuses, as well as to pressure for change in an ongoing struggle. The judicialisation of human rights at the European level renders international supervision of state actions more consequential. Court judgments are a most authoritative source of pressure that are continuously monitored by the EU, the Committee for the Prevention of Torture, and other international and European organisations that draw upon them to define their policies and positions vis-à-vis different states. In sum, the ECtHR judgments do matter in multifaceted ways even if their implementation is at times resisted or evaded by national authorities. Today, the battles over the rights of individual citizens and the interests of state security in Europe have as an inescapable frame of reference the transnational human rights regime centring in the ECtHR to an extent and in a manner far more pervasive and consequential than was originally intended or anticipated.

[105] 'Response to the Committee of Ministers Resolution of 18 September 2008, on the Execution of ECtHR Judgments in Relation to Turkish Security Forces', KHRP Public Statement.

[106] See House of Lords House of Commons Joint Committee on Human Rights, 'Monitoring the Government's Response to Human Rights Judgments: Annual Report 2008', 27–29; see also Anthony and Mageean (n 80) 192–94.

8

Activists and Lawyers in the ECtHR: The Struggle for Gay Rights

LOVEDAY HODSON

THE EUROPEAN COURT of Human Rights (ECtHR) has emerged as a central site upon which important social and political struggles are played out in Europe. Activism in litigation before it though has largely been overlooked; the Court is an institution typically studied through a legalistic lens. While academics such as Upendra Baxi[1] and Neil Stammers[2] have long insisted that rights have their genesis in social movements rather than formal legal documents, only recently have writers such as Dembour[3] begun to pay special attention to the European Convention on Human Rights (ECHR) as a site upon which social activists conduct their struggles. In this chapter, I suggest that whilst litigation before the Court is still heavily individualistic and consequently the role that NGOs play in shaping it should not be exaggerated, there are notable spaces or niches in it in which NGOs are prominent in claiming rights. In particular, this study examines how lawyers and activists have used litigation before the ECtHR as a tool through which to mobilise on behalf of LGBT (lesbian, gay, bisexual and transgender) minorities. It also highlights the transformative role of NGOs in framing and shaping rights claims in circumstances where their very nature is contested.

The history of legal struggles by gay rights activists has shaped the Court's interpretation of the Convention's rights. As Bunch notes, 'The concept of human rights, like all vibrant visions, is not static or the property of any one group: rather, its meaning expands as people reconceive of their needs and hopes in relation to it'.[4] Hence our understanding of the rights protected

[1] U Baxi, *The Future of Human Rights* (Oxford, Oxford University Press, 2002).

[2] See, for example, N Stammers, *Human Rights and Social Movements* (London, Pluto Press, 2009).

[3] M Dembour, *Who Believes in Human Rights? Reflections on the European Convention* (Cambridge, Cambridge University Press, 2006).

[4] C Bunch, 'Women's Rights as Human Rights: Towards a Re-vision of Human Rights' (1990) 12 *Human Rights Quarterly* 486, 487.

under the ECHR is subject to continual change. The ECtHR's adopted process of teleological interpretation requires it to pronounce upon legal, social, political and cultural developments as it establishes the scope of the Convention's rights, regardless of whether or not it is adequately equipped to do so. The questions raised in many of the cases that come before it have no immediately obvious answer that can be derived from universally accepted human rights standards. In recent cases—which serve only as examples of the myriad important and complex issues that have been placed before the Court for resolution—the Court has been asked to address questions relating to the pre-implantation screening of embryos at risk of inheriting cystic fibrosis,[5] extending testimonial privilege in criminal proceedings to long-term co-habiting partners,[6] the refusal of parental leave to military servicemen when such leave is available to servicewomen.[7] In delivering judgments upon issues such as these, the Court has the potential to play a dynamic role in sculpting the social landscape of Europe.

While the Court has typically been viewed through a legal lens, the ramifications of its judgments are clearly not constrained to the legal sphere. NGOs in particular recognise that the ECtHR's judgments have the potential to foster social transformation—albeit on a modest and incremental scale—and several organisations have consequently become involved in applications to the Court with this aim in mind. It is particularly noteworthy that groups that have a narrow political focus and a clear agenda to promote social change ('pressure groups' or 'single-issue groups') have a tendency to instigate litigation that demands a (re)interpretation of the Convention's rights. This chapter presents an issue-based case study that focuses on 'gay rights'[8] cases before the Court and considers the role that NGOs have played in them. By presenting data relating to LGBT rights claims that have been heard by the Court (concentrating on admissible cases only), I examine the level and nature of NGO involvement in these cases and analyse the impact of this involvement in shaping the Court's jurisprudence. The analysis raises questions about the impact that gay rights activists have had on the nature and direction of the Court's jurisprudence, as well as about the effectiveness of ECHR litigation strategies as a means of securing gay rights.

I. THE ECHR AND RIGHTS MOBILISATION

The ECtHR, I suggest, does not predominantly operate as a forum for rights mobilisation. In many respects the European system of rights protection

[5] *Costa and Pavan v Italy* App no 54270/10 (ECtHR, 28 August 2012).
[6] *van der Heijden v Netherlands* App no 42857/05 (ECtHR, 3 April 2012).
[7] *Konstantin Markin v Russia* App no 30078/06 (ECtHR, 22 March 2012).
[8] Using the catch-all term 'gay rights', I mean to refer to all LGBT rights claims.

epitomises the liberal ideal of resolving discrete individual rights claims that have no significance beyond the applicant and state concerned. Indeed, the Court's procedures have been adapted over the years with the specific purpose of placing the individual victim in a more central position. As is noted, the Court has generally 'refrained from considering the broader laws and institutional structures, to which the issues raised by the individual case at hand may be linked'.[9] The Court's proceedings are technocratic and legalistic in nature, rendering it meaningfully accessible to an elite few. Taking a case to Strasbourg is costly and slow—and thus it is a high-risk strategy for time-poor, cash-strapped organisations.

Thus there are a number of reasons why social activists' engagement with the Court's litigation is limited from a quantitative perspective.[10] However, certainly some activists and lawyers *have* used it in their struggles to effect, and the transformative potential of its judgments are now starting to be better appreciated. This coincides with the Court's constitutional role recently being stressed by a number of commentators, most notably Steven Greer, as the individualistic model of justice comes under growing strain.[11] In recent years the Court has shown greater willingness to look behind the individual facts presented in a case and to acknowledge the broader systemic issues that place those facts in a meaningful context. Alongside this trend towards 'constitutionalisation', the Convention's enforcement mechanisms have been strengthened, which makes it a more attractive focal point for the limited resources of NGOs. In particular, the Committee of Ministers supervises more intensely the execution of judgments since the amendment of Article 46 under Protocol 11. This inevitably adds considerable political authority to the Court's judgments, whose legal authority is already rated highly by many commentators.

As the Court gains confidence in its 'constitutional' role and flexes its jurisprudential muscles in order to breathe life into the Convention's

[9] D Anagnostou, 'Does European Human Rights Law Matter? Implementation and Domestic Impact of Strasbourg Court Judgments on Minority-Related Policies' (2010) 14 *International Journal of Human Rights* 721, 724.

[10] See L Hodson, *NGOs and the Struggle for Human Rights in Europe* (Oxford, Hart Publishing, 2010), especially chapter 3.

[11] S Greer, *The European Convention on Human Rights: Achievements, Problems and Prospects* (Cambridge, Cambridge University Press, 2006); S Greer, 'What's Wrong with the European Convention on Human Rights?' (2008) 30 *Human Rights Quarterly* 680. See also: R Berhardt, 'Human Rights and Judicial Review: The European Court of Human Rights' in DM Beatty (ed), *Human Rights and Judicial Review: A Comparative Perspective* (Dordrecht, Kluwer, 1994); R Ryssdal, 'On the Road to a European Constitutional Court' (1992) 12 *Collected Courses of the Academy of European Law* 1; C Warbrick, '"Federal" Aspects of the European Convention on Human Rights' (1989) 10 *Michigan Journal of International Law* 698. The Court itself has referred to the Convention as a constitutional 'instrument of European public order' on several occasions. See, for example, *Loizidou v Turkey* (preliminary objections) Series A no 310 (1995) 20 EHRR 99 [75] and *Cyprus v Turkey* ECHR 2001-IV (2002) 35 EHRR 30 [78].

decades-old language, so, inevitably, the social and political—as well as legal—impact of its decisions is greater. This is not to argue that the Court no longer demonstrates a cautious approach in its decision making; rather, it is to suggest that when the Court finds itself adopting a 'controversial' or 'radical' judgment, the ensuing ripples *can* spread very widely. In the words of Anagnostou, the '... ECtHR case law does matter and it matters in a variety of ways. Its potential to exert influence over domestic laws and policies ranges from negligible to substantial'.[12]

NGOs are playing a significant role in this trend towards constitutionalisation. In particular, those NGOs wishing to expand and reframe human rights norms have increasingly paid attention to the task of reshaping the Court's jurisprudence. Such involvement typically takes place 'behind the scenes' in a supportive or advisory role, although NGOs can also intervene as a third party, submitting written (and occasionally oral) observations as a non-party.[13] From the perspective of activists, the potential gains that come from a 'win' in Strasbourg are considerable. In short, in recent years there has been greater awareness of the important opportunity that the ECHR provides for activists and lawyers to mobilise and to make rights claims. This realisation has opened the door to studies of social movements and activists before it.

While the degree of NGOs' involvement should not be exaggerated, it is clear that they play a prominent part in 'issue emergence' in the Court's litigation.[14] In a recent study of NGO involvement in ECHR litigation I found that one area in which NGOs 'cluster' is at the 'margins' of the Court's litigation, in those difficult grey areas in which battles over the Convention's meaning are fought.[15] While some NGOs aim to have a stabilising role that seeks to support the status quo established under the Convention system, the primary aims of others is to expand the Convention's meaning or to challenge the Court's established case law and take the Convention in new directions. This is the more radical and potentially transformative role that NGOs play in litigation before the Court and one usually performed

[12] Anagnostou (n 9) 735.

[13] Article 36 of the Convention provides:

1. In all cases before a Chamber or the Grand Chamber, a High Contracting Party one of whose nationals is an applicant shall have the right to submit written comments and to take part in hearings.
2. The President of the Court may, in the interest of the proper administration of justice, invite any High Contracting Party which is not a party to the proceedings or any person concerned who is not the applicant to submit written comments or take part in hearings.
3. In all cases before a Chamber or the Grand Chamber, the Council of Europe Commissioner for Human Rights may submit written comments and take part in hearings.

[14] Issue emergence 'is the conceptual link between the myriad bad things out there and the persuasive machinery of advocacy politics in world affairs'. RC Carpenter, 'Setting the Advocacy Agenda: Theorizing Issue Emergence and Nonemergence in Transnational Advocacy' (2007) 51 *International Studies Quarterly* 99, 102.

[15] Hodson (n 10).

by 'single-issue' groups or pressure groups. Such trangressive activities are particularly challenging because they highlight the potentially radical implications of NGO involvement in human rights law, raising hard questions about the nature and legitimacy of organisations and strategies that aim to transform rather than entrench the Court's case law. The ethical questions raised by any shift away from a victim-centred focus in the Court's litigation are also deeply challenging.

Conversely, for those NGOs that look to the Convention with transformation in mind, the question will be how far transformation is actually possible within the confines of the Strasbourg system. If the Court is sought by social actors as a place to challenge entrenched legal and political norms, how successful can such challenges be, given the notoriously conservative nature of the institution in question? If the Court is a place where hegemonic and counter-hegemonic forces meet, what outcome can be expected from such a potentially combustible collision point? I turn now to consider this question through an examination of ECHR cases aimed at furthering gay rights.

II. MOBILISING FOR GAY RIGHTS BEFORE THE ECTHR

Rapid legal and social developments have taken place in recent years throughout Europe concerning sexual minorities, developments that have been associated with organised activism and legal mobilisation on the part of pressure groups.[16] Human rights discourse has become 'one of the most effective vehicles for mobilizing a range of moral and political claims that contest the widespread social and legal discrimination experienced by sexual minorities'.[17] A number of activist organisations have recognised the potential the Court's judgments have to bring pressure to bear on Council of Europe Member States to establish equal rights for sexual minorities. Consequently, there have been a number of key ECHR cases in which the struggle for gay rights has been played out, and that have resulted in significant victories for those mobilising for change.[18] From the table included at the end of this chapter, the scale of NGO involvement can be assessed. In short, of the 45 key LGBT cases in which the Court has delivered a judgment at the time of writing, I identified NGO involvement in 29. That figure, naturally, is *far* higher than would be found in a random selection

[16] Anagnostou (n 9).

[17] P Johnson, *Homosexuality and the European Court of Human Rights* (Abingdon, Routledge, 2013) 2.

[18] For a full discussion, see, eg: R Wintermute, *Sexual Orientation and Human Rights: The United States Constitution, the European Convention and the Canadian Charter* (Oxford, Clarendon Press, 1995); E Heinze, *Sexual Orientation: A Human Right. An Essay on International Human Rights Law* (Dordrecht, Martinus Nijhoff Publishers, 1995); L Thomas, *Sexual Orientation and Human Rights* (Lanham, MD, Rowman & Littlefield, 1999).

of the Court's cases.[19] I turn now to consider the role that some of these NGOs have played in greater depth.

A. Privacy Rights: Out of the Closet and into the Court

Initially, the Court was engaged with cases involving criminal law provisions that discriminated against gay men, the first of which was *Dudgeon v UK*.[20] In that case the Court held that the criminalisation of male homosexual acts under the Offences against the Person Act 1861 in Northern Ireland amounted to a violation of Article 8 of the Convention. Jeffrey Dudgeon, who brought that case before the Court after being interrogated by the Ulster Constabulary about his sexual activities, is a prominent activist and politician in Belfast. The Court noted of Mr Dudgeon that 'he and others have been conducting a campaign aimed at bringing the law in Northern Ireland into line with that in force in England and Wales and, if possible, achieving a minimum age of consent lower than 21 years'.[21] Specifically, the case was initiated by the Northern Ireland Gay Rights Association—an organisation established in 1975—which had chosen one member to act as the named victim.[22] We can therefore see in this case evidence of the central role law has played in the framing of gay rights mobilisation: here embryonic activist groups were specifically organised around the task of challenging particular discriminatory laws. Significantly, counsel in this case was the prominent human rights academic and activist, Kevin Boyle, who would go on to represent applicants in a huge number of Strasbourg cases, perhaps most prominently supporting Kurdish victims of gross human rights violations by the Turkish State.

The early use made of those versed in the technocratic legalistic language of human rights illustrates the perceived need gay rights activists had to at once root their campaign in the current core of human rights discourse while at the same time articulating an alternative vision of that core. Indeed, there is some evidence that the supporting networks behind the *Dudgeon* case had a transnational dimension (albeit limited): while no formal third party intervention was submitted, the applicant, although under the Rules of Court at the time not formally party to the proceedings, requested the Court to hear evidence from Dr Dannacker, Assistant Professor at the University of Frankfurt in the field of human sexuality (although no further

[19] Hodson (n 10) chapter 3.

[20] *Dudgeon v UK*, Series A/49 23 September 1981, (1982) 4 EHRR 149.

[21] Ibid, para 32.

[22] S Jeffery-Poulter, *Peers, Queers & Commons: The Struggle for Gay Law Reform from 1950 to the Present* (London, Routledge, 1991) 148.

reference to this person is made in the judgment). Following Mr Dudgeon's case, homosexuality was decriminalised in Northern Ireland.[23]

South of the border, the campaigning baton passed to David Norris, another high-profile politician and activist.[24] The Court described the applicant as 'an active homosexual [who] has been a campaigner for homosexual rights in Ireland since 1971; in 1974 he became a founder member and chairman of the Irish Gay Rights Movement'.[25] Significantly, he was also a founder of the Campaign for Homosexual Law Reform in Ireland, signalling his recognition of the transformative potential of campaigning strategies with a legal dimension. His application to Strasbourg, similarly to Mr Dudgeon's, challenged legislation criminalising male homosexual activity (although, unlike Mr Dudgeon, the relevant legislation had not been enforced in any way against him personally). Illustrating the difficulties that organisations have in being accommodated within the formal confines of the ECHR framework, it is interesting to note and little reported that the National Gay Federation was joined in the application at the Commission stage, although complaints made on its behalf were dismissed.[26] The applicant was represented by Mary Robinson, herself a member of the Campaign for Homosexual Law Reform. The Criminal Law (Sexual Offences) Act 1993, which entered into force on 7 July 1993, modified the Irish criminal legislation regarding homosexual acts. These cases were followed by *Modinos v Cyprus*,[27] in which the anti-sodomy provision in Section 171 of the Cypriot Criminal Code was successfully challenged. Similarly to the Irish cases preceding it, the applicant is referred to by the Court as the President of the 'Liberation Movement of Homosexuals in Cyprus'. While the Cypriot response to the judgment was rather slow, homosexual acts were eventually decriminalised in 1998.

These cases represent a kind of legal awakening; they are the product of driven individuals supported by embryonic campaigning organisations. They serve to demonstrate why gay rights legal campaigns might have emerged: the potential impact of a 'win' in Strasbourg for these movements was considerable and transnational in effect. The Court's individualistic procedures inevitably shaped these early gay rights campaigns into isolated individual complaints; behind the scenes of these cases, however, were numerous nameless others driving the mobilisation efforts. While the cost of litigation was in personal terms for the named applicants undoubtedly

[23] The Homosexual Offences (Northern Ireland) Order 1982, No 1536 (NI 19).

[24] *Norris v Ireland*, Series A/142 26 October 1988, (1991) 13 EHRR 186. At the time his case was before the Court, Mr Norris was a member of the Seanad Eireann (the second chamber of the Irish Parliament), where he continues to hold a seat. In 2011 he stood for election as President of Ireland.

[25] Ibid, para 9.

[26] *Norris v Ireland*, Decision of 16 May 1985 (1986) 8 EHRR CD75 135.

[27] *Modinos v Cyprus*, Series A/259 22 April 1993, (1993) 16 EHRR 485.

high (David Norris continued to face questions about his homosexuality during his 2011 Presidential campaign), the gains were considerable. These cases heralded the start of an ongoing relationship between gay rights organisations and the ECtHR. Although the Court did not embrace the involvement of NGOs and organised social movements (we see the NGOs, of which the applicants were a part, only operating behind the scenes of the cases), locating their campaigns both in the human rights core and in a counter-hegemonic vision of rights was nonetheless critical in getting gay rights on to the Court's agenda.

However, the outcome of these cases was not invariably positive, at least not immediately, and it is clear that the Court's judgments are not a panacea. Following *Modinos*, for example, the government's response was not approved by the Committee of Ministers until December 2001,[28] pursuant to legislative changes adopted on 16 June 2000 (under Amending Law 77(1)/2000). Trimikliniotis and Karayanni note that 'the significant delay in responding to the recommendations of the European Court of Human Rights was the result of strong opposition from some Christian organisations and church leaders'.[29] Revealingly, Mr Dudgeon was less than enthusiastic about his personal experience before the Strasbourg Court, describing the process as one in which governments export power to a system free from democratic constraints, yet maintain the capacity to stall progress.[30] This perhaps reflects the too-heavy demands that the individualistic procedures of the Courts make on the individual applicant. The psychological discomfort experienced by many rights litigants may also raise questions about the choice of strategy that these early gay rights campaigners adopted, in which the individual applicant is effectively reduced through the process of rights articulation to a single—essential, yet private—aspect of his being. On a normative level, Johnson notes that the Court's early tendency to conceptualise the claims of sexual minorities as a matter concerning private life has a 'tendency to reinforce the social relations of the closet'.[31]

B. Professionalising Dissent: Stonewall and the ECtHR[32]

Stonewall was formed in 1989 as a professional lobby organisation that would strive to achieve legal equality and social justice for LGBT people

[28] Resolution ResDH(2001)152.

[29] N Trimikliniotis and S Stavrou Karayanni, *The situation concerning homophobia and discrimination on grounds of sexual orientation* (SIMFILIOSI Policy Paper, Cyprus, March 2008).

[30] Jeffery-Poulter (n 22) 154.

[31] Johnson (n 17) 212.

[32] An earlier version of this discussion of Stonewall's litigation was published in Hodson (n 10) chapter 6.

in the UK.[33] The experience of those who had campaigned against the introduction of the notorious 'Section 28', which prohibited local authorities from intentionally 'promoting homosexuality', highlighted the need for such an organisation.[34] Stephen Jeffery-Poulter, in his study of the UK movement for gay law reform, writes:

> The establishment of Stonewall as a modern, streamlined, professional non-partisan lobbying outfit designed to react quickly and effectively without being hamstrung by reference to a mass membership and yet aiming to work within the broad consensus of its constituency, suggests that the campaigning movement has finally come of age.[35]

Jeffery-Poulter suggests that the section 28 debate was something of a watershed as it was the 'first time, every politician opposed to Clause 28 had framed their arguments in the context of gay rights being a matter of basic civil liberties'.[36]

What is interesting about Stonewall is its professionalism as a lobby group and the naturalness with which it has engaged with human rights. Stonewall certainly used rights-based arguments as a lobbying tactic from very early on, and one of its first actions was to draft an Equality Bill.[37] The adoption of a rights-based approach has led Stonewall to challenge discriminatory legislative provisions through a limited programme of human rights litigation, alongside more traditional lobbying methods. Although Stonewall is not a public interest litigation organisation, it sometimes brings its expertise and resources to bear in strategically important cases. Stonewall does not have in-house lawyers working on these cases; it relies instead upon a network of lawyers who are prepared to do pro bono work on its behalf. Neither does Stonewall have a dedicated legal advice helpline, which might be used to identify potentially important cases. Nevertheless, it is a relatively large and high-profile organisation with a wide membership body and it is regularly contacted for help and advice by people who have faced discrimination, which appears to be the primary means by which potential test cases are identified. In particular, Stonewall has a short but impressive history of challenging legislative provisions that criminalise homosexual activity, some of which has been done through litigation before the ECtHR. It was, for example, involved in *Wilde, Greenhalgh and Parry v UK*[38] and

[33] For more information, see Stonewall's website at www.stonewall.org.uk.

[34] The Local Government Act 1986, s 2A(1) (as amended by Local Government Act 1988, s 28). It was repealed in September 2003.

[35] Jeffery-Poulter (n 22) 260.

[36] Ibid, 240.

[37] Ibid, 246.

[38] *Wilde, Greenhalgh and Parry v UK* (Cm dec), App no 22382/93 (ECtHR, 19 January 1995) (1995) 19 EHRR CD86.

Sutherland v UK,[39] both of which challenged the higher age of consent for sexual activity between men before the Commission. *ADT v UK*,[40] the first Stonewall case to reach the Court, followed this pattern of challenging specific pieces of discriminatory legislation through human rights litigation.

The *ADT* case arose following the applicant's conviction for gross indecency between men contrary to section 13 of the Sexual Offences Act 1956. Although sexual acts between men in England and Wales were partially decriminalised under the Sexual Offences Act 1967, this did not extend to acts committed when two or more persons take part or are present. The applicant's conviction was primarily based on videotapes that showed him and up to four other men engaging in sexual acts, which were found during a police search of his home. Although the acts in question were consensual and had taken place in a private residence, because they involved more than two men they fell foul of the Sexual Offences Act. Following his conviction the applicant was sentenced and conditionally discharged for two years and he was advised that there were no prospects for a successful appeal. He immediately turned to Stonewall for help. The application to the European Commission on Human Rights (EcommHR) and the resulting proceedings before the ECtHR (in which a violation of Article 8 was found) were financed by Stonewall, which was assisted by lawyers acting pro bono. By this stage of the proceedings the domestic lawyer, although named as the applicant's representative, was not really involved. Angela Mason, then Executive Director of Stonewall, is referred to in the judgment as 'adviser' to the applicant.

Repeal of section 13 of the Sexual Offences Act 1956 was a central part of Stonewall's 'Equality 2000' campaign, which was launched in June 1997 to eradicate specific areas of legislative discrimination against gay people. Gross indecency laws, Stonewall argued, 'led to the use of "pretty policemen" acting as agents provocateurs and often poisoned relationships between the police and the gay community'.[41] Indeed, the *ADT* litigation undoubtedly made a considerable contribution to the British government's decision in January 1999 to conduct a major review of sexual offences, which was undertaken by a diverse team that included representatives from Stonewall. The review team, noting the discriminatory nature of the gross indecency laws, recommended their repeal. Behind this recommendation was a belief that 'the criminal law should not treat people differently on the basis of their sexual orientation'.[42] The review team's conclusion was

[39] *Sutherland v UK* App no 25186/94 (Commission decision, 21 May 1996; ECtHR, 27 March 2001).

[40] *ADT v UK*, 31 July 2000, (2001) 31 EHRR 33.

[41] Stonewall Press Release, 'Anti-Gay Law Now a Dead Letter', 31 July 2000 (on file with author).

[42] Home Office, *Setting the Boundaries: Reforming the Law on Sex Offences* Volume 1 (London, Home Office Communication Directorate, July 2000), Recommendation 44.

based—at least in part—on the 'indications of greater openness towards and acceptance of differing sexual orientation'.[43] The Sexual Offences Act 2003, which was implemented in May 2004, repealed the gross indecency provisions of the earlier Sexual Offences Act and brought this particular campaign to its conclusion.

Although on a restrictive reading the *ADT* case addressed a rather narrow legal provision prohibiting certain sexual acts between men, it goes without saying that its significance lies in the fact that it was a small but important step in gay rights organisations' (ongoing) journey towards eradicating all forms of discrimination against LGBT people and achieving social inclusion for this group. It demonstrates the potentially destabilising impact of legal mobilisation strategies: whilst LGBT people in Europe are not subjected to the same levels of discrimination and marginalisation as the Roma, for example, it is clear that they have frequently been constructed as 'undesirable' and 'the other' in Europe.[44]

Stonewall's rooting of its struggle for gay rights in the core of human rights discourse certainly reaped many rewards in terms of legislative change. It also coincided with gay rights discrimination issues being picked up by more mainstream human rights organisation, such as Liberty,[45] which intervened in *Smith and Grady v UK*[46] (the 'gays in the military' case, ending the prohibition on homosexual men and women serving in the armed forces) and in *Goodwin v UK*[47] (leading to the rights of trans persons to have their gender recognised). Nevertheless, with the involvement of professional gay rights lobby groups the struggle for gay rights became increasingly technocratic and distanced from the grassroots. In the process of professionalising dissent, the task of destabilising the rights core looked occasionally more akin to refining—and perhaps even reaffirming—the rights core.

C. ILGA-Europe: A Transnational Network is Established

The International Lesbian, Gay, Bisexual, Trans and Intersex Association (formerly the International Gay Association) was founded in 1978 and brings together hundreds of LGBT groups (and transgender, intersex and queer) to

[43] Ibid, 98.

[44] C Stychin, *A Nation by Rights: National Cultures, Sexual Identity Politics, and the Discourse of Rights* (Philadelphia, Temple University Press, 1998) 13. Herman makes the similar point that 'the demand for lesbian and gay rights is a struggle for membership in the "human community"'. See D Herman, 'The Politics of Law Reform: Lesbian and Gay Rights Struggles into the 1990s' in J Bristow and AR Wilson (eds), *Activating Theory: Lesbian, Gay, Bisexual Politics* (London, Lawrence & Wishart, 1993) 250.

[45] For more information about Liberty, see Hodson (n 10) chapter 5.

[46] *Smith and Grady v UK*, Reports of Judgments and Decisions 1999-VI, (1999) 27 EHRR CD42.

[47] *Christine Goodwin v UK*, no 28957/95, ECHR 2002-VI.

unite in the struggle for rights. Its relationship with the United Nations has been long and complex, and the organisation continues to struggle to find an effective platform there.[48] The European region of the organisation (ILGA-Europe) was established as a separate organisation in 1996 and has enjoyed participative status at the Council of Europe since 1997. It brings together 294 organisations from 40 Council of Europe states, and has been notably more influential than its parent body in instigating legal and social reform.

Part of ILGA-Europe's strategy is to develop strategic litigation targeted at identified 'gap' areas. To this end it encourages potential organisations and litigants to approach them with suitable cases, in which they can assist. Much of its litigation activity takes place in the background, and for the purposes of this research it was therefore sometimes hard to identity its role in ECtHR cases. Nonetheless, its presence as a unifying force for European gay rights organisations, a resource centre, and a centre of expertise in strategic litigation is unquestionably highly significant. ILGA-Europe's strategy of mobilisation of rights norms 'has spread transnationally, coordinating national initiatives, and transmitting relevant legal expertise, political skills, and advocacy work across states'.[49]

ILGA-Europe's most visible presence before the Court is as a third party intervener, in which role it provides comments in key cases, invariably joining other major human rights organisations to add weight to its arguments. Interestingly, its interventions have usually been in the area of LGBT family rights, suggesting that ILGA-Europe prefers to focus its legal expertise on those 'gap areas' in which the Court's approach has been, at best, ambiguous. For example, in *Schalk and Kopf v Austria* it argued (partly successfully) that same-sex couples can establish family life and that they have a right to relationship recognition. Previously, in *EB v France*,[50] it argued (successfully) that France was not entitled to exclude a single lesbian woman from the opportunity of applying to adopt a child; in *Karner v Austria*[51] it argued (partly successfully) that discrimination between unmarried same-sex and opposite-sex couples in relation to tenancy succession was unlawful and that same-sex couples enjoy family life under the Convention. These cases strikingly demonstrate mobilisation strategies that continue to imagine what the Convention might mean for LGBT people and to re-imagine ways in which their rights might be argued before the Court.

Transnational networks are also important in supporting those engaged in old struggles (from an ECHR perspective) that continue to be played out in less receptive political climates. Further to effective transnational

[48] J Swiebel 'Lesbian, Gay, Bisexual And Transgender Human Rights: The Search For An International Strategy' (2009) 15 *Contemporary Politics* 19.

[49] Anagnostou (n 9) 736.

[50] *EB v France* App no 43546/02 (ECtHR, 22 January 2008), (2008) 47 EHRR 21.

[51] *Karner v Austria* App no 40016/98 (ECtHR, 24 July 2003), (2004) 38 EHRR 24.

networking among gay rights organisations, litigation strategies developed in Western European countries have spread to newer Member States and are currently being used to challenge the treatment of sexual minorities in hostile and oppressive climates. Taking the lead in this is Project GayRussia. The organisation says it has initiated over 200 court cases in Russia but, with domestic courts typically unreceptive to its claims, it is making its presence felt in a number of applications to the ECtHR.[52] In *Alekseyev v Russia*,[53] which was brought by the founder and leader of GayRussia, the authorities' repeated ban on the holding of a gay pride march in Moscow was successfully challenged. By the time this case was heard, there was, of course, established case law prohibiting discrimination on the basis of sexual orientation. In short, the legal argument was effectively already won. But cases such as this highlight the importance of transnational networks in the face of regimes reluctant to keep pace with the advances in gay rights made in recent years in Europe. Thus, networks help to extend the platform that has already been built by the pioneers. However, once again it can be seen that activists' experience of the Court, even when ultimately successful, is rather mixed: prior to his win, in February 2009, Mr Alekseyev held a demonstration outside the Court building to protest against the delays to cases involving suppression of gay pride marches.[54] Individualised litigation still comes at considerable personal cost: the applicant in this case continues to experience harassment at the hands of the Russian authorities.[55]

III. NGOS AS LEGAL AND SOCIAL CHANGE ACTORS

NGOs are far from being the 'lifeblood' of the ECtHR. Nevertheless, in this chapter I have suggested that while the dominant form of litigation before the Court is individualistic, this should not cloud the fact that the pursuit of individual justice is not the only model for understanding the Court's litigation. Gay rights organisations have clearly been central to the Court's framing of the Convention in respect of sexual minorities' claims. The involvement of pressure groups in the Court's litigation has previously received little attention from legal academics, primarily because such involvement tends to be small-scale and infrequent. However, this chapter suggests that this is an unfortunate oversight. Single-issue groups, as the gay rights cases outlined in this chapter have shown, can generate momentum towards new understandings of human rights. Their litigation offers

[52] www.gayrussia.eu/en/campaigns/legal-court-cases-by-gayrussia.php.

[53] *Alekseyev v Russia* App nos 4916/07, 25924/08, 14599/09 (ECtHR, 21 October 2010).

[54] 'Gay Activists Protest Inaction of European Human Rights Court in Strasbourg Demo', available at www.ukgaynews.org.uk/Archive/09/Feb/1401.htm.

[55] BBC News, 'Gay Rights Campaigner Fined in Russia for 'Propaganda', 4 May 2012. Available at www.bbc.co.uk/news/world-europe-17955794.

a pertinent reminder of the dynamism of human rights and the Court's role, albeit tempered by the restraints of State sovereignty. Pressure groups can consequently create an interesting tension between their own utopian struggles and the Court's more cautious interpretive conventions. By infusing their litigation with comparatively radical politics they contribute to the Court's awareness of social changes and have pointed to an alternative understanding of rights. Having identified the importance of gay rights activists in reframing the Convention's rights, it might now be useful to draw together the central strands of my analysis and consider the limitations under which NGOs operate as litigators.

A. A Lack of Democratic Accountability?

Julie Mertus has framed the 'dangers of NGOs' in terms of democracy and good governance. She notes that while considerable power is wielded by NGOs within the global human rights movement, they are democratically unaccountable in the exercise of that power.[56] The decisions of NGOs, she notes, are often taken in an opaque manner and without pluralist participation.[57] Certainly, none of the gay rights groups discussed in this chapter operate in a manner that could be termed democratic. Furthermore, they are typically marginal political actors who have little leverage in more democratic arenas. As Galanter has noted, 'Those who seek change through the courts tend to represent relatively isolated interests, unable to carry the day in more political forums'.[58] In relation to this research, this raises the spectre of gay rights organisations influencing the Court's agenda without popular support and without being answerable to others for their actions. Certainly even relatively uncontroversial judgments such as *Modinos* raised problems of implementation at the domestic level because of its conflict with dominant morality.

A related concern is that activists' involvement in litigation can unhelpfully reduce genuinely complex political disputes into simplistic rights-based arguments. Away from the consensus that tends to emerge in more democratic fora, gay rights activists in their litigation might appear in principle to be free to pursue their ends without reference to the real concerns and dissent of others. This is likely to be of particular concern to those who understand

[56] J Mertus, 'From Legal Transplants to Transformative Justice: Human Rights and the Promise of Transnational Civil Society' (1998–9) 14 *American University International Law Review* 1335. See also K Anderson, 'The Ottawa Convention Banning Landmines, the Role of International Non-Governmental Organizations and the Idea of International Civil Society' (2000) 11 *European Journal of International Law* 91.

[57] Mertus (n 56) 1372–74.

[58] M Galanter, 'Why the "Haves" Come out Ahead: Speculations on the Limits of Legal Change' (1974) 9 *Law and Society Review* 95, 135.

human rights claims to be the unbending and limitless pursuit of power. Costas Douzinas argues that solutions to complex problems are unlikely to be forged through human rights arguments because 'it removes the fight from the terrain of warring interests into that of allegedly absolute truths and uncompromising entitlements'.[59] In other words, one could argue that cases such as *X v Austria* (calling for second-parent adoption for same-sex couples),[60] for example, represent baldly stated claims to entitlement that unhelpfully reduce the complex myriad interests as stake in such matters, and which are more likely to result in antagonism rather than conciliation.

No attempt has been made to judge the value of the claims made by the gay rights organisations discussed in this contribution (although I am by inclination sympathetic to them). Nevertheless, it is worth noting that the making of human rights claims requires only the barest of nods to liberal values, and the role of NGOs in ECtHR litigation is therefore not inevitably benign. In response to counter-hegemonic challenges from gay rights organisations, it has been noted that more conservative organisations have attempted to influence the Court's agenda.[61] This chapter demonstrates too that even progressive organisations have been, for example, very slow to represent the concerns of lesbian women before the ECtHR and to help them to articulate their claims. The lack of organisational support for trans men and women in their litigation is also apparent.

How, then, can we respond to the questions raised by gay rights activists' lack of democratic accountability? We might at least begin by acknowledging that these concerns reflect a tension within the human rights movement itself. Although human rights can assist in securing democratic participation, they are also fundamentally anti-majoritarian. During the drafting of the Convention, it will be recalled, the individual application procedure itself was criticised for being anti-democratic (ie anti-Statist). One need only refer to decisions such as *Tyrer v UK*,[62] in which the Court found the practice of judicial birching—popularly supported at the time in the Isle of Man—to be a violation of the Convention, to see that human rights can conflict with beliefs held by the majority. And this, of course, is one of the acknowledged strengths of human rights: they provide a platform for those that would dissent from majoritarian views. So it is at least questionable whether actors in human rights litigation should be judged on the extent to which they are accountable to a popular will: the argument that the views of human rights NGOs are not democratically representative rather misses this point.

[59] C Douzinas, *The End of Human Rights: Critical Legal Thought at the Turn of the Century* (Oxford, Hart Publishing, 2000) 251.

[60] *X and Ors v Austria* App no 19010/07 (ECtHR, 19 February 2013).

[61] See, for example, the third party intervention by the 'Alliance Defending Freedom' in the *X and Ors v Austria* case, ibid.

[62] *Tyrer v UK* Series A no 26 (1979–80) 2 EHRR 1.

If human rights litigation is a space in which conflicting claims are put forward, this does not mean that NGOs involved in ECtHR litigation wield power anarchically. The cases outlined in this chapter have demonstrated that while the NGOs concerned may not have been democratically accountable, they were nonetheless constrained within the ECHR system. In practice, this served to considerably curb and modify their more radical claims and to 'professionalise' dissent. Rather than being major power-players in ECtHR litigation, gay rights activists articulate their demands in a forum that accommodates many influences and whose judgments are invariably incremental. In *Schalk and Kopf*, for example, we saw that the careful claims of third party interveners assisted the Court to take the small but important step of recognising the right of same-sex couples to enjoy family life, while at the same time failing to articulate states' positive obligations in respect of that right. It is therefore unhelpful to exaggerate the conditional and contingent power that NGOs have; rather, they should be acknowledged as contributors to the inevitably continuous reframing of the Convention's rights. Gay rights organisations themselves are generally pragmatist and well aware of the limitations under which they operate, and most treat litigation as a welcome opportunity to present their position as coherently and convincingly as possible. As the cases in this chapter have demonstrated, they would be foolish and mistaken to believe that their views unquestioningly prevail in litigation.

B. A Lack of Accountability to Applicants?

An associated question is the nature of the relationship between NGOs and those whose interests they seek to represent in ECtHR cases. While the early cases discussed in this chapter, *Dudgeon*, *Norris* and *Modinos*, emerged from authentic grassroots movements and the applicants were intimately involved in mobilisation efforts, as the efforts became more professionalised, this close connection between applicant and movement became less marked. It might consequently be argued that the struggle for gay rights has moved in a direction that renders activists less able to articulate the authentic voice of those on whose behalf they profess to litigate. Baxi's concern that 'Injustice and human violation is headline news only as the pornography of power'[63] is of particular relevance to those who seek to use the suffering of others to further political campaigns. The inherent danger in NGO litigation strategies is that the individual's humanity is overlooked.

Although the NGOs discussed in this chapter may make no claims to democratic accountability, many do claim to represent the interests of the groups

[63] Baxi (n 1) 125.

on whose behalf they litigate. Because ECHR cases are usually brought in the name of individual applicants, NGOs also have a real and direct impact on the lives of people in whose name they litigate. Without having close contact with applicants and without making attempts to be sensitive to their multifaceted characters, human rights litigation is likely to caricature the applicants in whose name a case is brought. One might reach the conclusion that in NGO litigation, the applicant, and by implication her case, cannot be released from the constraints of the ambition that NGOs have for it. As gay rights mobilisation strategies become more professionalised and distant from the communities on whose behalf they work, so the divergence in aims between organisation and community is likely to increase.

There is clearly room for gay rights organisations to take the issue of accountability to their 'constituents' more seriously. Julie Mertus suggests that NGOs should concentrate on building close relationships with the communities they seek to represent. She argues that the closer an organisation is with the 'grassroots', 'the greater its chances at promoting positive social change because it is more likely to represent a highly engaged constituency'.[64] Human rights, she goes on to suggest, are most effective when they are internalised, and they generally will not succeed if they represent 'forced impositions of outside ideas'.[65] The emphasis in this research on human rights as a space for dialogue between local and global actors, then, is important: it directs NGOs to build as many lines of communications as possible between themselves and the local actors they would seek to represent. As Mertus notes, this demands from NGOs a willingness to listen 'to their less powerful counterparts'.[66] This is of particular relevance to international organisations such as ILGA-Europe and suggests that the move from the grassroots we have witnessed in this chapter is not unproblematic.

C. The Ineffectiveness of NGO Litigation?

Perhaps most important from the perspective of NGOs themselves is the danger in exaggerating the transformation that can be achieved through human rights litigation. Baxi has remarked upon the 'human rights romanticism' that 'leads NGOs to be over-optimistic about their achievements'.[67] Certainly, the litigation strategies of ILGA-Europe suggest that NGOs are well aware of the confines in which they operate, when they are active in a legal field. The ECtHR is an institution in which transformation can happen, but the individual nature of Strasbourg justice means it is a slow, incremental,

64 Mertus (n 56) 1373.
65 Ibid, 1345.
66 Ibid, 1385–86.
67 Baxi (n 1) 62.

and somewhat erratic process. The Court's fragmentary approach to the question of LGBT family rights is a case in point.[68] Cases are in any event often subject to forces outside of the control of the organisations pursuing them. Despite the relative success of gay rights in Strasbourg, litigation strategies are piecemeal attempts at reform that cannot be a substitute for coherent policy making.

Galanter has noted that even where a judgment is delivered that challenges institutional power relations, courts are usually not in a strong position to implement the changes they instigate. Consequently, he concludes that litigation is unlikely to be transformative.[69] Certainly the ongoing dialogue between the Committee of Ministers and Russia in respect of the *Alekseyev v Russia* judgment might hint at the truth of this.[70] Scheingold's analysis of what he refers to as 'the myth of rights' is even bleaker:

> The continued vitality of litigation may be read as a triumph of myth over reality—as a lesson in false consciousness. Or perhaps it is symptomatic of the willingness of middle class lawyers to settle for half a loaf—at least for their clients. Either way, litigation emerges as a strategy of desperation rather than hope.[71]

In the context of ECtHR litigation, it seems logical to conclude that respondent states are, almost by definition, going to be reluctant to embrace any change that results from the Court's judgments.

There are, then, many reasons to be cautious when assessing the likely impact that NGO litigation can ultimately have. While this chapter establishes NGOs as important actors in gay rights cases brought under the ECHR, the litigation discussed herein is far from being a panacea. However, given the numerous factors that are outside NGOs' control when taking a deliberately targeted test case, one might argue that that makes the considerable success of gay rights litigation all the more noteworthy. In fact, this research shows that, despite its drawbacks, ECtHR litigation is a highly valuable tool in the area of gay rights.

This research points to a number of reasons why gay rights litigation strategies before the ECtHR have been effective. First, mechanisms for enforcing the Court's judgments are relatively strong; the Committee of Ministers has the political authority to hold Member States to account, which is *generally* respected. Secondly, international human rights standards—in which gay rights claims are rooted—have a moral authority that makes the finding of

[68] For a discussion of the court's approach to LGBT families, see, for example, L Hodson, 'Ties That Bind: Towards a Child-Centred Approach to Lesbian, Gay, Bi-Sexual and Transgender Families under the ECHR' (2012) 20 *The International Journal of Children's Rights* 501.

[69] Galanter (n 58) 151.

[70] P Johnson, 'Gay Rights in Russia: Alekseyev v Russia Update', 5 March 2013 at http://echrso.blogspot.co.uk/2013/03/gay-rights-in-russia-alekseyev-v-russia_5.html.

[71] S Scheingold, *The Politics of Rights: Lawyers, Public Policy and Political Change* (New Haven, Yale University Press, 1974) 95.

a violation particularly persuasive and may generate international pressure for reform. Thirdly, gay rights organisations as litigators can pursue implementation, through non-legal measures, of the transformation that has been indicated in the Court's judgments. Fourthly, gay rights organisations are characterised by their single-minded focus on, and commitment to, principled causes.[72]

IV. CONCLUDING OBSERVATIONS

Although a radical liberal individualism remains deeply embedded in our understanding of the Convention, an attempt has been made in this chapter to place the Convention in an alternative analytical framework. I established a clear connection between the developing law of the ECtHR on sexual minorities and the gay rights movement, a connection that is often overlooked by lawyerly analysis of the Convention. The Convention's rights arose out of the struggles of the past, and will be shaped and determined by the struggles of the future. Human rights norms, including those developed in the jurisprudence of the ECtHR, emerge in order to challenge conventional political structures. Gay rights activists emerge in this study as important actors whose struggles have contributed to the shaping of ECHR norms. Their role, however, is contingent and they are presented as compromised actors in a symbiotic relationship with the centre of human rights power, whose claims are themselves shaped by the language of the Convention as the strictures of the Convention's institutions.

[72] S Ahmed and D Potter, *NGOs in International Politics* (Bloomfield, Kumarian Press, 2006) 243.

Table 1: NGO Involvement in Key ECHR Gay Rights Cases

Date of judgment	Name of case & nature of issue	NGO(s) involved	Nature of involvement
22 October 1981	**Dudgeon v UK (7525/76)** Criminalisation of sexual activity	Northern Ireland Gay Rights Association	Background support
17 October 1986	**Rees v UK (9532/81)** Trans gender recognition		
26 October 1988	**Norris v Ireland (10581/83)** Criminalisation of sexual activity	1. National Gay Federation 2. Campaign for Homosexual Law Reform 3. Irish Gay Rights Movement	1. Joined as applicant (before Commission) 2. Legal support and background support. 3. Background support
27 September 1990	**Cossey v UK (10843/84)** Trans gender recognition		
25 March 1992	**B v France (13343/87)**		
22 April 1993	**Modinos v Cyprus (15070/89)** Criminalisation of sexual activity	Liberation Movement of Homosexuals in Cyprus	Background support
20 January 1997	**Laskey & Ors v UK (21627/93, 21826/93 & 21974/93)** Criminalisation of sexual activity	Rights International	Third party intervention
22 April 1997	**X,Y & Z v UK (21830/93)** Trans parental rights.	Press for Change?	Possible background support (not mentioned in judgment, but X co-founded PFC in 1992)
30 July 1998	**Sheffield & Horsham v UK (22985/93; 23390/94)** Trans gender recognition	Liberty	Third party intervention
27 September 1999	**Smith & Grady v UK (33985/96, 33986/96)** 'Gays in the military'	Liberty	Legal representation
27 September 1999	**Lustig-Prean & Beckett v UK (31417/96, 32377/96)** 'Gays in the military'		

Date of judgment	Name of case & nature of issue	NGO(s) involved	Nature of involvement
21 December 1999	**Salgueiro da Silva Mouta v Portugal (33290/96)** Parental rights of gay man		.
31 July 2000	**ADT v UK (35765/97)** Criminalisation of sexual activity	Stonewall	Background support
26 February 2002	**Fretté v France (36515/97)** Adoption rights	ILGA-Europe	Third party intervention (possible legal representation?)
11 July 2002	**Christine Goodwin v UK (28957/95)** Trans gender recognition	Liberty	Third party intervention
11 July 2002	**I v UK (25680/94)** Trans recognition	Liberty	Third party intervention
22 October 2002	**Beck & Others v UK (48535/99, 48536/99, 48537/99)** 'Gays in the military'		
22 October 2002	**Perkins & R v UK (43208/98, 44875/98)** 'Gays in the military'		.
9 January 2003	**SL v Austria (45330/99)** Unequal age of consent	Rechtskomittee LAMBDA	Background support and legal representation
9 January 2003	**L & V v Austria (39392/98, 39829/98)** Unequal age of consent	Rechtskomittee LAMBDA	Background support and legal representation
24 July 2003	**Karner v Austria (40016/98)** Property rights for same-sex couples	ILGA-Europe, Liberty, and Stonewall	Third party intervention (joint)
12 June 2003	**Van Kück v Germany (35968/97)** Trans privacy and fair trial rights		
10 February 2004	**BB v UK (53760/00)** Unequal age of consent		
21 October 2004	**Woditschka & Wilfling v Austria (69756/01 and 6306/02)** Unequal age of consent	Rechtskomittee LAMBDA	Background support and legal representation
3 February 2005	**Ladner v Austria (18297/03)** Unequal age of consent	Rechtskomittee LAMBDA	Background support and legal representation

(*Continued*)

Table 1: (*Continued*)

Date of judgment	Name of case & nature of issue	NGO(s) involved	Nature of involvement
26 May 2005	**Wolfmeyer v Austria (5263/03)** Unequal age of consent.	Rechtskomittee LAMBDA	Background support and legal representation
2 June 2005	**HG & GB v Austria (11084/02 and 15306/02)** Unequal age of consent	Rechtskomittee LAMBDA	Background support and legal representation
23 May 2006	**Grant v UK (32570/03)** Trans gender recognition and pension rights	Liberty	Legal representation
19 January 2006	**RH v Austria (7336/03)** Unequal age of consent	Rechtskomittee LAMBDA	Background support and legal representation
3 May 2007	**Bączkowski & Others v Poland (1543/06)** Freedom of assembly	Foundation for Equality	Joined as applicant
11 September 2007	**L v Lithuania (27527/03)** Trans recognition		
22 January 2008	**EB v France (43546/02)** Adoption rights	Fédération internationale des Ligues des Droits de l'Homme (FIDH); ILGA–Europe; British Association for Adoption and Fostering (BAAF); and Association des Parents et futurs parents Gays et Lesbiens (APGL)	Third party intervention (joint)
8 January 2009	**Schlumpf v Switzerland (29002/06)** Trans person's right to fair hearing		
2 March 2010	**Kozak v Poland (13102/02)** Property rights, same-sex couple		
24 June 2010	**Schalk and Kopf v Austria (30141/04)** Marriage/partnership rights for same-sex couples	FIDH, ICJ (International Commission of Jurists) AIRE Centre (Advice on Individual Rights in Europe) and ILGA-Europe	Third party intervention (joint)
22 July 2010	**PB & JS v Austria (18984/02)** Employment benefits discrimination—same-sex couple		

Date of judgment	Name of case & nature of issue	NGO(s) involved	Nature of involvement
28 September 2010	**JM v UK (37060/06)** Non-discrimination (maintenance payments, lesbian parent)	1. Liberty 2. Equality and Human Rights Commission	1. Legal representation 2. Third party intervention
21 October 2010	**Alekseyev v Russia (4916/07, 25924/08 and 14599/09)** Freedom of assembly	LGBT Human Rights Project GayRussia	Background support. Mr A is founder and leader
30 November 2010	**PV v Spain (35159/09)** Trans family rights (contact with child)		
9 February 2012	**Vejdeland and Ors v Sweden (1813/07)** Conviction for distributing anti-homosexual leaflets in schools	Interights and ICJ	Joint third party intervention
15 March 2012	**Gas and Dubois v France (25951/07)** Second-parent adoption for same-sex couples	ICJ; ILGA-Europe; BAAF; Network of European LGBT Families Associations; FIDH.	Joint third party intervention
12 June 2012	**Genderdoc-M v Moldova (9106/06)** Freedom of assembly	1. Genderdoc-M 2. ICJ	1. Applicant 2. Third party intervention
9 October 2012	**X v Turkey (24626/09)** Conditions of detention of homosexual prisoner representing inhuman or degrading treatment		
13 November 2012	**H v Finland (37359/09)** Trans marriage rights		
19 February 2013	**X v Austria** Second-parent adoption for same-sex couples	1. ICJ; ILGA-Europe; BAAF; Network of European LGBT Families Associations; FIDH; European Commission on Sexual Orientation Law. 2. European Centre for Law and Justice 3. Attorney-General for Northern Ireland 4. Amnesty International 5. Alliance Defending Freedom	1. Joint third party intervention 2. Third party intervention 3. Third party intervention 4. Third party intervention 5. Third party intervention

9

Law and Rights as Opportunity and Promise for Minorities in Europe? Concluding Observations and Research Agendas

DIA ANAGNOSTOU

THE PROLIFERATION OF legally codified rights at different levels of law and government in Europe has primarily been understood in relation to the growing role of courts and the spread of rights review. Scholarly research though has left largely unexplored the socio-legal processes that underpin the expansion of legal and judicially pronounced norms, as well as the salience of law and rights for the politics of minorities and social reform. From a variety of different disciplinary angles from law, political science and sociology, the case and comparative studies in this volume have explored the relationship between rights mobilisation and legal action in pursuit of social goals in the multi-level European system. They are especially interested in how and why law and legal entitlements are employed, often strategically, by and on behalf of marginalised groups and minorities, as well as by various kinds of actors who seek to influence social change on their behalf. While the volume's analytical frame does not fully depart from a court-centred perspective, most of the case studies pay close attention to the social-legal processes that shape rights claiming on behalf of vulnerable individuals and minorities in court.

In the European system, multiple layers of normative, legal and public order interact and at times contest one another, without, however, a predetermined line of hierarchy and an ultimate point of reference and authority. For a long time now EU law has established its direct effect and supremacy over national law, yet this exists side by side with national legal and constitutional systems that continue to proclaim their sovereignty and ultimate authority. This goes against the grain of traditional constitutional theory built upon the assumption of a clear and universally accepted hierarchy of legal norms and judicial structures, existing within given state boundaries and having an ultimate source of authority. In view of the limits of the constitutional paradigm in depicting EU and ECHR law, European law scholars have analysed the dynamics of the multi-level system by highlighting pluralism as its central structuring property.[1] While the existence of different levels of government and legal jurisdictions is well known in federated systems, the nature and extent of such pluralism in the EU and in Europe at large is far greater and more complex.

In a parallel fashion that complements the legal pluralist narrative, this volume conceptualises the multi-level legal and judicial system in Europe as a holistic, albeit diverse and fragmented, frame of norms and social-legal action. The interaction between the national, supranational and international legal spheres is so dense and extensive that the different normative and judicial frames for rights protection must be seen as components of an integrated transnational structure par excellence. At the same time, the contributions in this book move beyond conceptual, legal pluralist theorising to explore the variety of legal and social mobilisation processes that underpin and constitute the European decentralised legal system. Individual and collective actors can draw from a multiplicity of legal rules and entitlements to invoke in court in disputes with private or state parties, or in the course of struggle for social reform. Judges also have significant leeway in choosing which norms to appeal to and enforce.[2]

The aim of this last chapter is to provide an overview and discuss the findings of the case studies included in this volume and to suggest directions for future research. In the following four brief sections, it discusses (a) the factors that influence litigation and legal mobilisation on behalf of minorities and vulnerable groups (at the national and European level, Sections I and II), (b) the role of lawyers and civil society actors (Section III), and (c) the effects of legal mobilisation and court decisions for state policy and social reform (Section IV).

I. LEGAL OPPORTUNITIES AND JUDICIAL ARENAS BETWEEN THE NATIONAL AND EUROPEAN LEVELS

Over the past 20 years or so, Europe has undoubtedly witnessed a proliferation of rights frames that have expanded the possibilities and opportunities to

[1] For an overview of the post-national constitutionalist debate, see N Walker, 'Taking Constitutionalism Beyond the State' (2008) *Political Studies* 56, 519–43. See also N Krisch, 'The Open Architecture of European Human Rights Law' (2007) LSE Law, Society and Economy Working Papers 11; and A Torres Pérez, *Conflicts of Rights in the European Union: A Theory of Supranational Adjudication* (Oxford, Oxford University Press, 2009).

[2] A Stone Sweet, 'A Cosmopolitan Legal Order: Constitutional Pluralism and Rights Adjudication in Europe' (2012) 1 *Global Constitutionalism* 53, 61. See also G de Búrca and O Gerstenberg, 'The Denationalization of Constitutional Law' (2006) 47 *Harvard International Law Journal* 243, 257–59.

raise normative claims in court. At least three avenues for seeking fundamental rights protection exist: (1) before national courts by invoking constitutional rights and principles, (2) in the ECtHR once domestic remedies are exhausted, and (3) before national courts or the CJEU when there is a matter that falls within the EU's competence and a relevant claim can be raised under EU law.[3] Dawson, Muir and Claes in this volume elaborate on the third avenue, by outlining and analysing the distinct processes through which EU rights can be claimed in national courts and in the CJEU, both by public and private actors, and vis-à-vis state and private parties. Along with others writing on the subject, the authors concede that the adoption of the Charter of Fundamental Rights (CFR) with the Lisbon Treaty has added a great deal of complexity to the existing multi-level system of rights protection in Europe.

Legal opportunity structures for rights mobilisation in Europe are as great as they are complex, and taking full advantage of them is often a highly resource-demanding task. For those who can find their way through the juridical maze, the EU and ECHR law present varying advantages to human rights litigators. In the first place, EU law is arguably advantageous in so far as it may provide a speedier and more direct process of contesting and setting aside national law provisions that conflict with EU norms through a preliminary reference ruling. Litigants can also appeal to an expanded and up-to-date body of EU fundamental rights contained in the Charter, which extend well beyond those contained in the ECHR. Prospective litigants in the ECtHR on the other hand, must take a 'long and arduous road' to Strasbourg, having to exhaust domestic remedies first before being able to lodge a claim.[4]

At the same time, it could be argued that claimants, their counsel and supporters have little control or influence in pursuing a preliminary reference ruling, which significantly depends on national judges deciding whether an issue raised by a case merits such a request. Furthermore, in preliminary reference rulings, rights claims invoking the Charter can only be raised in law and policy areas pertaining to EU law, rather than to state policy and action more broadly. As a consequence, in most litigation that comes through a preliminary reference ruling, fundamental rights tend to be pleaded in a tangential manner within the EU's largely market-dominated competences. By contrast, in petitions in the ECtHR, appeal to and consideration of rights, is the centrepiece of the adjudicatory process, in which Convention rights are applied as freestanding public goods.[5] Notwithstanding the various pros and cons of taking recourse in Luxembourg and in Strasbourg, the contribution by Psychogiopoulou shows that each rights review system is likely to be more appropriate and accessible depending on the issue at hand; the

[3] S Douglas-Scott, 'The European Union and Human Rights after the Treaty of Lisbon' (2011) 11 *Human Rights Law Review* 645, 647.

[4] Ibid, 656–57.

[5] Ibid, 680.

two are more likely to be seen as complementary, rather than as conflicting alternatives.

The extent to which the expansion of European legal norms in practice increases meaningful opportunities for individual and social actors to claim entitlements and enhanced protection in courts is thoroughly mediated and shaped by national variables. Disparities or 'lack of fit' between the scope and procedural rules of EU equality rights on the one hand, and entrenched national social, legal and institutional conditions and practices on the other, render actual opportunities for legal mobilisation highly conditional, and perhaps for the time being circumscribed. For instance, concepts such as indirect discrimination, the use of statistics to prove it, and the shift in the burden of proof, which are introduced with the EU anti-discrimination directives, are unfamiliar to jurists across several national legal systems, an obstacle that must be overcome in order to generate litigation.[6]

Furthermore, despite a degree of convergence that the above-mentioned EU directives and other European norms bring about, persistent national differences fragment rights protection in Europe.[7] Significant variation in litigation across Member States points to the variable national legal, social and institutional factors that enhance or restrict the ability of individual and social actors to mobilise the law and access the justice system across European countries.[8] As the chapter by Dawson, Muir and Claes shows, variable procedural rules of access and rules of standing across national legal systems shape the overall structure that facilitates or constrains the ability of individual and other social actors to bring a lawsuit, including before European courts. Victims of discrimination are constrained in accessing justice, due to substantial cross-national diversity in procedural rules, but also due to the overall weak position of collective enforcement mechanisms in the EU Member States. Generally, there is a vast uncharted space for single and comparative case studies to research the extent and ways in which national legal, social, institutional and political factors facilitate or constrain rights litigation and legal mobilisation in Europe.

II. PURSUING RIGHTS MOBILISATION: DO ISSUES AND NATURE OF MINORITY GROUP MATTER?

Beyond the above general observations, consideration of the opportunities and motives for legal mobilisation of rights has to take an issue-specific, as

[6] V Guiraudon, 'Equality in the Making: Implementing European Non-discrimination Law' (2009) 13 *Citizenship Studies* 527, 535–37.

[7] M Bell, 'The Implementation of European Anti-Discrimination Directives: Converging towards a Common Model?' (2008) 79 *Political Quarterly* 36.

[8] K Alter and J Vargas, 'Explaining Variation in the Use of European Litigation Strategies' (2000) 33(4) *Comparative Political Studies* 452–82.

well as group-specific approach. From the perspective of those mobilising the law on behalf of various kinds of minorities, immigrants and asylum seekers, the national, subnational and European legal norms and courts appear as alternative venues of a single system. The conceptual frame adopted in this volume has stressed the importance and appropriateness of pursuing a multi-level and multi-sited approach on how law and legal mobilisation matter to a group seeking to challenge different aspects of discrimination, marginalisation and social injustice, perhaps more so in Europe than anywhere else. Legal opportunities available at different levels are distinctly configured from the point of view of various minority groups, and in regard to the particular social conditions and issues that affect them.

A crucial precondition for legal mobilisation in respect to a particular issue is the existence of legally codified rights that can be enforced through courts, whether in constitutional or international law. With regard to historical minorities and the issue of language rights, the chapters by de Witte and (partly) by Arzoz show that the nature of the relevant international and constitutional norms is for the most part unpropitious for the pursuit of such rights through courts, which explains the 'rights without litigation' paradox. Judicial interpretations at the European, national or subnational levels have found little ground to expand the scope of minority language rights and to render them justiciable. Democratic states generally tolerate the use of minority languages in private relations and protect their speakers from discrimination and assimilation. The promotion of a minority language though further presupposes 'positive' rights to enable its use in the public administration, in education and in relations with the governments and the courts.

Minority language rights (MLR) are generally drafted in constitutions as programmatic provisions that place legislatures and other public authorities under a duty to act in order to enable minority citizens to promote their language (notwithstanding exceptions, such as Canada and Finland where MLR are constitutionally recognised). However, individuals cannot oblige a state to act if it refuses to make rights effective through law.[9] International law in this area takes the form of general 'soft' law provisions. Even an advanced text like the European Charter for Regional and Minority Languages does not guarantee enforceable rights, individual or collective. It only encourages states to take measures to protect regional and minority languages, which can be developed through domestic constitutional and legislative instruments.[10] In the case of Spain, while the Charter did not create new rights, it has exerted an important influence in encouraging legal mobilisation of minority language activists in Navarre, who have sought to

[9] X Arzoz, 'Language Rights as Legal Norms' (2009) 15 *European Public Law* 541, 545–48.
[10] Ibid, 555.

realise to a fuller extent the scope of the respective rights envisioned in the constitution.

Rights cannot always be translated into universal models and generalised standards. This is the case for MLR because they depend on the size and density of minority populations in given territories, which greatly varies across states and regions. This also explains their limited enforceability through courts. In addition, the implementation of MLR demands substantial resources from public authorities, and for this reason requires a flexible, pragmatic and context-specific approach[11] that is not compatible with a rights-based, adjudicatory process.[12] Therefore, the construction and concretisation of MLR in each region and country, as de Witte argues, is highly dependent on the domestic political process and deliberation. Far from being fundamental rights in the sense of being universal, MLR are local, historically rooted claims. As Arzoz states:

> Even if formulated as fundamental rights, constitutional language rights are not accorded for the sake of freedom and equality of all individuals and groups living in the state, but for the sake of basically protecting certain language communities (for instance, Swedish- and French-speaking citizens in Finland and Canada respectively).[13]

The case of Spain, where significant litigation around MLR has taken place, along with the case of Belgium (examined in de Witte's chapter), suggest that minority language litigation may be more likely to take place in federated or decentralised states, not only on behalf of those wishing to expand rights and/or local autonomy, but also on the part of the central government seeking to curb the latter. In these states, conflicts over MLR often get entangled with questions of jurisdiction and competence between different and antagonistic levels of government. Legal mobilisation around MLR is also more likely to take place on behalf of highly mobilised and politicised minorities, such as the Basques of Spain, or the French-speakers of Canada.

The possibilities for legal mobilisation are not only shaped by the extent to which particular rights are inherently (non)justiciable, but also by their relevance and appropriateness with respect to the social conditions and characteristics of a minority group. The contribution by Dawson, Muir and Claes suggests that existing legal provisions of EU law may be less favourable to, and less favourably perceived by, communities such as the Roma. This is

[11] On the advantages of a flexible, non-judicial approach to minority rights enforcement, see G Pentassuglia, 'Minority Rights, Human Rights: A Review of Basic Concepts, Entitlements and Implementation Procedures under International Law'in *Mechanisms for the Implementation of Minority Rights* (Strasbourg, Council of Europe Publishing, 2004) 24.

[12] R Hofmann, 'The Framework Convention for the Protection of National Minorities: an Introduction' in M Weller (ed), *The Rights of Minorities in Europe* (Oxford, Oxford University Press, 2005) 6.

[13] Arzoz (n 9) 573.

in line with assessments by other scholars who see the EU Race Directive's prescriptions as being less suitable for addressing the issues posed by individuals from national (or historical) minorities or the Roma, who are predominantly found in Central-East and South-East Europe (CESE). Instead, the provisions of the EU Race Directive are more in tune with the issues and problems affecting immigrant communities like those in West Europe. Structural problems such as racial segregation in education, affecting the Roma in a number of countries, are not mentioned in the directives, which can only be invoked before a court by an identifiable victim. The absence of admissible references to the CJEU from courts in the 12 East European states that joined the EU in 2004, under any of the 2000 directives (at least until 2008) has been attributed to this lacuna.[14]

At the same, judicially expansive or innovative interpretations may over time render general provisions of human rights increasingly relevant for highly marginalised individuals and groups, such as refugees and asylum seekers. The seminal case of *MSS v Belgium and Greece* examined by Psychogiopoulou was the result of strategic legal action. It was prompted by and followed along an incremental and expansive conceptualisation of the nature and scope of Articles 3 (prohibition of inhuman or degrading treatment) and 5 (right to liberty and security) ECHR. In response to this case, the Strasbourg Court further enlarged the scope of what constitutes degrading treatment, by extending it beyond instances of purposeful harm by state agents. For the first time, it acknowledged that removal of an asylum seeker to conditions of absolute poverty may amount to a breach of Article 3 ECHR.[15] The legal actors involved in the case thoroughly relied on a wealth of reports by human rights NGOs. In exposing and criticising reception and detention conditions in Greece, as well as the destitution often facing released individuals while waiting for the processing of their asylum application, they rendered the legal claim compelling.

The litigation on behalf of individual asylum seekers in the CJEU, which is examined by Psychogiopoulou, was conjoined with the strategic goal to challenge EU policy related to asylum management. Significantly, recourse to the ECtHR in this case was not only a means to exert pressure for altering national laws and practices but also to stress the importance of developing policies at the EU level that promote the protection of migrants' rights. The *MSS v Belgium and Greece* case was specifically aimed at challenging the assumption of all EU Member States as 'safe countries'. It also challenged the highly uneven manner in which existing EU policy under the Dublin II Regulation assigns responsibility for asylum petitions between states on the EU's southern and eastern borders and the remaining states.

[14] Bell (n 7) 38.

[15] G Clayton, 'Asylum Seekers in Europe: *MSS v Belgium and Greece*' (2011) 11 *Human Rights Law Review* 758, 769.

As a strategic litigation case, the counter-part of the *MSS* case in the CJEU, the *Saeedi* case (*NS and ME and Others v UK*), primarily contested a point of judicial-legal competence between the EU and national levels—it was about the extent to which the UK and Poland had an effective, general opt-out from the applicability of the CFR by virtue of Protocol 30 to the Lisbon Treaty on the Application of the CFR of the EU to Poland and the UK.[16] This aspect of the contestation was paramount for a transnationally active segment of UK-based human rights lawyers who had been involved in this case one way or another, or were closely following it. The decision of the CJEU was that Protocol 30 lacked any impact as an effective opt-out, a clarification that was eagerly sought and welcomed by human rights lawyers planning their future litigation strategies.

In turn, the chapter by Israël is a sober reminder to attend to the importance of legal and social developments since the 1970s at the national level. As others also show, the legal mobilisation of immigrants' rights in France must be traced back to the rise of leftist and immigrant-support social movements, as well as the turn to the restrictionist immigration policies in the 1970s.[17] The fascination with the growth of rights and judicial review at the European level has led us to neglect the fact that many of these European legal developments were gestated domestically, and they were national in origin; the relevant developments were possibly more important and far reaching in some countries than in others. It is well known that the coalition of lawyers, experts and activists that pushed for the adoption of the EU's anti-discrimination law in the 1990s predominantly originated from particular national contexts, and it emulated legal developments in the UK and the Netherlands.[18] Important national differences also characterise the construction of particular minority populations, such as immigrants, as rights-bearing individuals.[19]

Legal mobilisation on behalf of marginalised groups and minorities both reflects and reinforces shifts in the social place and political significance of law, including the development of new kinds of legal practices across different European countries. Besides France, the UK has also witnessed since the 1970s and 1980s the blossoming of group-based litigation and pressure activity through the law, which grew in domestic courts while also expanding in the ECtHR and in the CJEU.[20] The study of how law and legal action became increasingly incorporated in social reform goals and movement

[16] Douglas-Scott (n 3) 655.

[17] L Kawar, 'Legal Mobilization in the Terrain of the State: Creating a Field of Immigrant Rights Lawyering in France and the United States' (2011) 2 *Law and Social Inquiry* 354.

[18] A Geddes and V Guiraudon, 'Britain, France, and EU Anti-Discrimination Policy: The Emergence of an EU Policy Paradigm' (2004) 27 *West European Politics* 334, 340.

[19] L Kawar, 'Juridical Framings of Immigrants in the United States and France: Courts, Social Movements, and Symbolic Politics' (2012) 46 *International Migration Review* 414, 420.

[20] C Harlow, 'Public Law and Popular Justice' (2002) 65 *Modern Law Review* 1.

strategies in the European countries that experienced the social protests of the 1960s, the diverse socio-legal pathways of south European countries that underwent democratisation in the 1970s, and the human rights legal activism that has emerged in many ex-communist countries since the 1990s all present a major gap in European socio-legal research, about which we know very little.

III. CAUSE LAWYERS, NGOS AND TRANSNATIONAL NETWORKS

Scholarly research has increasingly paid attention to the important and growing role of civil society actors in international law and courts, including in Europe.[21] The third part of the volume has explored how social movement organisations, like Stonewall and ILGA in the area of LGBT rights, as well as looser but expanding synergies between human rights groups and lawyers committed to a social cause, have become increasingly engaged in litigation in the ECtHR. Human rights activists and organisations have embraced litigation in the ECtHR as a way of bringing to the international limelight gross violations such as those occurring in contexts of armed conflict. They have pursued systematic legal mobilisation, defending individual applicants, while also pressing the Strasbourg Court on particular points of law, influencing in this way notable shifts and expansive interpretations of Convention provisions in its case law.

Social movement actors in the area of LGBT rights, including individual activists and organisations, have increasingly leveraged human rights law to pursue national-level legal and policy reform. They have incorporated litigation in domestic and European courts as an important component of their strategies and activism. In this area, strategic legal mobilisation in the ECtHR initially to condemn and dismantle legal discrimination against gays, and subsequently to claim further family life and privacy rights evolved from the engagement of a few committed individuals and groups to become increasingly international and professionalised. Expertise by lawyers combined with resources (financial, knowledge of local or national conditions, among others) supplied by social movement and human rights organisations have augmented the support structures enabling litigation and legal mobilisation of gays and lesbians at the European level.

The legalisation of various kinds of social activism that we have witnessed over the past 20 years has resulted in advancements in European human rights law. This is the case with regard to the transnational legal

[21] R Cichowski, 'Civil Society and the European Court of Human Rights' in J Christoffersen and MR Madsen (eds), *The European Court of Human Rights between Law and Politics* (Oxford, Oxford University Press, 2011) 77–97; L Hodson, *NGOs and the Struggle for Human Rights in Europe* (Oxford, Hart Publishing, 2010).

action in Strasbourg, which developed to redress violations under a state of emergency, analysed by Anagnostou. The contributions of Anagnostou and Hodson both show that litigation pursued by networks and synergies between lawyers, social movement and human rights actors has tended to exert notable influence over the jurisprudential and adjudicatory process in Strasbourg. Supported by networks of lawyers and activists extending across different states and regions, legal mobilisation over time prompted the ECtHR to be increasingly attentive to alleged gross violations, and to expand the rights of individual victims under a state of emergency. Hodson also argues that by strategically targeting litigation to issues and points of law where there is potential for expanding the scope and content of human rights, NGOs, activists and lawyers have inadvertently contributed to the constitutionalisation of the Convention.

In some areas, legal action in Strasbourg has emerged through the forging of close ties and synergies between lawyers, often a nucleus of more committed ones, with human rights NGOs and social activists across different states. Transnational networks of lawyers, human rights and social movement organisations have specifically supported litigation in the ECtHR originating in countries and regions where political conditions are unreceptive or hostile, such as with regard to gay rights in Russia and the plight of civilians caught in the Chechen conflict between the Russian forces and the Chechen separatists. In this way, the creation of networks and alliances across states enabled litigation by supplying an external source of support in places where egregious violations occur. It also served as a guarantee that local and national intimidation and persecution would not be buried in silence but would be exposed, and that resources and advocacy would be marshalled to condemn them in the international and European community.

Systematic contacts and collaboration between lawyers and organisations at the local and national level and others abroad also made it possible to engage in the kind of facts-intensive and evidence-based litigation at the ECtHR, which is usually necessary to convince a high court to enunciate new principles that depart from precedent. Such facts-intensive and evidence-based litigation, for instance, is reflected in the Article 2 (right to life) and Article 3 (prohibition of inhuman and degrading treatment) ECHR cases in regard to disappearances and ill-treatment by security forces, explored in the contribution by Anagnostou. Another example of facts-intensive litigation are the Strasbourg Court cases of Roma segregation in education and cases of ill-treatment of individuals of Roma ethnic origin by the police. The bulk of those cases have been supported by the European Roma Rights Centre (EERC) with the cooperation of lawyers and NGOs at the local and national level in different countries such as Romania, Bulgaria, Hungary and Greece, among others. As one of the founders of the EERC and former director describes, documenting the widespread and often systematic nature of these violations was crucial, even in systems that do not formally recognise class actions or group remedies. The factual information that it was possible to gather by engaging legal-human rights networks was crucial in exposing violations and in convincing the ECtHR that these had a profound structural and systemic nature.[22]

While NGO activity is not extensive in litigation in the ECtHR, it is nonetheless significant because it is clustered in areas and issues where battles over the meaning as well as the boundaries of the Convention are being fought. For activists though, the emergence of professional organisations with a rights-based approach and legal strategy in the service of social reform goals, such as NGOs in the area of LGBT, generates concerns. It raises classic social movement dilemmas and tensions between a more technocratic and institutionally integrated (and for many co-opted and compromised) approach on the one hand, and the connection with grass-roots membership and action on the other. These two forms of engagement for social reform often entail conflicting priorities and commitments that render their coexistence difficult.

The expansion of NGOs, pressure groups, and social movement organisations' activity in the legal process and the courts has also raised profound questions concerning how representative of broader public interests the NGOs pursuing particular issues are, as well as their lack of accountability vis-à-vis the public. Hodson's contribution takes stock of such concerns voiced by scholars about the anti-majoritarian elements of NGO-driven legal activism. Broadening access to courts by giving more groups standing to sue would arguably exacerbate such concerns, and undermine judicial independence by drawing courts into pressure group politics.[23] Such concerns further feed into the broader scepticism about the 'judicialisation of politics' on the part of those who dwell on the democratic deficit of judicial decision making. The growing authority of transnational courts is especially seen to pose a major challenge to parliamentary democracy, national legal traditions and sovereignty as it surfaces in the scathing critique of the ECtHR by Lord Hoffman.[24]

IV. DO LEGAL MOBILISATION AND COURT DECISIONS PROMOTE SOCIAL REFORM AND JUSTICE?

Scholars studying legal mobilisation and courts have questioned the ability of judicial decisions to bring actual social and policy change on the ground, an

[22] J Goldston, 'The Struggle for Roma Rights' (2010) 32 *Human Rights Quarterly* 311, 323.
[23] Harlow (n 20).
[24] Lord Hoffmann, 'The Universality of Human Rights', Judicial Studies Board Annual Lecture, 19 March 2009.

outcome that they view as highly conditional and clearly bounded.[25] Courts may pronounce rights in an expansive and progressive direction, but they may also vindicate actors who counter-mobilise to resist change. Even judicial decisions that are favourable to minority claims can hope to influence policy reform only when there is sufficient societal support, as well as support from legislative and executive officials.[26] The dependent and conditional policy impact of court decisions though, should in no way lead us to dismiss their importance. It is well known that strategic litigation is often employed '... as part of a multi-pronged strategy designed to gain leverage in *extra-judicial* negotiations', a goal that is not strictly linked to policy implementation.[27] After all, why expect courts, which often rule on specific and narrow points of law and rights, to mandate policy outcomes that tend to involve complex accommodation and pragmatic choices about resource allocation?

Both from within but also beyond a policy approach of judicial impact, scholars have significantly broadened their understanding of the kinds of effects that court decisions can have on politics. From a distinct constitutive perspective, rights are primarily understood as discursive logics that shape the normative and political frames through which individual and collective actors conceptualise social problems.[28] From this perspective, legal norms and their interpretation by courts may have various unintended, but nonetheless important, constitutive effects in regard to the political context of social struggles, as well as the social actors themselves. Court decisions can act as catalysts in reshaping the context of a social and political struggle, and recast the contours of public debates on an issue, by imparting legitimacy on, or enhancing the salience of, particular kinds of rights claims. They can also expose systemic inequalities, making targeted authorities (or employers) more vulnerable and thus more willing to negotiate. From an actor-centred approach McCann argues that court decisions can influence the discursive frames and strategies of social movement actors, they can reconstruct their interests and identities, and at times empower them. In these ways, they can contribute to the emergence, growth or decline of social movements.[29]

Alternatively, from a constitutive perspective focusing on institutional contexts, courts can be seen to act in complex policy settings as one set

[25] G Rosenberg, *The Hollow Hope: Can Courts Bring About Social Change?* (Chicago, University of Chicago Press, 1991).

[26] Ibid, 31.

[27] K Alter and J Vargas, 'Explaining Variation in the Use of European Litigation Strategies' (2000) 33(4) *Comparative Political Studies* 455.

[28] MW McCann, *Rights At Work* (Chicago, University of Chicago Press, 1994). See also the debate with Rosenberg in G Rosenberg, 'Hollow Hopes and Other Aspirations: A Reply to Feely and McCann' (1992) 17 *Law and Social Inquiry* 761.

[29] M McCann, 'Law and Social Movements: Contemporary Perspectives' (2006) 2 *Annual Review of Law and Social Science* 17.

of actors among others, such as legislatures, local governments, media, and state administration. Under particular conditions, their decisions can influence policy outcomes by virtue of how they are interpreted, leveraged or circumvented by different institutional and societal actors. This is evidently a highly contingent and variable effect. In studying the impact of legal mobilisation and court decisions on minority language policy in Canada, Riddell argues that over time these had a cumulative effect in promoting policy change in the direction of expanding French-speaking education outside of Quebec. They did so by critically influencing the political parameters, within which policy formulation was debated, contested and deliberated.[30] From this approach, which sees courts as participants in broader institutional and policy settings, the impact of their decisions is likely to be mediated and shaped differently by different forms of government, judicial structures, constitutional rules and federal structures, across countries.

Even if government authorities shy away from or resist rights-expansive reform, judicial rulings may still augment the salience of a particular reformist agenda, as the US Supreme Court decisions did in regard to the civil rights agenda in the 1960s.[31] Similarly, the progressive pronouncements of the Conseil d'Etat in the second half of the 1970s, a result of legal mobilisation pursued by the GISTI, explored in the contribution by Israël, promoted the right to family life for legally residing immigrants, and had a long-lasting impact on French immigration policies. Besides limiting administrative discretion, the court decisions critically contributed to a discursive frame that constructed immigrants as rights-bearing legal subjects, and bolstered the emerging socialist programme to strengthen immigrants' rights in the 1980s.[32]

The effects of judicial decisions have not been specifically or substantially explored in this volume. The contribution by Arzoz points to the limited impact that legal mobilisation and the resulting court decisions have had in changing the regional government's policy concerning the use of Basque language in the mixed and the non-Basque-speaking zones of Navarre. Legal mobilisation was mainly a defensive strategy to uphold language rights that were already guaranteed in law and provided for in the constitution. Yet, Arzoz also concedes that legal mobilisation and court decisions have had important indirect effects, most importantly in changing the political climate in favour of a more proactive approach to preserve the Basque language and the right to use it in Navarre. They had an incremental, limited, and yet significant impact in tilting the balance towards those

[30] TQ Riddell, 'The Impact of Legal Mobilization and Judicial Decisions: The Case of Official Minority-Language Education Policy in Canada for Francophones Outside Quebec' (2004) 38 *Law and Society Review* 583.

[31] McCann (n 29) 27.

[32] Kawar (n 19).

political forces with more progressive views on MLR. In this way, courts played an important part in a multifaceted process of struggle to redefine the parameters of minority language policy in Navarre.

Beyond theoretical and analytical debates about the role and impact on legal mobilisation and courts of policy and social reform, scholars have debated the use and effectiveness of individual-based litigation in redressing structural inequalities and situations of pervasive minority marginalisation. In questioning the effectiveness of litigation as such, the chapter by Dawson, Muir and Claes argues for a strategy of fundamental rights protection in the EU and the Member States that combines judicial approaches with non-judicial ones. This strategy would focus on monitoring rights violations, awareness raising, as well as empowering equality bodies to speak and act on behalf of vulnerable groups.[33] Undoubtedly, much needs to be done in this direction and others, in order to provide meaningful and effective rights-based mechanisms and remedies in Europe. Altogether though, this volume makes abundantly clear that today rights litigation is very different from the privately motivated and individualised form of engagement that prevailed in the 1970s, including in the civil law traditions of continental Europe.[34] Instead, it has been increasingly implicated, directly or indirectly, in important social struggles and policy debates, and it involves the building of synergies and alliances between legal, social and political actors within and across state borders.

[33] See also M Dawson and E Muir, 'Individual, Institutional and Collective Vigilance in Protecting Fundamental Rights in the EU: Lessons from the Roma' (2011) 48 *Common Market Law Review* 751, 766.

[34] JB Grossman and A Sarat, 'Litigation in Federal Courts: A Comparative Perspective' (1975) 9 *Law and Society Review* 321.

Bibliography

Abel R, 'Speaking Law to Power: Occasions for Cause Lawyering' in Austin Sarat and S Scheingold (eds), *Cause Lawyering. Political Commitments and Political Responsibilities* (Oxford, Oxford University Press, 1998) 69–117.

Abott A, *The System of Professions. An Essay on the Division of Expert Labor* (Chicago, University of Chicago Press, 1988).

Acosta D, 'The Good, the Bad and the Ugly in EU Migration Law: Is the European Parliament Becoming Bad and Ugly?' (2009) 11 *European Journal of Migration and Law* 1.

Agirreazkuenaga I, 'Dictamen jurídico emitido a requerimiento del Alcalde del Ayuntamiento de Lekunberri (en representación de otras Administraciones e instituciones) sobre la legalidad del Decreto Foral 372/2000, de 11 de diciembre, por el que se regula el uso del vascuence en las Administraciones públicas de Navarra (BON de 5 de enero de 2001)' (2001) 59 *Revista Vasca de Administración Pública*.

——— *Diversidad y convivencia lingüística* (Diputación Foral de Gipuzkoa, 2003).

Agrikoliansky E, *La ligue française des droits de l'homme et du citoyen depuis 1945. Sociologie d'un engagement civique* (Paris, L'Harmattan, 2002).

Ahmed S and D Potter, *NGOs in International Politics* (Bloomfield, Kumarian Press, 2006).

Amireaux V and V Guiraudon, 'Discrimination in Comparative Perspective' (2010) 53(12) *American Behavioral Scientist* 1691–714.

Amnesty International, Amnesty International Report 2009, http://report2009.amnesty.org/sites/report2009.amnesty.org/files/documents/air09-en.pdf, accessed 5 January 2013, 156.

Anagnostou D (ed), 'Does European Human Rights Law Matter? Implementation and Domestic Impact of Strasbourg Court Judgments on Minority-related Policies' (2010) 14 *The International Journal of Human Rights* 721.

——— 'Politics, Courts and Society in the Domestic Implementation and Practice of the ECtHR's Case Law' in D Anagnostou (ed), *Domesticating the European Court of Human Rights* (Edinburgh, Edinburgh University Press, 2013).

——— *The European Court of Human Rights: Implementing Strasbourg's Judgments on Domestic Policy* (Edinburgh, Edinburgh University Press, 2013).

——— and Y Grozev, 'Human Rights Litigation and Restrictive State Implementation of Strasbourg Court Judgments: the Case of Ethnic Minorities from Southeast Europe' (2010) 16 *European Public Law* 401.

——— and S Millns, 'Gender Equality, Legal Mobilisation and Feminism in the European Multi-level System' (2013) 28 *Canadian Journal of Law and Society* 1.

——— and E Psychogiopoulou (eds), *The European Court of Human Rights and the Rights of Marginalised Individuals and Minorities in National Context* (Leiden, Martinus Nijhoff Publishers, 2010).

——— and ——— 'Under What Conditions Do National Authorities Implement the European Court of Human Rights' Rulings? Religious and Ethnic Minorities in Greece' in D Anagnostou (ed), *The European Court of Human Rights: Implementing Strasbourg's Judgments on Domestic Policy* (Edinburgh, Edinburgh University Press, 2013) 143–65.

Alter K, *The European Court's Political Power: Selected Essays* (Oxford, Oxford University Press, 2009).

——— and J Vargas, 'Explaining Variation in the Use of European Litigation Strategies' (2000) 33(4) *Comparative Political Studies* 454.

Andersen EA, *Out of the Closets and Into the Courts—Legal Opportunity Structure and Gay Rights Litigation* (Ann Arbor, University of Michigan Press, 2006).

Anderson K, 'The Ottawa Convention Banning Landmines, the Role of International Non-Governmental Organizations and the Idea of International Civil Society' (2000) 11 *European Journal of International Law* 91.

Anthony G and P Mageean, 'Habits of Mind and "Truth Telling": Article 2 ECHR in Post-Conflict Northern Ireland' in J Morison et al (eds), *Judges, Transition, and Human Rights* (Oxford, Oxford University Press, 2007) 181–200.

Aolain FN, 'The European Convention on Human Rights and Its Prohibition on Torture' in S Levision (ed), *Torture: A Collection* (Oxford, Oxford University Press, 2004), 213–28.

——— 'Transitional Emergency Jurisprudence: Derogation and Transition' in A Buyse and M Hamilton (eds), *Transitional Jurisprudence and the ECHR* (Cambridge, Cambridge University Press, 2011) 24–50.

Artières P and M Zancarini-Fournel (eds), *68, Une histoire collective* (Paris, La Découverte, 2008).

Arzoz X, 'La convivencia lingüística en Navarra' (2004) 69(II) *Revista Vasca de Administración Pública* 35.

——— 'Die geschichtlichen Autonomien der Basken, Galizier und Katalanen als Beispiel eines multinationalen "Quasi-Föderalismus" im Einheitsstaat' in C Pan and B Sybille Pfeil (eds), *Zur Entstehung des modernen Minderheitenschutzes in Europa* (Vienna, Springer, 2006) 387–412.

——— 'Estatuto jurídico del euskera en Navarra' in JM Pérez Fernández (ed), *Estudios sobre el estatuto jurídico de las lenguas en España* (Barcelona, Atelier, 2006) 387–416.

——— (ed), *Respecting Linguistic Diversity in the European Union* (Amsterdam, John Benjamins Publishing Co, 2008).

——— 'The Implementation of the European Charter for Regional or Minority Languages in Spain' in *The European Charter for Regional or Minority Languages: Legal Challenges and Opportunities*, No 8 (Strasbourg, Council of Europe Publishing, 2008) 83–107.

——— 'Language Rights as Legal Norms' (2009) 15 *European Public Law* 541.

——— 'Lenguas y modalidades lingüísticas en la Constitución Española: ¿dos regímenes jurídicos diferenciados?' in A Milian Massana (ed), *El plurilingüisme a la Constitució española* (Barcelona, Institut d'Estudis Autonòmics, 2009) 61–122.

——— 'Accommodating Linguistic Difference: Five Normative Models of Language Rights' (2010) 6 *European Constitutional Law Review* 102.

——— 'Linguistic Minorities in Spain' in D Richter et al (eds), *Language Rights Revisited—The Challenge of Global Migration and Communication* (Berlin, Berliner WissenschaftsVerlag-Wolf Legal Publishers, 2012) 271–85.

Ayerdi Etxeberri PM, 'Actitudes políticas y resultados electorales de Navarra desde 1977' (2010) 7 *Iura Vasconiae: Revista de Derecho Histórico y Autonómico de Vasconia* 117.

Badinter R, *L'abolition* (Paris, Seuil, 2000).

Bartholomeusz L, 'The Amicus Curiae before International Courts and Tribunals' (2005) 5 *Non-State Actors and International Law* 209.

Bates E, *The Evolution of the European Convention on Human Rights: From its Inception to the Creation of a Permanent Court of Human Rights* (Oxford, Oxford University Press, 2010).

Baxi U, *The Future of Human Rights* (Oxford, Oxford University Press, 2002).

Beirne M and A Hegarty, 'A View From the Coal Face: Northern Ireland, Human Rights Activism, and the War on Terror' in J Morison, K McEvoy and G Anthony (eds), *Judges, Transition, and Human Rights* (Oxford, Oxford University Press, 2007).

Bell M, *Anti-Discrimination Law and the EU* (Oxford, Oxford University Press, 2002).

——— 'Walking in the Same Direction? The Contribution of the European Social Charter and the European Union to Combating Discrimination' in G de Búrca and B de Witte (eds), *Social Rights in Europe* (Oxford, Oxford University Press, 2005) 273.

——— 'The Implementation of European Anti-Discrimination Directives: Converging Towards a Common Model?' (2008) 79 *Political Quarterly* 36.

Benoit-Rohmer F and H Hardeman, *The Minority Question in Europe: Towards the Creation of a Coherent European Regime* (Brussels, Centre for European Policy Studies, 1994).

Berhardt R, 'Human Rights and Judicial Review: The European Court of Human Rights' in DM Beatty (ed), *Human Rights and Judicial Review: A Comparative Perspective* (Dordrecht, Kluwer, 1994) 297–319.

Bernard N, 'L'arrêt Wooncode de la Cour constitutionnelle du 10 juillet 2008: quand l'arbre (linguistique) cache la forêt' (2008) *Journal des Tribunaux* 689.

Bertile V, *Langues régionales ou minoritaires et Constitution: France, Espagne et Italie* (Brussels, Bruylant, 2008).

Blätte A, 'The Kurdish Movement. Ethnic Mobilization and Europeanization' in H Kleinschmidt (ed), *Migration, Regional Integration and Human Security* (Aldershot, Ashgate, 2006) 181–202.

Boigeol A, 'La formation des magistrats: de l'apprentissage sur le tas à l'école professionnelle' (1989) 76–77 *Actes de la Recherche en Sciences Sociales* 49.

Bonbled N and S Weerts, 'La liberté linguistique' in M Verdussen and N Bonbled (eds), *Les droits constitutionnels en Belgique*, vol 2 (Brussels, Bruylant, 2011) 1097–147.

Börzel T, 'Participation Through Law Enforcement—The Case of the EU' (2006) 39 *Comparative Political Studies* 128.

Boyle K, 'Human Rights and Political Resolution in Northern Ireland' (1982–83) 9 *Yale Journal of World and Public Order* 156.

——— 'Article 14 Bites at Last' (2006) 5 *EHRAC Bulletin* 1, available at www.londonmet.ac.uk/library/x29082_3.pdf.

———, T Hadden and P Hillyard, *Law and State—The Case of Northern Ireland* (London, Martin Robertson and Co, 1975).

Buckley C, *Turkey and the ECHR—A Report on the Litigation Programme of the Kurdish Human Rights Project* (London, KHRP, 2000).

Bunch C, 'Women's Rights as Human Rights: Towards a Re-vision of Human Rights' (1990) 12 *Human Rights Quarterly* 486.

Burstein P, 'Legal Mobilization as a Social Movement Tactic: The Struggle for Equal Employment Opportunity' (1991) 96 *American Journal of Sociology* 1201.

Cain, B, RJ Dalton and S Scarrow (eds), *Democracy Transformed? Expanding Political Opportunities in Advanced Industrial Democracies* (Oxford, Oxford University Press, 2003) 192–219.

Cardi V, 'Regional or Minority Language Use before Judicial Authorities: Provisions and Facts' (2007) 6 *JEMIE.*

Carpenter CR, 'Setting the Advocacy Agenda: Theorizing Issue Emergence and Nonemergence in Transnational Advocacy' (2007) 51 *International Studies Quarterly* 99.

Carrera S and B Petkova, 'The Role and Potential of Civil Society and Human Rights Organizations Through Third Party Interventions before the European Courts: The Case of the EU's Area of Freedom, Security and Justice' in M Dawson, B de Witte and E Muir, *Judicial Activism at the Court of Justice* (Cheltenham, Edward Elgar, 2013) 233–63.

Carrozza P, 'Minoranze linguistiche' in S Cassese (ed), *Annuario delle autonomie locali* (Rome, Edizioni delle Autonomie, 1981).

Chalmers D, 'The Positioning of EU Judicial Politics within the United Kingdom' (2000) 23 *West European Politics* 169.

Chevalier-Watts J, 'Effective Investigations under Article 2 of the ECHR: Securing the Right to Life or an Onerous Burden on a State?' (2010) 21 *European Journal of International Law* 701.

——— 'The Phenomena of Enforced Disappearances in Turkey and Chechnya: Strasbourg's Noble Cause?' (2010) 11 *Human Rights Review* 469.

Cichowski R, 'Courts, Rights and Democratic Participation' (2006) 39 *Comparative Political Studies* 50.

——— Introduction. Courts, Democracy, and Governance' (2006) 39 *Comparative Political Studies* 3.

——— *The European Court and Civil Society: Litigation, Mobilization and Governance* (Cambridge: Cambridge University Press, 2007).

——— 'Civil Society and the European Court of Human Rights' in J Christoffersen and MR Madsen (eds), *The European Court of Human Rights between Law and Politics* (Oxford, Oxford University Press, 2011) 77–97.

——— and A Stone Sweet, 'Participation, Representative Democracy and the Courts' in Claes M, *The National Courts' Mandate in the European Constitution* (Oxford, Hart Publishing, 2006).

Clarke K and N Denti, 'The Nascent Impact of the "Greek Transfer" Cases', http://www.legalaidboard.ie/lab/publishing.nsf/content/The_Researcher_April_2012_Article_6, accessed 5 January 2013.

Claverie E, 'Procès, affaire, cause. Voltaire et l'innovation critique' (1994) 7 *Politix*.

Clayton G, 'Asylum Seekers in Europe: *MSS v Belgium and Greece*' (2011) 11 *Human Rights Law Review* 758.

Clement J, *Taalvrijheid, bestuurstaal en minderheidsrechten. Het Belgisch model* (Morstel, Intersentia, 2003).

Cohen A and A Vauchez, 'Introduction: Law, Lawyers, and Transnational Politics in the Production of Europe' (2007) 32 *Law and Social Inquiry* 75.

Commaille J and M Kaluszynski (eds), *La fonction politique de la justice* (Paris, La Découverte, 2007).

Conant L, *Justice Contained: Law and Politics in the European Union* (Ithaca, Cornell University Press, 2002).

—— 'Individuals, Courts and the Development of European Social Rights' (2006) 39 *Comparative Political Studies* 76.

Cornell SE, 'The Kurdish Question in Turkish Politics' (2001) 45 *Orbis* 31.

Council of Europe. *Shaping Language Rights. Commentary on the European Charter for Regional or Minority Languages in the Light of the Committee of Experts' Evaluation*, No 9 (Strasbourg, Council of Europe Publishing, 2012).

Daftary F, 'Experimenting with Territorial Administrative Autonomy in Corsica: Exception or Pilot Region?' (2008) 15 *International Journal on Minority and Group Rights* 273.

Dawson M and E Muir, 'Individual, Institutional and Collective Vigilance in Protecting Fundamental Rights in the EU: Lessons from the Roma' (2011) 48 *Common Market Law Review* 751.

—— and —— 'Enforcing Fundamental Values: EU Law and Governance in Hungary and Romania' (2012) 19 *Maastricht Journal of European and Comparative Law* 469.

——, —— and M Claes, 'Enforcing the EU's Rights Revolution: The Case of Equality' (2012) 13 *European Human Rights Law Review* 276.

De Beco G and E Lantschner, 'The Advisory Committee on the Framework Convention for the Protection of National Minorities (the ACFSC)' in G De Beco (ed), *Human Rights Monitoring Mechanisms of the Council of Europe* (London, Routledge, 2011).

De Búrca G, 'EU Race Discrimination Law: a Hybrid Model?' in G de Búrca and J Scott (eds), *Law and New Governance in the EU and the US* (Oxford, Hart Publishing, 2006) 97–120.

—— 'Stumbling into Experimentalism: The EU Anti-Discrimination Regime' in C Sabel and J Zeitlin (eds), *Experimentalist Governance in the EU* (Oxford, Oxford University Press, 2010) 215–31.

—— and O Gerstenberg, 'The Denationalization of Constitutional Law' (2006) 47 *Harvard International Law Journal* 243.

De Fazio G, 'Legal Opportunity Structure and Social Movement Strategy in Northern Ireland and Southern United States' (2012) 53 *International Journal of Comparative Sociology* 3.

De Mol M, 'The Novel Approach of the ECJ Towards the Horizontal Direct Effect of the EU Principle of Non-discrimination: (Unbridled) Expansionism of EU Law?' (2011) 48 *Maastricht Journal of European and Comparative Law* 109.

De Schutter O, 'Recognition of the Rights of Minorities and the EU's Equal Opportunities Agenda' (2010) 11 *European Anti-Discrimination Law Review* 23.

De Varennes F, 'Using the ECtHR to Protect the Rights of Minorities' in *Mechanisms for the Implementation of Minority Rights* (Strasbourg, Council of Europe Publishing, 2004) 101–02.

De Witte B, 'From a "Common Principle of Equality" to EU Equality Law' (2010) 53 *American Behavioral Scientist* 1715.

——— 'National Equality Institutions and the Domestication of EU Non-discrimination Law' (2011) 18 *Maastricht Journal of European and Comparative Law* 157.

——— and Enikő Horváth, 'The Many Faces of Minority Policy in the European Union' in K Henrard and R Dunbar (eds), *Synergies in Minority Protection—European and International Law Perspectives* (Cambridge, Cambridge University Press, 2008).

Della Porta D, *Social Movements, Political Violence, and the State. A Comparative Analysis of Italy and Germany* (Cambridge, Cambridge University Press, 2006).

Dembour M, *Who Believes in Human Rights? Reflections on the European Convention* (Cambridge, Cambridge University Press, 2006).

Den Heijer M, 'Joined Cases C-411 & 493/10, N.S. v. Secretary of State for the Home Department and M.E. and Others v. Refugee Applications Commissioner, Minister for Justice, Equality and Law Reform, Judgment of the Court (Grand Chamber) of 21 December 2011, nyr' (2012) 49 *Common Market Law Review* 1735.

Déplaude M-O, 'Une mobilization contre-révolutionnaire: la refondatin du Syndicat autonome des enseignants de médecine en mai 1968 et sa lutte pour la "selection"' (2009) 73 *Sociétés contemporaines* 21.

Devillé A, 'L'entrée du syndicat de la magistrature dans le champ juridique en 1968' (1992) 22 *Droit et Société* 639.

Dezalay Y and BG Garth, 'Introduction—Constructing transnational justice' in Y Dezalay and BG Garth (eds), *Lawyers and the Construction of Transnational Justice* (London, Routledge, 2011) 3–13.

Dhavernas O, *Droit des femmes, pouvoir des hommes* (Paris, Seuil, 1977).

Dickson B, *The European Convention on Human Rights and the Conflict in Northern Ireland* (Oxford, Oxford University Press, 2010).

Doppelbauer M, *València im Sprachenstreit. Sprachlicher Sezessionismus als sozialpsychologisches Phänomen* (Vienna, Braumüller, 2006).

Doughty Street Chambers, 'Government Concedes in the Court of Appeal that UK Has No Opt-out from the EU Charter of Fundamental Rights', 13 July 2010, www.doughtystreet.co.uk/news/news_detail.cfm?iNewsID=405, accessed 5 January 2013.

Douglas-Scott S, 'The European Union and Human Rights after the Treaty of Lisbon' (2011) 11 *Human Rights Law Review* 645.

Douzinas C, *The End of Human Rights: Critical Legal Thought at the Turn of the Century* (Oxford, Hart Publishing, 2000).

Doward J, 'Funding Crisis over Legal Aid Threatens UK Asylum Chaos, Ministers are Warned', *The Guardian*, www.guardian.co.uk/uk/2010/may/30/asylum-refugee-migrant-justice, accessed 25 March 2013.

Duchêne A and M Heller (eds), *Discourses of Endangerment* (London, Continuum, 2007).

Dunbar R, 'Language Legislation and Language Rights in the United Kingdom' [2002/3] *European Yearbook of Minority Issues* 95.
——— 'The Gaelic Language (Scotland) Act 2005' (2005) 9 *Edinburgh Law Review* 466.
——— 'The Committee of Experts of the European Charter for Regional or Minority Languages (the CECL)' in G de Beco (ed), *Human Rights Monitoring Mechanisms of the Council of Europe* (London, Routledge, 2011) 150–70.
Edel F, *The Prohibition of Discrimination under the ECHR*, Human Rights files no 22 (Strasbourg, Council of Europe Publishing, 2010).
Edelman L, G Leachman and D McAdam, 'On Law, Organizations and Social Movements' (2010) 6 *Annual Review of Law and Social Science* 653.
Elbaz S and L Israël, 'L'invention du droit comme arme politique dans le communisme français: l'Association Juridique Internationale' (2005) 85 *Vingtième siècle* 31.
Epp C, *The Rights Revolution* (Chicago, The University of Chicago Press, 1998).
Erize Etxegarai X, *Nafarroako euskararen historia soziolinguistikoa (1863–1936)* (Pamplona, Gobierno de Navarra, 1997).
——— *Vascohablantes y castellanohablantes en la historia del euskera de Navarra* (Pamplona, Gobierno de Navarra, 1999).
——— 'El discurso contrario a la 'normalización' de la lengua vasca en Navarra (1997–2002)' (2001) 46 *Revista Internacional de Estudios Vascos* 661.
European Commission, 'A Common European Asylum System', MEMO/13/532, 12 June 2013, http://europa.eu/rapid/press-release_MEMO-13-532_en.htm, accessed 13 June 2013.
European Committee for the Prevention of Torture and Inhuman or Degrading Treatment or Punishment, Report to the Government of Greece on the visit to Greece from 27 August to 9 September 2005, CPT/Inf(2006)41, www.cpt.coe.int/documents/grc/2006-41-inf-eng.pdf, accessed 5 January 2013.
European Roma Rights Centre and the Migration Policy Group, 'Strategic litigation of race discrimination in Europe: from principle to practice', available at http://www.migpolgroup.org/public/docs/57.StrategicLitigationofRaceDiscriminationinEurope-fromPrinciplestoPractice_2004.pdf.
Evans Case R and TE Givens, 'Re-engineering Legal Opportunity Structures in the European Union? The Starting Line Group and the Politics of the Racial Equality Directive' (2010) 48 *Journal of Common Market Studies* 222.
Ewick R and SS Silbey, *The Common Place of Law. Stories from Everyday Life* (Chicago, University of Chicago Press, 1998).
Favoreu L, 'La décision "Statut de la Corse" du 9 mai 1991' (1991) 6 *Revue française de droit constitutionnel* 305.
Fraisseix P, 'La France, les langues régionales et la Charte européenne des langues régionales et minoritaires' (2001) 1 *Revue française de droit administratif* 59.
Galanter M, 'Why the "Haves" Come out Ahead: Speculations on the Limits of Legal Change' (1974) 9 *Law & Society Review* 95.
Geddes A and V Guiraudon, 'Britain, France, and EU Anti-Discrimination Policy: The Emergence of an EU Policy Paradigm' (2004) 27 *West European Politics* 334.
Gheda P, 'Les droits de l'homme au service de la lutte politique. Les avocats dans le conflit nord-irlandais (1970–2000)' (2012) 3 *Le mouvement social* 49.
Gilbert G, 'The Burgeoning Minority Jurisprudence of the ECtHR (2002) 24 *Human Rights Quarterly* 736.

Gilligan E, *Terror in Chechnya: Russia and the Tragedy of Civilians in War* (Princeton, Princeton University Press, 2009).

GISTI, *Le petit livre juridique des travailleurs immigrés* (Paris, Maspero, 1974).

Goldhaber M, *A People's History of the European Court of Human Rights* (New Brunswick, Rutgers University Press, 2007).

Goldston J, 'The Struggle for Roma Rights: Arguments that Have Worked' (2010) 32 *Human Rights Quarterly* 311.

——— and M Adjami, 'The Opportunities and Challenges of Using Public Interest Litigation to Secure Access to Justice for Roma in Central and Eastern Europe' in Y Ghai and J Cottrell (eds), *Marginalized Communities and Access to Justice* (Abingdon, Taylor and Francis, 2009) 205–31.

Government of Navarre, *Estudio sociolingüístico sobre el vascuence en Navarra. 2003* (Pamplona, Gobierno de Navarra, 2004).

Gragl P, 'The Shortcomings of Dublin II: Strasbourg's M.S.S. Judgment and its Implications for the European Union's Legal Order' in W Benedek, F Benoît-Rohmer, W Karl and M Nowak (eds), *European Yearbook on Human Rights* (Mortsel, Intersentia, 2012).

Granata-Menghini S, 'The Application of the Framework Convention for the Protection of National Minorities in Belgium—The Opinion of the European Commission for Democracy through Law' [2002/3] *European Yearbook of Minority Issues* 359.

Greek Ministry of Citizen Protection, 'Greece sends its National Action Plan for Migration Management to the European Commission', 25 August 2010, www.ydt.gr/index.php?option=ozo_content&perform=view&id=3246&Itemid=443&lang=EN, accessed 5 January 2013.

Greek Ombudsman, 'Έκθεση αυτοψίας στους χώρους κράτησης παρανόμως εισερχομένων αλλοδαπών και αιτούντων άσυλο στην περιοχή του Ν. Έβρου και Ροδόπης' [Report concerning the detention premises of irregular migrants and asylum seekers in the prefectures of Evros and Rodopi], 29 October 2007, www.synigoros.gr/resources/_autopsia_thraki_29_01.pdf, accessed 5 January 2013.

Greer S, *The ECHR—Achievements, Problems and Prospects* (Cambridge, Cambridge University Press, 2006).

——— 'What's Wrong with the European Convention on Human Rights?' (2008) 30 *Human Rights Quarterly* 680.

Grossman J and A Sarat, 'Litigation in the Federal Courts: A Comparative Perspective' (1975) 9 *Law and Society Review* 321.

Guarnieri C, 'Courts and Marginalized Groups: Perspectives from Continental Europe' (2007) 5 *International Journal of Constitutional Law* 187.

Guia Conca A, *La llengua negociada* (Valencia, Edicions 3 i 4, 2001).

Guild E and P Minderhoud (eds), *The First Decade of EU Migration and Asylum Law* (Leiden, Brill, 2012).

Guiraudon V, 'Weak Weapon of the Weak? Mobilizing around Migration at the EU-level' in D Imig and S Tarrow (eds), *Contentious Europeans: Protest and Politics in an Emerging Polity* (Lanham MD, Rowman and Littlefield, 2001).

——— 'Equality in the Making: Implementing European Non-discrimination Law' (2009) 13 *Citizenship Studies* 527.

Hadden T, K Boyle and C Campbell, 'Emergency Law in Northern Ireland: The Context' in A Jennings (ed), *Justice Under Fire—The Abuse of Civil Liberties in Northern Ireland* (London, Pluto Press, 1988) 1–26.

Halimi G, *Le procès de Bobigny: Choisir la cause des femmes* (Paris, Gallimard, 2006).

Hammarberg T, Council of Europe Commissioner for Human Rights, Report following his visit to Greece, 8–10 December 2008, Issue reviewed: Human rights of asylum seekers, CommDH(2009)6, 4 February 2009, wcd.coe.int/ViewDoc.jsp?id=1401927&Site=CommDH&BackColorInternet=FEC65B&BackColorIntranet=FEC65B&BackColorLogged=FFC679, accessed 5 January 2013.

Harlow C, 'Public Law and Popular Justice' (2002) 65 *Modern Law Review* 13.

——— and R Rawlings, *Pressure Through Law* (London, Routledge, 1992).

Harmsen R, 'The Reform of the Convention System: Institutional Restructuring and the (Geo-) Politics of Human Rights' in J Christoffersen and MR Madsen (eds), *The European Court of Human Rights Between Law and Politics* (Oxford, Oxford University Press, 2011) 119–43.

Heinze E, *Sexual Orientation: A Human Right. An Essay on International Human Rights Law* (Dordrecht, Martinus Nijhoff Publishers, 1995).

Henrard K, 'A Patchwork of "Successful" and "Missed" Synergies in the Jurisprudence of the ECHR' in K Henrard and R Dunbar (eds), *Synergies in Minority Protection—European and International Law Perspectives* (Cambridge, Cambridge University Press, 2008) 314–64.

——— (ed), *Double Standards Pertaining to Minority Protection* (Leiden, Brill, 2010).

——— and R Dunbar (eds), *Synergies in Minority Protection—European and International Law Perspectives* (Cambridge, Cambridge University Press, 2008).

Herman D, 'The Politics of Law Reform: Lesbian and Gay Rights Struggles into the 1990s' in J Bristow and AR Wilson (eds), *Activating Theory: Lesbian, Gay, Bisexual Politics* (London, Lawrence & Wishart, 1993) 245–62.

Hilbink T, 'The Profession, the Grassroots and the Elite: Cause Lawyering for Civil Rights and Freedom in the Direct Action Era' in A Sarat and S Scheingold (eds), *Cause Lawyers and Social Movements* (Stanford, Stanford University Press, 2006) 60–83.

Hilpold P, 'Minderheitenschutz in Italien: völkerrechtliche und verfassungsrechtliche Grundlagen' in P Hilpold (ed), *Minderheitenschutz in Italien* (Vienna, Braumüller, 2009) 3–35.

Hilson C, 'New Social Movements: the Role of Legal Opportunity' (2002) 9 *Journal of European Public Policy* 238.

Hodson L, *NGOs and the Struggle for Human Rights in Europe* (Oxford, Hart Publishing, 2010).

——— 'Ties That Bind: Towards a Child-Centred Approach to Lesbian, Gay, Bi-Sexual and Transgender Families under the ECHR' (2012) 20 *The International Journal of Children's Rights* 501.

Hofmann R, 'The Framework Convention for the Protection of National Minorities: an Introduction' in M Weller (ed), *The Rights of Minorities in Europe* (Oxford, Oxford University Press, 2005) 1–25.

Hogan-Brun G, C Mar-Molinero and P Stevenson (eds), *Discourses on Language and Integration: Critical Perspectives on Language Testing Regimes in Europe* (Amsterdam, John Benjamins Publishers Co, 2009).

Home Office, *Setting the Boundaries: Reforming the Law on Sex Offences*, vol 1 (London, Home Office Communication Directorate, July 2000).

Human Rights Watch, 'Stuck in a Revolving Door. Iraqis and Other Asylum Seekers and Migrants at the Greece/Turkey Entrance to the European Union', November 2008, www.hrw.org/sites/default/files/reports/greeceturkey1108web_0.pdf, accessed 5 January 2013.

Ignatieff M, *The Rights Revolution*, 2nd edn (Toronto, House of Anansi Ltd, 2007).

Ilieva M, 'Legal Standing for Civil Society Legal Entities to Litigate Against Discrimination in the Member States of the European Union and Candidate Countries'. Paper presented at the Jean Monnet Conference 'One for all and all for one? The role of collective actors in enforcing European Law', Hertie School of Governance, Berlin, 23 May 2013.

Israël L, 'Faire émerger le droit des étrangers en le contestant, ou l'histoire paradoxale des premières années du GISTI' (2003) 16 *Politix* 115.

Jeffery-Poulter S, *Peers, Queers & Commons: The Struggle for Gay Law Reform from 1950 to the Present* (London, Routledge, 1991).

Jennings A, 'Bullets Above the Law' in A Jennings (ed), *Justice Under Fire—The Abuse of Civil Liberties in Northern Ireland* (London, Pluto Press, 1988).

Johnson P, 'Gay Rights in Russia: Alekseyev v Russia Update', available at echrso.blogspot.co.uk/2013/03/gay-rights-in-russia-alekseyev-v-russia_5.html, accessed 5 March 2013.

—— *Homosexuality and the European Court of Human Rights* (Abingdon, Routledge, 2013).

Joppke C and E Marzal, 'The New Constitutionalism and Immigrant Rights: The Case of the French Conseil Constitutionnel' (2004) 43 *European Journal of Political Research* 823.

Judson P, *Guardians of the Nation—Activists on the Language Frontiers of Imperial Austria* (Cambridge, MA, Harvard University Press, 2006).

Kahn Zemans F, 'Legal Mobilization: The Neglected Role of the Law in the Political System' (1983) 77 *American Political Science Review* 690.

Karpik L, 'Lawyers and Politics in France, 1814–1950: the State, the Market, and the Public' (1988) 13 *Law & Social Inquiry* 707.

—— *French Lawyers. A Study in Collective Action, 1274–1994* (Oxford, Clarendon Press, 2000).

Kawar L, 'Legal Mobilization in the Terrain of the State: Creating a Field of Immigrant Rights Lawyering in France and the United States' (2011) 2 *Law and Social Inquiry* 354.

—— 'Juridical Framings of Immigrants in the United States and France: Courts, Social Movements, and Symbolic Politics' (2012) 46 *International Migration Review* 414.

Kay T, 'Legal Transnationalism: The Relationship between Transnational Social Movement Building and International Law' (2011) 36 *Law and Social Inquiry* 419.

Keck M and K Sikkink, *Activists Beyond Borders* (Ithaca, Cornell University Press, 1998).

Kelemen D, 'Suing for Europe: Adversarial Legalism and European Governance' (2006) 39 *Comparative Political Studies* 101.

—— 'Eurolegalism and Democracy' (2012) 50 *Journal of Common Market Studies* 55.

Keller H and A Stone Sweet (eds), *A Europe of Rights—The Reception of the ECHR in National Legal Systems* (Cambridge, Cambridge University Press, 2008).

Keohane R, A Moravscik and A-M Slaughter, 'Legalized Dispute Resolution: Interstate and Transnational' (2000) 54 *International Organization* 457.

Kilpatrick C, 'Gender Equality: A Fundamental Dialogue' in S Sciarra (ed), *Labour Law in the Courts—National Judges and the ECJ* (Oxford, Hart Publishing, 2001) 31–130.

Krisch N, 'The Open Architecture of European Human Rights Law' (2007) 11 LSE Law, Society and Economy Working Papers.

Kurban D, 'Protecting Marginalised Individuals and Minorities in ECtHR: Litigation and Jurisprudence in Turkey' in D Anagnostou and E Psychogiopoulou (eds), *The European Court of Human Rights and the Rights of Marginalised Individuals and Minorities in National Context* (Leiden, Martinus Nijhoff Publishers, 2010) 159–82.

——, O Erözden and H Gülalp, 'Supranational rights litigation, implementation and the domestic impact of Strasbourg Court jurisprudence: A case study of Turkey', Report of the JURISTRAS Project, 2008, 4, available at http://www.juristras.eliamep.gr/wp-content/uploads/2008/10/casestudyreportturkeyfinal.pdf, accessed 22 July 2013.

—— and H Gülalp, 'A Complicated Affair: Turkey's Kurds and the ECtHR' in D Anagnostou (ed), *The ECtHR—Implementing Strasbourg's Judgments on Domestic Policy* (Edinburgh, Edinburgh University Press, 2013) 166–87.

Lambert H, 'The European Convention on Human Rights and the Protection of Refugees: Limits and Opportunities' (2005) 24 *Refugee Survey Quarterly* 39.

Lantschner E, *Soft Jurisprudence im Minderheitenrecht. Standardsetzung und Konfliktbearbeitung durch Kontrollmechanismen bi- und multilateraler Instrumente* (Baden-Baden, Nomos, 2009).

Lasser de S-O-l'E M, *Judicial Transformations: The Rights Revolution in the Courts of Europe* (Oxford, Oxford University Press, 2009).

Latour B, *La fabrique du droit. Une ethnographie du Conseil d'État* (Paris, La Découverte, 2002).

Lavialle C, 'Du nominalisme juridique. Le nouvel article 75-1 de la Constitution du 4 octobre 1958' [2008] *Revue française de droit administratif* 1110.

Leach P, 'The Chechen Conflict: Analysing the Oversight of the ECtHR' (2008) 6 *European Human Rights Law Review* 732.

Leclerc H, *Un combat pour la justice, Entretiens avec Marc Heurgon* (Paris, La Découverte, 1994).

Lhernoud J-P, 'L'éloignement des Roms et la directive 2004/38 relative au droit de séjour des citoyens de l'UE' (2010) 11 *Droit Social* 1024.

Livingstone S, 'And Justice for All? The Judiciary and the Legal Profession in Transition' in C Harvey (ed), *Human Rights Equality and Democratic Renewal in Northern Ireland* (Oxford, Hart Publishing, 2001) 131–62.

López Basaguren A, 'The Spanish Constitution: Problems in Applying the Charter' in Council of Europe, *Minority Language Protection in Europe: Into a New Decade*, No 8 (Strasbourg, Council of Europe Publishing, 2010) 117–38.

Macfarlane LJ, *Human Rights: Realities and Possibilities* (Basingstoke, Macmillan, 1990).

Madsen MR, 'France, the UK, and the "Boomerang" of the Internationalisation of Human Rights (1945–2000)' in S Halliday and P Schmidt (eds), *Human Rights Brought Home: Socio-legal Perspectives on Human Rights in the National Context* (Oxford, Hart Publishing, 2004).

——— 'From Cold War Instrument to Supreme European Court: the ECtHR at the Crossroads of International and National Politics' (2007) 32 *Law and Social Inquiry* 137.

——— 'The Protracted Institutionalization of the Strasbourg Court: From Legal Diplomacy to Integrationist Jurisprudence' in J Christoffersen and MR Madsen (eds), *The European Court of Human Rights between Law and Politics* (Oxford, Oxford University Press, 2011) 43–60.

Mahoney P, 'Judicial Activism and Judicial Self-Restraint in the European Court of Human Rights: Two Sides of the Same Coin' (1990) 11 *Human Rights Law Journal* 57.

Maiman R J, '"We've had to Raise our Game": Liberty's Litigation Strategy under the Human Rights Act 1998' in S Halliday and P Schmidt (eds), *Human Rights Brought Home: Socio-Legal Perspectives on Human Rights in National Context* (Oxford, Hart Publishing, 2004) 94–95.

Malatesta M, *Professional Men, Professional Women. The European Professions from the 19th Century until Today* (Thousands Oaks, CA, Sage, 2010).

——— 'Défenses militantes. Avocats et et violence politique dans l'Italie des années 1970 et 1980' (2012) 3 *Le mouvement social* 85.

Malo L, 'Les langues régionales dans la Constitution française: à nouvelles donnes, nouvelle réponse?' [2011] *Revue française de droit constitutionnel* 69.

Mancini S and B de Witte, 'Language Rights as Cultural Rights: A European Perspective' in F Francioni and M Scheinin (eds), *Cultural Human Rights* (Leiden, Martinus Nijhoff, 2008) 247–84.

Marks S, 'Civil Liberties at the Margin: the UK Derogation and the ECtHR' (1995) 15 *Oxford Journal of Legal Studies* 69.

Martínez J, 'Der präföderale Staat: Das Beispiel Spaniens' in I Härtel (ed), *Handbuch Föderalismus*, Band IV (Berlin, Springer, 2012) 819–44.

Martinico G and O Pollicino, *The National Judicial Treatment of the ECHR and EU Laws* (Groningen, Europa Law Publishing, 2010).

Marx R, 'Sprachnachweis und Ehegattennachzug' (2011) *Zeitschrift für Ausländerrecht* 15–21.

Math A, 'Roms et autres: la protection sociale des ressortissants communautaires' (2010) 11 *Droit Social* 1037.

Maveety N and A Grosskopf, '"Constrained" Constitutional Courts as Conduits for Democratic Consolidation' (2004) 38 *Law and Society Review* 463.

McAdam D, S Tarrow and C Tilly, *Dynamics of Contention* (Cambridge, Cambridge University Press, 2001).

McCann M, *Rights At Work* (Chicago, University of Chicago Press, 1994).

——— 'How Does Law Matter for Social Movements?' in B Garth and A Sarat (eds), *How Does Law Matter?* (Evanston, IL, Northwestern University Press, 1998).

——— 'Law and Political Struggles for Social Change: Puzzles, Paradoxes and Promises in Future Research' in DA Schultz (ed), *Leveraging the Law. Using the Courts to Achieve Social Change* (New York, Peter Lang, 1998) 319–49.

—— 'Law and Social Movements: Contemporary Perspectives' (2006) 2 *Annual Review of Law and Social Science* 17.

McEvoy K, 'Law, Struggle and Political Transformation in Northern Ireland' (2000) 27 *Journal of Law in Society* 542.

—— and R Rebouche, 'Mobilizing the Professions: Lawyers, Politics, and the Collective Legal Conscience' in J Morison, K McEvoy and G Anthony (eds), *Judges, Transition and Human Rights* (Oxford, Oxford University Press, 2007).

McLeod W, 'A New Multilingual United Kingdom? The Impact of the European Charter for Regional or Minority Languages' in S Pertot T Priestly and C Williams (eds), *Rights, Promotion and Integration Issues for Minority Languages in Europe* (Hampshire, Palgrave, 2009) 44–59.

Medda-Windischer R, *Old and New Minorities: Reconciling Diversity and Cohesion* (Baden-Baden, Nomos, 2009).

Mélin-Soucramanien F, 'La République contre Babel—A propos de la décision du Conseil constitutionnel no. 99-412 DC du 15 juin 1999' (1999) *Revue du droit public* 985.

Mertus J, 'From Legal Transplants to Transformative Justice: Human Rights and the Promise of Transnational Civil Society' (1998–99) 14 *American University International Law Review* 1335.

Migrants at Sea, 'Cyprus, Greece, Italy, Malta, & Spain Issue Joint Communiqué Regarding Response to North African Migration', available at migrantsatsea.wordpress.com/2011/04/21/cyprus-greece-italy-malta-spain-issue-joint-communique-regarding-response-to-north-african-migration, accessed 5 January 2013.

Milieu, 'Synthesis report: Comparative study on access to justice in gender equality and anti-discrimination law' (February 2011), available at http://ec.europa.eu/justice/gender-equality/files/conference_sept_2011/final_report_access_to_justice_final_en.pdf, accessed 16 July 2013.

Ministère de l'Intérieur, de l'Outre-mer et des Collectivités Territoriales, Circulaire 'Evacuation des campements illicites' (5 August 2010) IOC/K/1017881/J.

Ministers' Deputies Information Documents, 'M.S.S. against Belgium and Greece, Assessment of the general measures presented in the action plans of Belgium and Greece, Memorandum prepared by the Department for the Execution of Judgments of the European Court of Human Rights', CM/Inf/DH(2012)19, 29 May 2012.

Mole N and C Meredith, *Asylum and the European Convention on Human Rights*, Human Rights Files, no 9 (Strasbourg, Council of Europe Publishing, 2010).

Morag-Levine N, 'The Politics of Imported Rights: Transplantation and Transformation in an Israeli Environmental Cause-Lawyering Organization' in A Sarat and S Scheingold (eds), *Cause Lawyering and the State in a Global Era* (Oxford, Oxford University Press, 2001) 334–53.

Moravscik A, 'The Origins of Human Rights Regimes: Democratic Delegation in Postwar Europe' (2000) 54 *International Organization* 217.

Mounier JP, 'Du corps judiciaire à la crise de la magistrature' (1986) 64 *Actes de la Recherche en Sciences Sociales* 20.

Mowbray A, 'The Creativity of the European Court of Human Rights' (2005) 5 *Human Rights Law Review* 57.

Muir E, 'Of Ages in—and Edges of—EU law' (2011) 48 *Common Market Law* Review 39.

Mulheron R, 'Reform of Collective Redress in England and Wales: A Perspective of Need', a research paper for submission to the Civil Justice Council of England and Wales (February 2008) at www.judiciary.gov.uk/JCO%2FDocuments%2FCJC%2FPublications%2FOther+papers%2Freform-of-collective-redress.pdf.

Muller J, *Language and Conflict in Northern Ireland and Canada—A Silent War* (Basingstoke, Palgrave Macmillan, 2010).

Ochoa Monzó J, 'Estatuto jurídico del valenciano' in JM Pérez Fernández (ed), *Estudios sobre el estatuto jurídico de las lenguas en España* (Barcelona, Atelier, 2006) 349–85.

O'Connell R, 'Cinderella Comes to the Ball: Article 14 and the Right to Non-discrimination in the ECHR' (2009) 29 *Legal Studies* 211.

Olson M, *The Logic of Collective Action* (Cambridge, MA, Harvard University Press, 1971).

Palermo F, 'Domestic Enforcement and Direct Effect of the Framework Convention for the Protection of National Minorities' in A Verstichel, A Alen, B de Witte and P Lemmens (eds), *The Framework Convention for the Protection of National Minorities: a Useful Pan-European Instrument?* (Antwerp, Intersentia, 2008) 187–214.

Pentassuglia G, 'Minority Rights, Human Rights: A Review of Basic Concepts, Entitlements and Implementation Procedures under International Law', *Mechanisms for the Implementation of Minority Rights* (Strasbourg, Council of Europe Publishing, 2004) 9–28.

—— 'The Strasbourg Court and Minority Groups: Shooting in the Dark or a New Interpretive Ethos?' (2012) 19 *International Journal on Minority and Group Rights* 1.

Pérez Fernández JM, 'La tutela de las lenguas regionales o minoritarias estatutarias y su encaje en el modelo constitucional español: ¿un tertium genus en el reconocimiento de los derechos lingüísticos?' (2008) 89 *Revista Española de Derecho Constitucional* 157.

Piergigli V, *Lingue minoritari e identità culturali* (Milan, A Giuffrè, 2001).

Poggeschi G, *I diritti linguistici: un'analisi comparata* (Rome, Carocci, 2010).

Pourquoi nous combattons, Déclaration d'Alain Geismar à son procès (20, 21, 22 Octobre 1970) (Paris, Maspero, 1970).

Pradilla MÀ, *El laberint valencià. Apuntes per a una sociolingüística del conflicto* (Benicarló, Onada edicions, 2004).

Prete L and B Smulders, 'The Coming of Age of Infringement Proceedings' (2010) 47 *Common Market Law Review* 23.

Psychogiopoulou E, 'The European Court of Human Rights in Greece: Litigation, Rights Protection and Vulnerable Groups' in D Anagnostou and E Psychogiopoulou (eds), *The European Court of Human Rights and the Rights of Marginalised Individuals and Minorities in National Context* (Leiden, Martinus Nijhoff Publishers, 2010) 115–36.

Rajfus M, *Mai 68. Sous le pavés, la répression (Mai 1968–1974)* (Paris, Cherche Midi, 1998).

Rawlings R, 'Engaged Elites: Citizen Action and Institutional Attitudes in Commission Enforcement' (2000) 6 *European Law Journal* 4.

Reding V, 'Observations on the EU Charter of Fundamental Rights and the Future of the European Union', XXV Congress of FIDE, Tallinn (30 May 2012).

Reidy A, F Hampson and K Boyle, 'Gross Violations of Human Rights: Invoking the European Convention on Human Rights in the Case of Turkey' (1997) 15 *Netherlands Quarterly of Human Rights* 161.

Report of the Compliance Committee (14 April 2011). Findings and recommendations with regard to communication ACCC/C/2008/32 (Part I) concerning compliance by the European Union.

Report of the High Level Group on Media Freedom and Pluralism, 'A free and pluralistic media to sustain European democracy' (January 2013).

Revon C, *Boutiques de Droit* (Paris, Éditions Solin, 1978).

Richter D, *Sprachenordnung und Minderheitenschutz im schweizerischen Bundesstaat* (Berlin, Springer, 2005).

——— 'The Model Character of Swiss Language Law' in AL Kjaer and S Adamo (eds), *Linguistic Diversity and European Democracy* (Aldershot, Ashgate, 2011) 189–204.

Riddell T, 'The Impact of Legal Mobilization and Judicial Decisions: The Case of Official Minority-Language Education Policy in Canada for Francophones Outside Quebec' (2004) 38 *Law and Society Review* 583.

Ringelheim J, *Diversité culturelle et droits de l'homme. La protection des minorités par la Convention européenne des droits de l'homme* (Brussels, Bruylant, 2006).

——— 'Minority Rights in a Time of Multiculturalism—The Evolving Scope of the Framework Convention on the Protection of National Minorities' (2010) 10 *Human Rights Law Review* 99.

Robins J, 'Legal Aid Cuts to Immigration Could Mean "Injustice, Hardship and even Loss of Life"', *The Guardian*, www.guardian.co.uk/law/2011/jul/15/immigration-advisory-service-legal-aid-cuts, accessed 25 March 2013.

Rosenberg G, *The Hollow Hope: Can Courts Bring About Social Change?* (Chicago, University of Chicago Press, 1991).

——— 'Hollow Hopes and Other Aspirations: A Reply to Feely and McCann' (1992) 17 *Law and Social Inquiry* 761.

Ross K, *May '68 and its Afterlives* (Chicago, University of Chicago Press, 2002).

Ryssdal R, 'On the Road to a European Constitutional Court' (1992) 12 *Collected Courses of the Academy of European Law* 1.

Sadurski W, *Rights Before Courts—A Study of Constitutional Courts in Postcommunist States of Central and Eastern Europe* (Dordrecht, Springer, 2008).

——— 'Partnering with Strasbourg: Constitutionalisation of the ECHR, the Accession of Central and East European States to the Council of Europe, and the Idea of Pilot Judgments' (2009) 9 *Human Rights Law Review* 397.

Sajo A and R Uitz, *The Constitution in Private Relations: Expanding Constitutionalism* (The Hague, Eleven International Publishing, 2005).

Sarat A and S Scheingold, *Cause Lawyering: Political Commitments and Professional Responsibilities* (Oxford, Oxford University Press, 1998).

——— and ——— 'What Cause Lawyers Do *For*, and *To*, Social Movements' in A Sarat and S Scheingold (eds), *Cause Lawyers and Social Movements* (Stanford, Stanford University Press, 2006).

Sayad A, *The Suffering of the Immigrant* (Cambridge, Polity Press, 2004).

Scheingold S, *The Politics of Rights—Lawyers, Public Policy and Political Change*, (New Haven, Yale University Press, 1974).

Shapiro M and A Stone Sweet, 'The New Constitutional Politics of Europe' (1994) 26 *Comparative Political Studies* 397.

Sikkink K, 'Patterns of Dynamic Multilevel Governance and the Insider-Outsider Coalition' in D della Porta and S Tarrow (eds), *Transnational Protest and Global Activism* (Oxford, Rowman & Littlefield, 2005) 151–74.

Sitaropoulos N, 'Η προστασία από την Ελλάδα θεμελιωδών δικαιωμάτων των αλλοδαπών μέσα από το πρίσμα της νομολογίας του Ευρωπαϊκού Δικαστηρίου Δικαιωμάτων του Ανθρώπου. Σχετικά ζητήματα ουσίας και εφαρμογής της ΕΣΔΑ στην Ελλάδα [The Greek State's Protection of Migrants' Fundamental Rights under the Jurisprudence of the European Court of Human Rights. Substantive Issues and the Application of the ECHR in Greece] (2003) 29 *To Syntagma* 233.

Snow D and R Benford, 'Ideology, Frame Resonance, and Participant Mobilization' (1988) 1 *International Social Movement Research* 197.

Snyder SB, *Human Rights Activism and the End of the Cold War* (Cambridge, Cambridge University Press, 2011).

Solvang O, 'Chechnya and the ECtHR: The Merits of Strategic Litigation' (2008) 3 *Security and Human Rights* 208.

Soysal YN, *Limits of Citizenship—Migrants and Postnational Membership in Europe* (Chicago, University of Chicago Press, 1994).

Stammers N, *Human Rights and Social Movements* (London, Pluto Press, 2009).

Stone Sweet A, 'The Birth and Development of Abstract Review in Western Europe: Constitutional Courts and Policy-making in Western Europe' (1990) 19 *Policy Studies Journal* 81.

—— *Governing with Judges. Constitutional Politics in Europe* (Oxford, Oxford University Press, 2000).

—— 'A Cosmopolitan Legal Order: Constitutional Pluralism and Rights Adjudication in Europe' (2012) 1 *Global Constitutionalism* 53.

Stradella E, 'La tutela delle minoranze linguistiche storiche tra Stato e Regioni davanti alla Corte costituzionale' (2009) 5 *Le Regioni* 1150.

Stychin C, *A Nation by Rights: National Cultures, Sexual Identity Politics, and the Discourse of Rights* (Philadelphia, Temple University Press, 1998).

Sunstein CR, *After the Rights Revolution: Reconceiving the Regulatory State* (Cambridge, MA, Harvard University Press, 1990).

Swenden W, 'Personality versus Territoriality: Belgium and the Framework Convention for the Protection of National Minorities' [2002–2003] *European Yearbook of Minority Issues* 331–56.

Swiebel J, 'Lesbian, Gay, Bisexual And Transgender Human Rights: The Search For An International Strategy' (2009) 15 *Contemporary Politics* 19.

Taqi I, 'Adjudicating Disappearance Cases in Turkey: An Argument for Adopting the Inter-American Court of Human Rights' Approach' (2000) 24 *Fordham International Law Journal* 940.

Teodoro i Peris M, 'La llengua a l'Estatut valencià. Comentaris a les disposicions lingüistiques del nou Estatut valencià' (2008) 49 *Revista de Llengua i Dret* 125.

Thomas A, 'Language Policy and Nationalism in Wales: A Comparative Analysis' (1997) 3 *Nations and Nationalism* 323.

Thomas L, *Sexual Orientation and Human Rights* (Lanham, MD, Rowman & Littlefield, 1999).

Thornberry P and M Amor Martin Estebanez, *Minority Rights in Europe* (Strasbourg, Council of Europe Publishing, 2004).

Toggenburg GN, 'Regional Autonomies Providing Minority Rights and the Law of European Integration: Experiences from South Tyrol' in J Woelk, F Palermo and J Marko (eds), *Tolerance through Law. Self-Governance and Group Rights in South Tyrol* (Leiden, Martinus Nijhoff, 2008) 177–200.

Toniatti R, 'Pluralismo sostenibile e interesse nazionale all'identità linguistica posti a fondamento di un nuovo modello di riparto delle competenze legislative tra Stato e Regioni' (2009) *Le Regioni* 1121.

Tonneau JP, 'Pratiquer le droit des étrangers, défendre une cause. Le syndicat des avocats de France initiateur d'un nouveau domaine du droit' (2010) 14 *Savoir/Agir* 29.

Torres Pérez A, *Conflicts of Rights in the European Union: A Theory of Supranational Adjudication* (Oxford, Oxford University Press, 2009).

Trimikliniotis N and S Karayanni, *The situation concerning homophobia and discrimination on grounds of sexual orientation* (SIMFILIOSI Policy Paper, Cyprus, March, 2008).

Tushnet M, 'Litigation Campaigns and the Search for Constitutional Rules' (2004) 6 *Journal of Appellate Practice & Process* 101.

UN High Commissioner for Refugees, 'Note on Access to the Asylum Procedure of Asylum-Seekers Returned to Greece, Inter Alia, Under Arrangements to Transfer Responsibility With Respect to Determining an Asylum Claim or Pursuant to Application of the Safe Third Country Concept', November 2004, www.unhcr.org/refworld/docid/46d52b3d2.html, accessed 5 January 2013.

UN High Commissioner for Refugees, 'UNHCR Position on the Return of Asylum-Seekers to Greece under the "Dublin Regulation"', 15 April 2008, www.unhcr.org/refworld/docid/4805bde42.html, accessed 5 January 2013.

UN High Commissioner for Refugees, 'UNHCR Information Note on National Practice in the Application of Article 3(2) of the Dublin II Regulation in particular in the context of intended transfers to Greece', 16 June 2010, www.refworld.org/cgi-bin/texis/vtx/rwmain?docid=4c18e6f92, accessed 5 January 2013.

UNEF-SNESup, *Le livre noir des journées de mai* (Paris, Seuil, 1968).

Van der Vet F, 'Seeking Life, Finding Justice: Russian NGO litigation and Chechen Disappearances before the ECtHR' (2012) 13 *Human Rights Review* 303.

Vanhala L, 'Anti-discrimination Policy Actors and their Use of Litigation Strategies: the Influence of Identity Politics' (2009) 16 *Journal of European Public Policy* 738.

Vauchez A, 'Democratic Empowerment Through Euro-law?' (2008) 7 *European Political Science* 444.

——— and B de Witte (eds), *Lawyering Europe: European Law as a Transnational Social Field* (Oxford, Hart Publishing, 2013).

Velaers J, 'Het Kaderverdrag tot bescherming van de nationale minderheden: een "non possumus" voor Vlaanderen?' in A Alen and S Sottiaux (eds), *Taaleisen juridisch getoetst* (Dordrecht, Kluwer Mechelen, 2009) 103–58.

Vernet J, E Pons, A Pou, JR Solé and AM Pla, *Dret Lingüístic* (Valls, Cossetània, 2003).

Verstichel A, 'Personal Scope of Application: An Open, Inclusive and Dynamic Approach—The FCNM as a Living Instrument' in A Verstichel, A Alen, B de Witte and P Lemmens (eds), *The Framework Convention for the Protection of National Minorities: a Useful Pan-European Instrument?* (Antwerp, Intersentia, 2008) 127–57.

Von Bogdandy A, 'The European Union as a Human Rights Organization? Human Rights and the Core of the European Union' (2000) 37 *Common Market Law Review* 1307.

Von Bogdandy A et al, 'Reverse *Solange*—Protecting the Essence of Fundamental Rights against EU Member States' (2012) 49 *Common Market Law Review* 489.

Waddington L and M Bell, 'More Equal Than Others: Distinguishing European Union Equality Directives' (2001) 38 *Common Market Law Review* 608.

Walker N, 'Taking Constitutionalism Beyond the State' (2008) *Political Studies* 56.

Warbrick C, '"Federal" Aspects of the European Convention on Human Rights' (1989) 10 *Michigan Journal of International Law* 698.

Wenneras P, 'A New Dawn for Commission Enforcement under Articles 226 and 228 EC. General and Persistent (GAP) Infringements, Lump Sums and Penalty Payments' (2006) 43 *Common Market Law Review* 1.

Willemez L, 'A Political-Professional Commitment? French Workers and Unions' Lawyers as Cause Lawyers' in A Sarat and S Scheingold, *The Worlds Cause Lawyers Make. Structure and Agency in Legal Practice* (Stanford, Stanford University Press, 2005).

Williams C, 'Governance without Conviction' in S Pertot, T Priestly and C Williams (eds), *Rights, Promotion and Integration Issues for Minority Languages in Europe* (Basingstoke, Palgrave Macmillan, 2009) 89–122.

Wintermute R, *Sexual Orientation and Human Rights: The United States Constitution, the European Convention and the Canadian Charter* (Oxford, Clarendon Press, 1995).

Woehrling J-M, *The European Charter for Regional or Minority Languages. A Critical Commentary* (Strasbourg, Council of Europe Publishing, 2005).

Yildiz K and C Brigham, *Human Rights Defenders in Turkey* (London, KHRP and Bar Human Rights Committee of England and Wales, 2006).

Index

Abbott, A 87
accountability *see under* gay rights activism
Actes–Cahiers d'Action Juridique (periodical) 86, 91, 102
Algerian war 91
armed conflict *see* state violations in armed conflict
asylum seekers *see under* third country nationals and asylum seekers, in Greece

Badinter, Robert 90
Baxi, U 181
Belgium, linguistic minorities 30, 42–46
  Convention issues 44–45
  ECHR cases 43–44
  language areas regime 42–43
  national litigation 45–46
Boyle, Kevin 169, 186
Bunch, C 181

Charrett, Patrice de 87–88
Charter of Fundamental Rights (CFR) 5
  equality law 105–06
Charter for Regional or Minority Languages 34–36
Chechnya *see under* state violations in armed conflict
Chevalier-Watts, J 160, 177
Cichowsky, R 163
Clerfayt, Georges 44
collective action 95–96
comparative studies 21–22
constitutional rights 6–8
Cornish language 48
Council of Europe, European Social Rights Committee (ESRC) 12
Court of Justice of the EU (CJEU) 5
  access route 17
  equality law, enforcement 126–27
  fundamental rights 129–30
  minority rights 11
  preliminary reference procedure 12
Croissant, Klaus 89–90

data protection 128
Dembour, M 181
Diyarbakir Human Rights Association 169–70
Douzinas, C 195
Dublin Regulation *see under* third country nationals and asylum seekers, in Greece
Dudgeon, Jeremy 186–87
Dujardin, Hubert 87

environmental protection 1
Epp, C 159
equality law, enforcement
  annulment actions 109–10, 115
  basic issues/conclusion 107–08, 127–28, 218
  collective actors 119–27
    and institutions 120–22
  complexity 127–28
  Court of Justice 126–27
  enforcement 108–15
  environmental law, contrast 119–20, 122, 124
  equality bodies 126–27
  ethnic-racial/sexual minorities 7
  fundamental law 105–08
  infringement proceedings 116–19
  institutions 115–19
  member states
    and collective actors 122–25
    and institutions 116–19
    and private parties 110–12
  minimum procedural rights 111–12
  opportunities 128
  political pressure 115–16
  private parties
    and collective actors 122–25
    and institutions 108–12
    and private parties 112–15
  private relationships 112–13
  Roma minority 114, 118–19, 125, 214–15
  summary 107
  validity of acts 109, 110–12
ethnic, linguistic and cultural minorities 7
European Charter for Regional and Minority Languages (ECRML) 15
European Convention on Human Rights (ECHR) 5, 6
  language rights 33–34
  minority rights 8–9
European Court of Human Rights (ECtHR) 5, 6
  access rout 17

contracting states 157–58
fundamental rights 129–30
language rights 33–34
migrants *see under* third country nationals and asylum seekers, in Greece
minority rights 9–11

family life 7
Felice, Jean-Jacques de 85
Finland, linguistic minorities 30–31
Finucane, P 168
Foucault, Michel 96
Framework Convention for the Protection of National Minorities (FCPNM) 15, 34, 36–37
Framework Directive for equal treatment in employment and occupation 11–12
France
lawyers *see* lawyers, France, post-1968
linguistic minorities
background 31, 40
Charter/Convention impacts 41–42
courts' role 40–41
Friuli-Venezia Giulia 38–39

Galanter, M 194, 198
gay rights activism
accountability to applicants 196–97
conclusions 199
constitutionalisation 183–84
democratic accountability 194–96
ECtHR 181–82
ILGA-Europe 191–93, 197
key cases 200–03 *Table*
legal mobilisation 185–93
LGBT groups 191–92
litigation effectiveness 197–99
NGOs as actors 182, 184–85, 193–99
post-ECHR 182–85
privacy rights 186–88
Stonewall 188–91
Geismar, Alain 84
gender equality 1
Germany, linguistic minorities 31
GIP (Groupe d'Information Prison–Information Group on Prison) 96
GISTI (Information and Support Group for Immigrant Workers)
background 80, 93–94, 102
birth of 94–96
choice of name 96
collective dimension 98–99
and Conseil d'État 99–100
law use 96–98
legal framing 94
legitimacy acquired 100–01
litigation use 98–101
official discourses, deconstruction 97–98
workers' living conditions 96–97, 98–99

Greece, migrants *see* third country nationals and asylum seekers, in Greece
Groupe d'Information Prison–Information Group on Prison (GIP) 96
Guarnieri, C 8

Halimi, Gisele 90–91
Hampson, F 169
Harlow, C 19
Hilbink, T 81
historical minorities *see under* linguistic minorities
Human Rights Advocacy Centre (EHRAC) 176

ILGA-Europe *see under* gay rights activism
immigrants *see* third country nationals and asylum seekers, in Greece
individuals
litigation 2–3
rights 7
Information and Support Group for Immigrant Workers *see* GISTI (Information and Support Group for Immigrant Workers)
International Convention on the Elimination of Racial Discrimination (ICERD) 13
international, supranational arenas
domestic courts 12–14
EU courts 9–12
Ireland, linguistic minorities 47–48
Italy, linguistic minorities 30, 37–40
constitutional rights 37–38
implementation 39–40
regional languages 38–39

Jeffery-Poulter, S 189
judicial power growth 5–7
multi-level structure 4–5
progressive associations 8

Karayanni, SS 188
Karpik, L 82
Keck, ME 163–64
Kurdish separatism *see under* state violations in armed conflict

lawyers, France, post-1968
basic issues 79–82, 101–02, 211–13
collective action 85–86, 91–92, 95–96
disciplinary procedures 87–89
Europeanisation 102
faculties of law 84–85
GIP 96
ideological commitment 90–93
innovative practices 85–93
left's approach 82
May events 79–80, 82–84, 102
organisations, distinctions 94

politicisation 82–85
politics of rights 79–80
role 80–81
self-image 86–87
terrorism 89–90
unions (legal) 86–90
legal opportunity structures (LOS)
access route 17
judicial precedent 17–18
main dimensions 16–17
reconceptualisation 16
resource mobilisation 18–19
LGBT groups *see under* gay rights activism
Liberty/NCCL 167, 168
linguistic minorities
background 27–30, 209–10
core right 29
Council of Europe Conventions 34–37
EU role 33–34
historical minorities 28–29
immigration-based 31–32
litigation role 27
national developments 30–32
official plurilingualism 30–31
political/legal mobilisation 32
private/official use of language 29–30
rights without litigation 51–52
summary 28
Western Europe 28
see also under individual countries
Lisbon Treaty 5

Magistrates' Union (France) 87–88, 95
Malatesta, M 102
Manx language 48
Mertus, J 194, 197
migrants *see* third country nationals and asylum seekers, in Greece
minority claims
European context 6–15
legal mobilisation 15–20
litigation 2, 4
rights revolution 1–6
summary of study 20–24
minority opportunities
holistic approach 206
interactions 205–06
legal rights mobilisation 208–13
national/European levels 206–08
social reform/justice promotion 215–18
transnational opportunities 213–15
Morag-Levine, N 81
multi-level system
background 1–6
legal opportunities *see* legal opportunity structures (LOS)
mobilising law and rights 15–20
rights/courts developments 6–15

Navarre, linguistic minorities
background 54–55
cultural organisations 67–68
ECHR/Charter rights 62–63, 69–71, 72–73, 75
educational effects 60–61
legal mobilisation 63–64, 71–73
legislation 57–58, 59–60
litigation 67–69
mixed zone 58–59, 65
municipalities 68–69
political effects 59, 73–77
Public University 64–65
regional courts 71–72
restrictive policies 64–67
summary 77
trade unions 68
zoning approach 57–60
see also Spain, linguistic minorities
NCCL/Liberty 167, 168
Norris, David 188
Northern Ireland
gay rights activism 186–87
see also under state violations in armed conflict

Olson, M 95–96

Racial Equality Directive (RED) 11–12
Rawlings, R 19
rights revolution 1, 4–5
Russia, gay rights activism 193

Sarat, A 79, 80
Scheingold, S 79, 80, 198
Scotland, linguistic minorities 30, 47–48
Sikkink, K 163–64
Snow, D 98
social actors 20
social rights 1
soft law instruments 14–15
Spain, linguistic minorities
background 30, 53–54, 210–11, 217–18
co-official languages 55–57
constitutional legal model 55
ECHR/Charter rights 61–62
intra-community conflict 54
legal mobilisation 57, 63–64
national/subnational institutions 53–54
see also Navarre, linguistic minorities
Stammers, N 181
state violations in armed conflict
admissibility rates 159
Chechnya 159, 161, 175–77
conclusion 177–80
derogations 167
detainees' ill-treatment 166
disappearances of individuals 176–77
domestic courts 165

ECtHR 157–62
Kurdish separatism 158, 161, 169–73, 186
lawyer activism 168–71, 175–76
legal mobilisation 177–78
margins of appreciation 160
NCCL/Liberty 167, 168
Northern Ireland 158, 164–68, 168, 173–75
socio-legal perspective 162–64
states of emergency 158–59, 161
transnationalisation 164, 168–77, 178–79
Stichting Russian Justice Initiative (SRJI) 175
Stonewall *see under* gay rights activism
supremacy doctrine 11
Switzerland, linguistic minorities 30, 48–50
Charter/Convention adoption 50
constitutional rights 48–49
territoriality principle 49–50
Syndicat des Avocats de France (SAF) 86, 88–89

third country nationals and asylum seekers, in Greece
asylum seekers 137–43, 144–49, 151–53, 211–12
background 129–30, 211–12
courts' role 129–33, 148–50, 151–52
cross-national support 136–37
detention conditions 134–35
Dublin Regulation 137–43, 146–47, 148–49
ECtHR litigation 131–32, 133–37
fundamental rights 129–30, 144–50
MSS case 131*N*, 137–38, 140–43
public interest litigation 132–33
unlawful detention 135–36
victims seeking redress 133–34
Tocqueville, Alexis de 80
Trimikliniotis, N 188

United Kingdom, linguistic minorities 30, 46–48
individual rights 47
pre/post-devolution 46–47
scope 47–48

Vanhala, L 20
Versnerndaroglu, Fevzi 169

Wales, linguistic minorities 30, 47–48
Western Europe *see under* linguistic minorities